A

This book traces the emergence of modernism in art in South Asia by exploring the work of the iconic artist George Keyt. Closely interwoven with his life, Keyt's art reflects the struggle and triumph of an artist with very little support or infrastructure. He painted as he lived: full of colour, turmoil and intensity. In this compelling account, the author examines the eventful course of Keyt's journey, bringing to light unknown and startling facts: the personal ferment that Keyt went through because of his tumultuous relationships with women; his close involvement with social events in India and Sri Lanka on the threshold of Independence; and his somewhat angular engagement with artists of the '43 Group.

A collector's delight, including colour plates and black and white photographs, reminiscences and intimate correspondences, this book reveals the portrait of an artist among the most charismatic figures of our time.

This book will be of interest to scholars and researchers of art and art history, modern South Asian studies, sociology, cultural studies as well as art aficionados.

Yashodhara Dalmia is an art historian and independent curator based in New Delhi, India. She has written several books including *Amrita Sher-Gil: A Life* (2006) that have received widespread international acclaim. She is also the author of *The Making of Modern Indian Art: The Progressives* (2001) and *Journeys: Four Generations of Indian Artists* (2011). She has curated many art shows, with the most recent being the centenary show 'Amrita Sher-Gil: The Passionate Quest' at the National Gallery of Modern Art in New Delhi, Mumbai and Bengaluru in 2014.

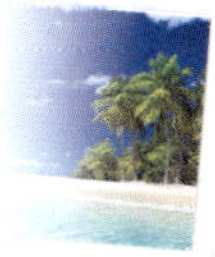

BUDDHA TO KRISHNA

Life and Times of George Keyt

Yashodhara Dalmia

Routledge
Taylor & Francis Group
LONDON AND NEW YORK

First published 2017
by Routledge

2 Park Square, Milton Park, Abingdon, Oxfordshire OX14 4RN
52 Vanderbilt Avenue, New York, NY 10017

Routledge is an imprint of the Taylor & Francis Group, an informa business

First issued in paperback 2019

British Library Cataloguing in Publication Data
A catalogue record for this book is available from the British Library

Library of Congress Cataloging in Publication Data
A catalog record for this book has been requested

ISBN: 978-1-138-23272-3 (hbk)
ISBN: 978-0-367-27978-3 (pbk)

Typeset in Goudy
by Apex CoVantage, LLC

FOR MY MOTHER

CONTENTS

PLATES

FIGURES

PREFACE

One of the most enigmatic of artists, George Keyt's paintings intrigue and tantalize. His bold, sensuous forms delineated with definitive strokes both reveal and conceal, are decorative yet edgy, modern but also ancient. A glimpse of these makes one wonder about the man behind these strangely captivating works. Yet to understand his persona is to take a path which criss-crosses other trajectories that are equally complex.

Mapping this uncharted terrain took me to Sri Lanka, the land of his birth, where it became evident that George Keyt was a charismatic figure and that his name aroused more than reverence. Covering a lifespan of 92 years (1901–93) Keyt, a Burgher, of Eurasian descent, is of importance not only because his work was to pioneer modernism in art in the subcontinent but also because he was the first modern Buddhist artist from South Asia and hence aroused interest in the international sphere. Keyt's painting of Buddha's life in the Gotami Vihara in Colombo is a lucid narration of a sensual, open-ended Buddhism that he suggested needs to be inscribed into the creation of an independent country. For this Keyt archived a gamut of artistic practices from the indigenous Sigiriya murals to the Cubist dissection of forms.

The artist's explorations in Hindu mythology and Indian literature led George to have close links with the cultural life of India, where he lived for long and short periods from 1939 right up to the late 1970s. To the Sri Lankan Buddhist sources were added the imagery of Hindu myth and legend as key influences that led to an art of great sensuality and lyricism. In their bold, robust forms and brilliant colours Keyt was to fuse the East and West and, not unlike Amrita Sher-Gil the Indo-Hungarian artist, was to influence successive generations of artists. In his close association with Indian painters like Francis Souza and M.F. Husain he was also to spearhead an emphatic modernism in the subcontinent.

The drama of Keyt's life is heightened by the fact that his ancestor, interestingly enough, was a British officer posted in Hyderabad where his liaison with a courtesan from the Nizam's court led to his expulsion from India and his basing himself in Ceylon. George's own tempestuous life, which infused his art, led him to renounce his wife and live with the maid who looked after his children and move to her village in Sri Lanka. Subsequently he was besotted by an Indian lady from Bombay and was to marry her and spend the last three decades of his life with her. Keyt's life acquires another dimension because of his close friendship with an Englishman, Martin Russell, who went back to London and was to interact with him over a prolific correspondence until the end. Russell (nephew of the famed Bertrand Russell) also popularized his work abroad and placed him firmly in the international arena.

The life and works of George Keyt, apart from their condensed energy that pioneered modernism, also reflect the social history of the period with all its dramatic upheavals. In his delineation of figures and their specific physiognomies and period costumes, in the archiving of mythology to reflect the struggle against colonialism and in the reflection of life lived by ordinary folk in colonial and post-colonial situations we have a telescopic view of events as they spanned the 20th century.

The Sri Lankan landscape embedded with a palimpsest of cultures provided the rich matrix for George's paintings. It was to lead him to India where the country was reverberating with all the energy of a newly found independence and George was to draw from it for many of his works. His international fame followed where Keyt's name resounded modernity in the subcontinent in a manner that was distinctive and specific. It was no wonder that the poet Pablo Neruda, writing of his works, mentions that 'These figures take on a strange expressive grandeur, and radiate an aura of intensely profound feeling.'

In tracking Keyt's journey I made my way to Melbourne and to a memorable visit to the oldest surviving member of the '43 Group, Richard Gabriel, in November 2011. He was in his late eighties, but his mind was vividly alive with narratives of the Group and his engagement with it. Richard took me around his studio in the outskirts of Melbourne, which was like a gallery of paintings, each one a Pandora's box of events. A sumptuous Sri Lankan meal followed, making it into a morning which one could not forget easily. I was fortunate to have met him just then for he passed away five years later, leaving behind everlasting memories.

In my visits to London and to Dorset to the home of his closest friend, Martin Russell, I was to find another rich source of correspondence and memorabilia. The paintings and drawings of Keyt lined the Dorset cottage, making his home a virtual museum of George Keyt. It was equally memorable to meet Martin's wife Anne who was on a wheelchair and in considerable ill health but was a gracious hostess and took pains to furnish us with essential details of the friendship. Her passing away in 2013 left very few people, barring his own family, who were close to George and remembered his days with such clarity.

In turning it over I think what drew me to work on this biography was to archive the embedded layers that brought about modern art in the subcontinent. The pioneering works of Keyt left behind a legacy that others were to follow. In unravelling some of the processes that went behind this journey I hope to also have uncovered his isolation, desolation and struggle to survive at a time of considerable personal ferment, some of it of his own making, which led him to the edge of an abyss. This was also a period when there was little infrastructure and almost no market for art and for his work. At that time, he had little money and until the end would be in need of it for ordinary day-to-day things. The contrast with his market today almost surpasses comparison. Yet he had to struggle without much support or recognition and with very little means to leave behind works that have considerable depth and grandeur.

It seems appropriate to end with a few lines from the poem on Keyt written by the poet Keki N. Daruwalla entitled *The World of George Keyt*:

For everything palpitates here.
The sandal coloured limbs pulse with ichor.
The green is brighter than a parrot's plumage
and takes off. The yellows are a quest for light.
The palette vibrates with the warmth of flesh tones
and overwhelms the senses
like the bursting of a musk-pod.

ACKNOWLEDGEMENTS

This work has been made possible with the help and support of the Martin Russell family and my heartfelt thanks to all of them. If Martin Russell was George Keyt's closest friend and supporter, it is his family whose open-hearted cooperation enabled me to write this biography on him. In particular, I would like to thank his son Julian Russell who opened his father's archives in London and allowed me to spend hours sifting through the papers and also generously took time off from his busy schedule to speak about the complex phenomena of this iconic artist. Julian also facilitated a visit to his mother, the late Anne Russell, in her picturesque cottage in Dorset. In a state of considerable ill health, she managed to sit up and speak to us for she pointed out that George was Martin's closest friend. The visit to the cottage where Martin had spent his last years also proved to be very helpful in the material it yielded for the book. I would also like to thank Julian's sisters, Laura and Emily, for their support.

George Keyt's own family has dispersed, but it was very useful to interact with his daughters Diana and Flavia for their many insights into George and their vivid memories of their growing-up years. Lionel Peiris and Damayanti Peiris, George's nephew and niece, are to be thanked for the many hours spent in divulging information about the family. I would also like to thank the solicitor Michael Sproule, George's nephew, for the useful information provided by him. I am grateful to Cedric de Silva, Chairman, George Keyt Foundation, and his wife Sita de Silva for their support. Heartfelt thanks to Deborah Philip for her meticulous research for this project. I am grateful to L.S.D. Peiris, Secretary of the Sapumal Foundation, for his help in introducing me to the Sri Lankan art scene and in particular the '43 *Group*.

It was very moving to meet the well-known film-maker Lester James Peries and his wife Sumitra at their ambient home in Colombo. Though he was over 90, his vivid recall of the formation of the '43 *Group*, where he was present, and its subsequent development as well as his memories of George proved immensely useful. The scholar Neloufer de Mel is to be thanked for her writings and for her generous help. I am also grateful to Kumari Jayawardena, the cultural theorist and writer, for her insights and her writings. Arjun Daraniyagala, Justin Daraniyagala's nephew, is to be thanked for his help in understanding his illustrious uncle.

The oldest surviving member of the '43 *Group*, the late Richard Gabriel, met us in his studio at Melbourne and is to be thanked posthumously for the immense trouble he took, despite his age and illness, to provide information and knowledge about the Group. I am grateful to Richard's daughter and her husband, Mr and Mrs Hiran Leidan, for facilitating this valuable meeting. Heartfelt thanks to the art historian and artist Neville Weeraratne, the author of the authoritative book, '43 *Group*, and his charming wife Sybil Keyt for the time spent at their home in Melbourne and for the information provided by them. I would also like to thank Esmeralda Claessen and her husband for the hours spent at their home, also George Claessen's studio in London, for their help. I owe a debt of gratitude to Nathan Sivasambu, the founder and the initiator of the *Ceylon Bloomsbury Group* and the '43 *Group Colombo London*, for his knowledgeable support and information provided on the Group.

Asha Seth and her daughter, the photographer Ketaki Seth, are to be thanked for their help and warm support for this project. I am grateful to the poet Keki N. Daruwalla, who was associated with George Keyt and has written a poem on him, for allowing me to use his poem and for his insights. The many writers and poets who have contributed to the making of this book by their writings are numerous and I would like to thank all of them for making this volume possible.

My heartfelt thanks to Dr Shashank Sinha, Publishing Director, Routledge India, and the entire team in Delhi for the immense care they have taken over this volume. I am also grateful to Routledge UK for bringing about this book.

This work is dedicated to my mother Saraswati Dalmia for her profound cultural and literary influence on me and the family. A writer and scholar herself, she sowed the first seed and lovingly nurtured its growth. My sister Vasudha Dalmia is to be thanked for her scholarly inputs and her warm encouragement for this project.

I would also like to thank my niece Gauri Agarwal, of Sotheby's, London, for her invaluable help for this book. My gratitude to the Sri Lankan artist Anoli Perera, based in Delhi, for her many insights into the art scene in Sri Lanka. Last and not least, I am grateful to Maseeh Rahman for his many insights and his constant intellectual and material support in making this book possible.

1

A FINE START

His life stretched across the entire 20th century and was witness to its triumphs and upheavals. Added to that was the drama of his own journey which was as intense as his creations in paint and poetry. George Keyt, the painter known for his voluptuous, sensual, spiritual and modern works, was born on April 1901 in Kandy, the Sri Lankan hill station, with its resplendent scenery and long tradition of history and culture. Kandy is Sri Lanka's second city after Colombo and was preferred by colonials because of its cooler climate and scenic beauty with its lakeland setting and hilly surroundings. Its many old colonial buildings and the tea plantations in its vicinity testify to their emphatic presence in the last century. Kandy's biggest draw, however, is the Temple of the Sacred Tooth, where a tooth relic of Lord Buddha is kept in a golden casket and a sumptuous annual festival takes place to celebrate this. Ironically enough it was the only town that did not have colonial rulers until it finally succumbed to the British in 1815.

The colonial encounter with Sri Lanka spanned four centuries, with the first ship of the Portuguese arriving around 1505 and the domination of the Western powers lasting till 1948. The Portuguese rule (1505/6–1658) was followed by the Dutch occupation (1658–1796) until the British (1796–1948) finally overpowered them and ruled till Independence in 1948. There have been few Asian countries that have had such a lengthy imperial rule under colonial powers as Sri Lanka, and it had a profound impact on its development and culture. But even when the British had occupied most of the country, the proud Kandyan chiefs did not succumb and it was only in 1815 and partly due to internal intrigue that the city gave in. The kingdom's remote location came to an end as roads were built from all cardinal directions into the city and plantations inhabited the surrounding landscape as the government set up its alternative headquarters here. The long and rich tradition of music, dance, drama and ritual however took its own course, as did the famous Buddhist temple that housed the Buddha's tooth relic. For most in Sri Lanka, traditional Kandyan culture is seen as representative of the country's indigenous wealth. The first king of Kandy, Vimaladharmasuriya, who came to power in the early days or in the 'year two thousand, one hundred and thirty-five from the nirvana of the Master' and had Buddha's tooth relic fetched from the province of Saparagamu and had a relic temple erected in the neighbourhood of the royal palace, may not have been pleased with the turn of history but would have been satisfied with the continuation of its culture.[1]

In many ways Kandy had not changed much since the days when the British writer Leonard Woolf had been posted there in 1907. In his time it had a population of 30,000 and was full of 'white men'. As he mentioned in his autobiographical account *Growing* about the time he spent in Sri Lanka,

> I'm glad that I spent a year of my life at twenty-seven in Kandy, for life there was unlike any that I had ever known elsewhere, but I did not like it in the way that I liked Jaffna or Hambantota, and it did a good deal to complete my education as an anti-imperialist.

His main observation about Kandy was that Europeanizing of the non-Europeans was a mistake. Leonard wrote to Lytton Strachey, his close friend from his Trinity College days in Cambridge:

> The Kandyan grovels on the ground and touches your boots, but has retained his independence and his manners . . . I certainly, all through my life in Ceylon enjoyed my position and the flattery of being the great man and the father of the people. That was why, as time went on, I became more and more ambivalent, politically schizophrenic, an anti-imperialist who enjoyed the flesh pots of imperialism, loved the subject peoples and their way of life, and knew from the inside how evil the system was beneath the surface for ordinary men and women.[2]

Leonard Woolf had joined the Civil Service and had been posted in Sri Lanka, or Ceylon as it was then known, in 1904. He moved in different parts of the country from Colombo to Jaffna and Kandy and it grew on him to his very bones. He returned to England in May 1911 and soon after married Virginia Stephen who was along with her husband a central figure in the Bloomsbury Group. He also wrote the famed novel *The Village in the Jungle* only two months after his return and it was published in 1913. It not only made record sales in the United Kingdom but was translated into Sinhalese and became an essential part of the literary culture of Sri Lanka. Leonard wrote in *Growing*:

> One of the charms of the island is its infinite variety. In the north, east and south-east you get the flat, dry, hot low country with a very small rainfall which comes mainly in a month or so of the north-east monsoon. It is a land of silent, sinister scrub jungle, or of great stretches of sand broken occasionally by clumps of low blackish shrubs, the vast dry lagoons in which, as you cross them under the blazing sun, you continually see in the thickening distance the mirage of water, a great non-existent lake sometimes surrounded by non-existent coconut or palmyra palms. This is a country of sand and sun, an enormous blue sky stretching away unbroken to an immensely distant horizon. Many people dislike the arid sterility of this kind of Asiatic low country. But I lived in it for many years . . . and it grows into my heart and my bones.[3]

Christopher Ondaatje mentions that after spending long hours at work Woolf while in Kandy would play tennis, squash and hockey. His day would end at the Kandy Club for a drink, bridge, billiards and dinner, and it was here that he experienced the centre of British imperialism with all its amplifications.[4]

George Keyt country

If Kandy was the last post of the white man where he was free to make much of his position and power and it is described graphically in Woolf's various writings, it was also George Keyt country and the landscape of his artistic world. George's origins themselves here were as colourful as his life. According to his biographer and close friend, the Englishman Martin Russell, his ancestor was John Thomas Keyt of the 51st Regiment of Foot, Yorkshire Regiment. While serving in the British army in India he eloped with a Begum's daughter in Hyderabad and escaped to Sri Lanka as her people were out to kill him. His son Henry Keyt (1802–67) served in the Ceylon civil service as assistant colonial secretary and married Louisa Elizabeth van der Smagt in the Dutch Reformed Church on 4 November 1839. Their son, Fredrick Theobald Keyt (1842–1904), was an MD from Aberdeen and served as a colonial surgeon in the Ceylon Medical Department and married Mary Elgin Dickman. But it was his second wife Elizabeth Henrietta Krickenbeeck, daughter of Frederick Justinus Krickenbeeck and Elizabeth Adrianne Toussaint, who was George's grandmother. The son born to them Henry Keyt (1867–1927), George's father, married Constance Evelyn Sproule, daughter of James Hugh Sproule, Proctor, and Gertrude Arabella Pierez. Their son, George Percival Sproule Keyt, was born on 17 April 1901.[5]

The family account, however, states that their first ancestor was working for the Dutch East India Company in India and fell in love with a courtesan from the court of the Nizam of Hyderabad. As a result his embarrassed employers asked him to leave the service. He then joined the British and was posted in Ceylon where he worked as a civil servant. He went with the English to fight the battle of Waterloo where he was killed. In recognition of his services, his wife and children were supported by the British. His Irish relatives, for he originally came from Drogheda in Ireland, came to Ceylon to ask for his children, but the dancing girl refused to give up the boy. The girl went with her father's family to Ireland and is lost to the family history.

This narrative which was provided by the eldest daughter of George, Diana Keyt, goes on to mention that their ancestry consisted of the Dutch Burghers of Ceylon who were descendants of French Huguenots, Portuguese settler families and citizens of the low countries. She states:

> As a child, I remember our government archivist, Jan Paulusz, showing us the huge leather bound books (Thombus) which held our family records. He showed me a name – Johanna van der Witt – and said 'She was your ancestor. She came here when she was 14 years old with her family', and then he showed me the family names I knew, the Krickenbeecks, the van der Smagts and so on. Through my mother and my father I am descended from two governors of Ceylon. When my sister was a student in Germany she became interested in our family tree and did some research from the church records in Europe. We had always been told by older family members that my father's curly black hair and pale blue eyes were 'his Jewish blood coming through'. Since the ancestor they claimed was a Jew was named 'Toussaint', we were skeptical. But my sister found that he had indeed once been Jew originally named Ari Goldenstein who had worked for Frederick the Great in Potsdam helping finance his battles. Somehow he

> decided not to be a Jew any longer and went to the low countries where he became a Christian and took the name of Harry (Henry) Toussaint.[6]

It seems that Constance, George's mother, belonged to an Irish Burgher family where there was a Portuguese connection as well. Flavia Keyt speaks of it and so does Diana when she states that:

> Many years ago there were still in Kandy, decaying mansions of the Portuguese gentry. On one of our afternoon calling days, Nana and I went to an area of dark little narrow streets and entered a large gloomy house. We went in to visit two ancient ladies, resplendent in outdated European clothes, who spoke with my grandmother in Portuguese. . . . These were maiden sisters of her mother, who had been a Pirez. . . . They were very slim and had grave aquiline faces with pale, olive skins . . .[7]

Little more is known of the daring ancestor who seems to have broken the iron curtain to elope with a Muslim girl, which was nothing short of courageous. The family account names him as Henry Keyt and that he was born in 1802, but in that case he could hardly have fought the battle of Waterloo in 1815. If we go by the fact that it was John Thomas Keyt who eloped with the Begum's daughter when serving in the British army in India he could then well have fought in the battle of Waterloo when he would be in his late twenties or early thirties. This would also tally with other narratives of similar incidents around the turn of the 18th century. In William Dalrymple's narrative in *The White Mughals* we have James Achilles Kirkpatrick, the British Resident at the court of Hyderabad between 1797 and 1805. He had apparently adopted Hyderabadi ways of living and clothes and shortly after arriving had fallen in love with the great niece of the diwan (Prime Minister) of Hyderabad. He married Khair un-Nissa, or 'Most Excellent Among Women', in 1800 according to Muslim law for he had converted to Islam to marry his bride. After a great deal of digging Dalrymple also stumbled on an account of a meeting between the young couple at the India Office Library which recounted in Kirkpatrick's own writing the fact that she was irrevocably in love with him and prepared to go through any fiery ordeal. The book recounts the tragic story of their relationship where in the end the daughter is taken away at the age of four to England and baptised and then completely cut off from her maternal relations. Absorbed into the upper crust of Victorian society as

Kitty Kirkpatrick she had fascinated her cousin's tutor, Thomas Carlyle, who in his novel *Sartor Resartus* had based his heroine Blumine on her, 'the fairest of Oriental light-bringers'. When Kitty finally is in contact with her grandmother the letters exchanged over continents revealed to her the narrative of her parents meeting and falling in love and the tragic fate of Khair un-Nissa.

That this was a period not widely acknowledged when the British mingled easily with the 'natives' and adopted their manners could make these cross-cultural marriages more common than is known. Dalrymple states in the Introduction of the book:

> The Kirkpatricks inhabited a world that was far more hybrid, and with far less clearly defined ethnic, national and religious borders, than we have been conditioned to expect, either by the conventional Imperial history books written by the British before 1947, or by the nationalist historiography of post-Independence India, . . . or for that matter by the post-colonial work coming from new generations of scholars, many of whom tend to follow the path opened up by Edward Said in 1978 with his pioneering Orientalism.[8]

If John Thomas Keyt did indeed fall in love with a dancing girl we must note that the courtesans of the period were a repository of knowledge and culture. Mekhala Sengupta states:

> The devdasi in ancient Hindu India who later morphed into the kothewali in Muslim India came to epitomise an independent woman artiste and connoisseur with a lifestyle encompassing both the erotic and artistry in not just the performing arts, but politics and persuasion as well.[9]

The case of the courtesan Umrao Jan immortalized in 1905 by Mirza Muhammad Hadi Ruswa in his novel is the narrative of a five-year-old girl who is kidnapped and sold to a tawaif in Lucknow. Ruswa describes the beautiful courtesan's mastery of Urdu poetry and her ability to write poetry and to her performances in dance and music as well as her wit and wisdom. Even more, according to Veena Talwar Oldenburg, the courtesan subverted male dominance and offered resistance to patriarchy where norms of traditional marriage reflected subjugation, denigration and exploitation.[10]

To revert to the genealogy of the Keyts, George turned all this on its head and stated that he descended from the Rajputs of North India and that their original name was 'Kirti'. The veracity of this fanciful belief need not be tested as it showed more than anything else his great desire to ally himself with India, a country whose cultural riches inspired him. But it also showed his disdain for the upper class and the stiff-upper lip Burgher culture which held itself above the rest.

Somebody to nobody

George belonged to precisely this culture. The Burghers before Sri Lanka became independent were by and large a privileged class and to belong to it would mean access to a comfortable life. The country's long history of colonial occupation meant there were more than one form of racial mix and the heterogeneity would invariably lead to differences: the 'Dutch Burghers' were the Dutch descendants the Burghers were the Dutch or the Portuguese where the latter were in some way considered inferior and the Eurasians were of British descent. To be a Euro-Asian was to be privileged and hence in politics many of them took a cautious, conservative stance on issues. Yet there were others who emerged as catalysts for modernization and democratization and would on occasion be on the vanguard of the early anti-colonial challenge. The most radical among them were inspired by the Enlightenment, the French Revolution, as well as with dissident intellectualism. As the scholar Kumari Jayawardena points out:

> Rather than being 'marginal' to society they were utopian-like visionaries and agitators, active on important political and social issues long before the time was ripe for major reforms or social change. Their support was for nascent nationalism, feminism, pluralism, secularism, and the rights of workers and peasants. They also opposed those South Asian hierarchical formations based on caste, ethnicity, patriarchy and semi-feudal class structures.[11]

All the more ironic then that in the later years the cultural resources of the Euro-Asians were not appreciated and a form of demonization took place which turned them into virtual outcastes. Jayawardena observes, 'In Sri Lanka, from the 1880's onwards, the preoccupation of the early nationalists with "Aryanness" meant a demonizing of the "lower races" of other ethnic and religious origins, the valorizing of Sinhala Buddhism, and a demeaning of the "impure" Christian Euro-Asian.'[12] Yet all that

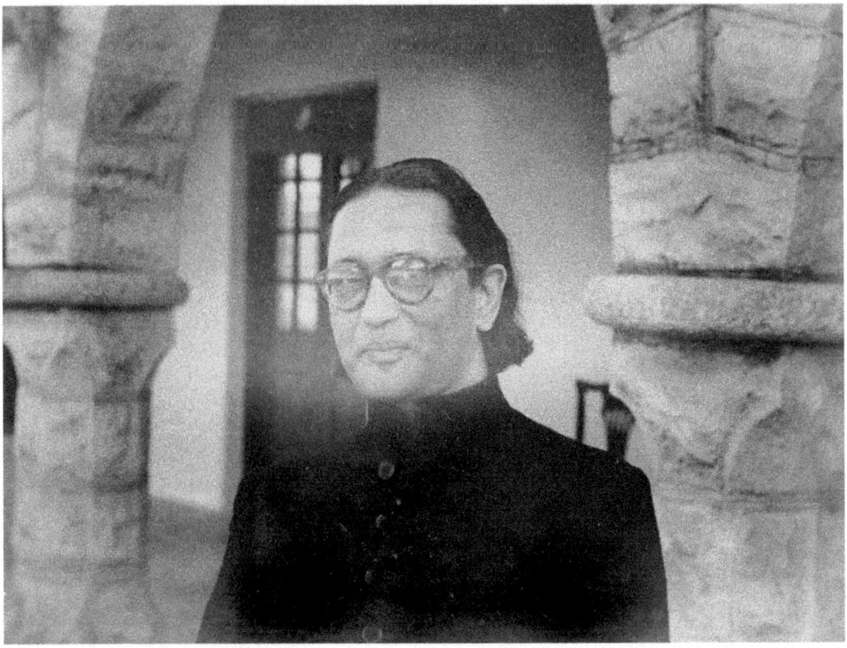

Figure 1.1 George Keyt.
Courtesy: Martin Russell Archives.

hybridity with its rich cultural and political overtones brought with it was the impossibility of essentialism.

Various accounts point to the colourful aura surrounding George's great-grandfather and the fact that he is mentioned as someone who eloped with a Begum's daughter and therefore had to flee India and seek refuge in Ceylon lend it some veracity if not historical accuracy. The first recorded introduction to his ancestors is his great-grandfather Henry Keyt who served in the Ceylon Civil Service and is mentioned by George himself in a letter to a close friend. He writes,

> my great grandfather was brought out by the British for the Civil Service here and was a 'native' and became Colonial Secretary and was knighted too. . . . He married into the aristocratic Dutch family – one of them opting to stay back when Ceylon was ceded to England in 1796 – the Van Krickenbeecks, who were counts. So the

> lineage included other noble families. And he married my grandfather into the same family. The name became Europeanised.[13]

His grandson Henry Keyt, possibly named after him, was a surveyor working in the Government Survey and Ordinance Department at Kandy. He seems to have been a man of learning and would read out both Shakespeare and Tennyson to young George who was both precocious and intelligent. George was known to make illustrations of Tennyson's *Idylls of the King*, a poem which his father would read aloud to him. As a child George would be seen doing drawings of the Crucifixion in which a finely detailed crowd would be pressing around. According to a friend,

> I remember that one of the Keyt pictures hanging in the drawing room of Harold's house at Alfred House Gardens, which was to be the last house in Colombo to which the family moved was a large canvas entitled 'Christ the King'. It showed Christ seated in an imposing and yet simple manner and I may be mistaken now, remembering it so many years later, but the Crown worn by him in some way recalled the Crown of thorns.[14]

George's mother, Constance, was according to family accounts very indulgent towards her son but he did not spare his view on her in his later years. He writes,

> My mother, the most impossible person on earth, and trying hard to no purpose to disentangle herself from the high mightiness and irresponsible frivolity of the 'high' society she lived in as a young woman is now past eighty, and though very difficult and troublesome, is nevertheless quite sane. But vain, inquisitive, suspicious and so irresponsible in her ways and her speech, and so incapable of looking after herself, which she never had to do in all her life, that my sister won't let her live away from her, and she lives on the premises, and is a constant source of worry and she alarms – not me anymore – the relatives, particularly abroad, by writing ghastly letters about accidents and so forth she's been having.[15]

The house George lived in as a child was one which had been built by his grandfather, 'heavy furnitured house . . . old style, built by my grandfather in 1860'.[16] He had a sunny childhood redolent with family love and richly endowed with folklore and animals, birds and friendships. He recalled how one morning his ayah Biso Menike, nostalgic for her village, smuggled him out of their residence and away to her village home. Until the end he remembered the aroma of cooking and wood smoke and the fond cuddling he received. He also remembered galloping around the garden on the strong shoulders of the Indian gardener, holding on to his turban and yelling with joy. Most of all he remembered his father presiding solemnly over the family dinners.[17] George was perhaps the closest to his Uncle Vere, who was a Casanova of sorts and had 'trysts with village maids with young George an intrigued bystander'. He also remembered a tearful governess being dismissed for being too familiar with his uncle.[18] Perhaps his uncle was a source of inspiration for him to have trysts with village maidens in his adult life.

George learnt to read and write only at the age of 10 and spent most of his time before that drawing and colouring. This would be a period of incubation where the rich subconscious sources of Keyt's art with their powerful drawing from mythology and folk tales took place.

The early years

As was inevitable with the upper classes in Kandy, George attended Trinity College where he met other boys of the principal families. His interest lay elsewhere though and he had little patience with the rigours of school discipline. His insubordination created a problem with the school authorities and by 1918 he wanted to leave school and could not be persuaded to return. Recognizing his unusual talent, however, the principal Reverend A.G. Fraser and another teacher, Canon Houlder, persuaded his father to let him remain at home and Reverend L.G. Gaster allowed him to use the school library, a facility George availed of in full measure.

In these early years George devoted himself to literary pursuits and always found it difficult to understand how the English colonial people he met at his father's house could have sprung from the race of Shakespeare, Milton and Shelley.

George had made sketches as a child but also focused on poetry. His leanings towards literature were well known and he spent many long years of his youth in reading the Classics. He constantly alludes to writers in his letters to friends. For instance, 'I've been reading a bit of Kafka's "Trial" and find I like it. Has that independent quality, free of time and space, like a dream, to me the true reality.'[19] He also spoke of numerous other writers.

In order to earn a little money Keyt worked for firms of photographers, where he would enhance the quality of negatives with his considerable skill with the brush. Seeing his talent his childhood friend, the culturally resourceful Lionel Wendt, encouraged him to devote himself solely to art.

It was in 1927 that Keyt began to give up his other interests and to work on paintings in a concentrated manner after a brief course in the rudiments of art with the painter George de Niese. It was through Lionel that George also met C.F. Winzer, the Ceylon Government's Inspector of art in the schools who was a painter himself. He was also a very vocal opponent of official art in Ceylon that consisted of replications of mediocre Victorian and Edwardian attempts in naturalism. Winzer in his own work strove to bring about a synthesis of the ancient art of Ceylon to modern needs and in some measure did succeed. As he stated in his last address to the Ceylon Art Club in 1931:

> Our materials are different, our conditions are different, the demands of the public are different, and the public must be trained and enlightened by us sufficiently, not only to appreciate our work, but also that of the past: which is appreciated actually as are relics, as signs of past greatness, but not out of time, as works of art. But in spite of all the differences of time, of condition, of presentment, the eternal qualities of art, as shown at Anuradhapura and Polonnaruwa, should be studied, adapted to our life, and a continuity with them achieved. I may add that this continuity is closer to the decorative conceptions of modern art than to the realistic, true-to-life prettiness and cheap harmonies of academic achievement.[20]

Ferment in art

A major contributory factor in the genesis of the modern art movement in Sri Lanka, Charles Freegrove Winzer (1886–1940) arrived in Colombo in 1920 and was to live and work there for eleven years. He was an artist himself who had spent his youth in Paris at the time when Picasso and Matisse held the art world in their sway. As the Inspector of Art for Sri Lanka his understanding of art therefore enabled him to lay the foundation for a more vital movement which moved away from the mechanical mimetic work that had existed and towards an archiving of indigenous traditions which he felt were aligned to modernism in art.

Winzer's approach to art was different from that of the Ceylon Society of Arts, which dominated artistic activity in the island along with its most enthusiastic supporter Mudaliyer A.C.G.S. Amarasekera, the art teacher and academic portraitist. He began the Ceylon Art Club in the 1920s, which was in operation for a few years and existed until he left Ceylon in 1931. Artists who were unhappy with the 'existing amenities' were able to exhibit their work at the Art Club and aside from Beling and Keyt, Justin Daraniyagala, David Paynter, D. Lokuge, R.W. Jayasinghe, R. Canagasaby and J.D.A. Perera were some of the other painters who displayed their work at the Club. Along with Lionel Wendt, Winzer stimulated and encouraged the talent he saw around him and this was to crystallize in the development of artists like George Keyt as well as the formation of the '43 Group. Winzer's vision was to leave an indelible mark on George Keyt's works particularly between the period from 1927 to 1929.

In Keyt's early works like the *Kandyan Scene* (1927) we have a load bearer in a sarong and a colourful fruit seller accurately depicted but rather like an ethnographic study. It is as if action has been frozen to allow for a momentary scanning of the lives of the common folk. *Panteru Dancers* (1927) reveals two muscular figures in close-up sitting erectly with their musical instruments and the suspended moment here is almost as if they will soon break into a performance. *The Kandyan Portrait* (1927) of two stately ladies in their traditional costume against a backdrop of trees, vegetation and hillocks reveals particular physiognomic characteristics while their body language is more fluid and seems to be breaking out of staticity into movement.

In many of the pictures we are reminded of the sitting Buddha posture from the ancient site of Anuradhapura, Polonnaruwa and Dambulla where the beneficent calm of his expression is matched by his body posture of absolute stillness. The emphasis on the folds of the dress in the painting *Kandyan Portrait* also resonates Buddhist sculptures with their treatment of incised lines and raised ridges. The squatting Buddhas in Anuradhpura in particular according to the art historian Benjamin Rowland are the best of their kind in Asia and far outmatch his looming forms in Sri Lanka, which are a bit awkward in comparison. 'The seated Buddha image from this early period of Singhalese sculpture are, if anything, more interesting and aesthetically moving than the examples of the standing type.'[21] Speaking of the Buddha in the *dyana mudra* in the Colombo museum which was originally located in Anuradhpura he states, 'In few other representations of the Buddha in yoga trance do we get such a sense of the complete self-absorption and serenity of the Enlightened One.'[22]

It is with his first nude study that George throws aside the Winzerian influence to make a stunning work that is almost classical in its depiction of feminine grace and dignity. All the more so as the difficulty of getting a model to pose nude in Ceylon, a conservative country, was considerable. In a letter written to his friend Van Geyzel in 1933 he mentions how a friend's niece who was Moorish suddenly lifted her dress in front of him and she was quite naked underneath. Although she was very embarrassed, 'This was very welcome because in those days I had not yet got models. It was in 1925'[23] (letter to Geyzel, from Senkadagalanuwa, 1933). With his *Portrait of Govindamma* (1928) where the nuanced tactile brown body creates an overpowering effect and her looming form is both human and god-like, we have the first of his studies of women which would later alter the course of his art. In contrast the fully clothed woman at the back is in repose and is contrasted with the frontal vividly alive Govindamma.

In his mind it was quite clear. When asked later what he felt about 'naked' and 'nude' he said:

> When you see, either in pictorial or sculptural depiction, a figure without clothing, and you just accept unquestioningly that figure to be just what it is, a thing in itself, naturally before you, like a tree or a flower; then it is a nude; e.g. unclothed women in Ingres, particularly the famous 'Odalisque', and in classical Helenistic sculpture etc. But on the other hand when you see the sort of painting or sculpture done in the raw, so to speak, direct and naturalistic, I should say, in some ways, a sort of art-expressed notice that they are just men and women who have taken off their clothes; then I think we use the term 'naked' e.g. some of Picasso's paintings and drawings, and Courbet, Rubens, Rembrandt, etc. and the erotic colour woodcuts of Utamaro, and Hindu erotic sculpture, and that truly horrible statue of 'David' by Michelangelo of which Florence is so proud, and put up in public.[24]

And it is precisely this difference that is evident in this work where the nude is transformed into a form of poetry. The almost caressing tenderness with which the woman emerges in this work would in some way be the predecessor to the many paintings of women, almost sublime in their nudity and without any artifice. This work marked the end of his naturalistic period. From now onwards there would be no looking back.

Notes

1 John Clifford Holt (ed.), *The Sri Lanka Reader, History, Culture, Politics*, Duke University Press, Durham, NC, 2011, p. 29.
2 Mentioned in 'Afterword' by Christopher Ondaattje, in *Village in the Jungle* by Leonard Woolf, originally published in 1913. Reprinted by Eland Publishing Limited, London, 2008, p. 205.
3 Mentioned in Woolf Ibid., p. 203.
4 Ondaatje, 'Afterword', op. cit., p. 205.
5 Martin Russell Archives, London.
6 Account sent by Diana Keyt by email on July 18, 2014.
7 *George Keyt: Nursery Rhymes for My Daughter Diana*, Vijitha Yapa Publications, Sri Lanka, 2013, no pagination.
8 William Dalrymple, *The White Mughals*, Penguin Books, India, 2002.
9 Courtesan Culture in India, IIC Quarterly Summer, 2014.
10 Veena Talwar Oldenburg, 'Lifestyle as Resistance: The Case of the Courtesans of Lucknow', *Feminist Studies*, Vol. 16, No. 2, Summer 1990, www.columbia.edu/itc/mealac/Pritchett/oourdu/umraojan/txt_veena_oldenburg.html.
11 Kumari Jayawardena, *Erasure of the Euro-Asian*, Women Unlimited, New Delhi, 2009, p. ii.
12 Ibid., p. 4.
13 Letter to Barbara from Gunnepana, June 14, probably 1953.
14 Sheelagh Goonewardene, *A Personal View of George Keyt*, publication not mentioned.
15 Letter to Barbara from Gunnepana, June 12, 1953.
16 Letter to Martin Russell from Sirimalwatta, April 20, 1985.
17 Mentioned in 'The Lives of Keyt' by Tissa Devendra, *Observer Pictorial*, Colombo, 1991, p. 19.
18 Ibid.
19 Letter to Len Van Geyzel, June 8, 1937.
20 Quoted in *George Keyt*, Martin Russell, Marg, Mumbai, 1950, p. 40.
21 Benjamin Rowland, *The Art and Architecture of India*, Penguin Books, Baltimore, MD, 1967, p. 364.
22 Ibid.
23 Letter to Geyzel from Senkadagalanuwa, 1933.
24 Letter to Martin Russell, March 22, 1982.

2

VALLEY OF ROMANCE

Most critical turning points are fortuitous and this was no exception. George's sister Peggy was a student at the teacher training school at Kandy and was friendly with a colleague, Noeline Jansz. On one of her frequent visits to the house Noeline came with her sister Gladys Ruth Jansz and it was then that she became acquainted with George. The two fell in love with each other and were married in 1930, at St. Mary's Church in Kurunegala for her family had left the Dutch Reformed Church and had converted to Roman Catholicism. George was not overly fond of Christianity but did not mind the Roman Catholic religion and agreed to get married there.

The light eyed, raven-haired bride, as their wedding photograph reveals, had considerable beauty and charm. Indeed the early years of marriage were of happy domesticity. A letter to his friend, the cultural theorist Len Van Geyzel, talks of recipes which he would like for his wife. He urges, 'How nice about the cooking. Please send the caju-nut-cream recipe! Ruth and Peggy are dying to do it. And I love caju nuts.'[1] As late as 1937 he was writing a letter every day to Ruth from Colombo despite the fact that it was not easy to communicate from there.

Of course George's far from commonplace interest in literature and art could not be matched by her training and hobbies and he seemed resigned to it.

George writes confiding in Geyzel,

> I am so very sorry I didn't write at once and acknowledge the lovely book you sent me . . . I kept the novel as Ruth wants to read it, in fact began it but invariably the crossword urge which is so deplorable an occupation among the less immoral of my women [took over].[2]

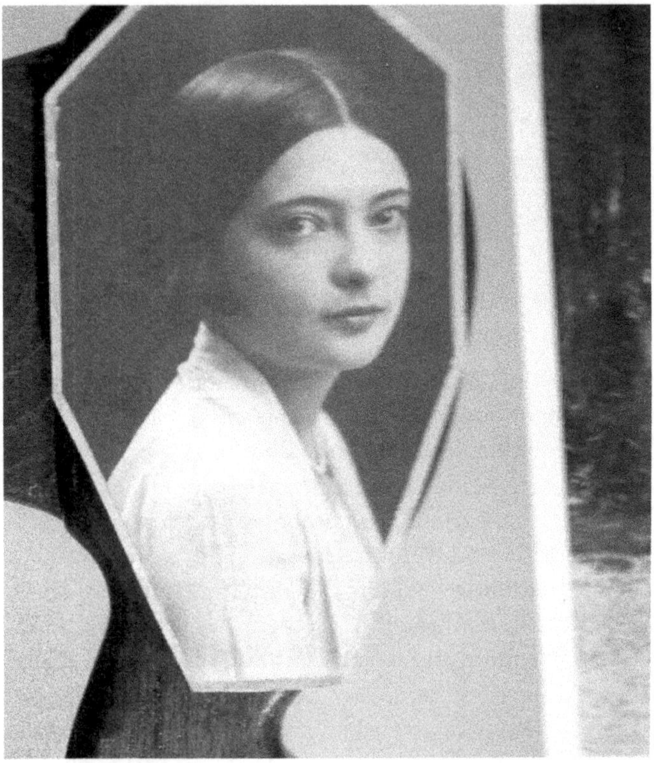

Figure 2.1 Ruth Keyt nee Jansz.
Courtesy: Martin Russell Archives.

But it was also true that it was her job which brought in the salary as a teacher and ran the house and left him free to practise his calling.

George's father had died young and relatives had helped his mother Constance to educate her three sons and daughter. He had left Trinity College to get a job but painting was his passion and Ruth decided that he should have more time for his art. She took a teaching position at Trinity College to allow George to paint all day in his studio. Their family now consisted of Peggy, the mother Connie and George and Ruth. Peggy Keyt, his sister, taught at Hillwood, Connie had a tiny pension, but it was Ruth's income which freed George from the drudgery of working at meaningless jobs. It might be added that she was an excellent and much loved teacher and as head of the kindergarten at Trinity evoked considerable respect.

Of cabbages and kings

A few years later in 1935 a daughter was born and christened Diana, and George spent happy days with her as he had the time while Ruth would be away at work. And it was here perhaps that George revealed his multi-faceted talent as he made nursery rhymes and drew them in a book which he presented to his three-year-old daughter on her birthday. Diana watched entranced and years later she writes 'Even now as I turn its pages I feel I am back in that happy place. In my mind I hear the wind in the rain trees and the sound of evening music floating over the water from the temple across the lake.'[3] There would be the dhobhi and the woman darning socks, the whimsical horse and the bull in the bathtub, the tortoise and the fish, frogs and stork and always plenty of snails. Diana writes: 'Villains of my childhood were snails (gombellas) who destroyed my grandmother's flower beds. Nightmares of "Gombees" disturbed my sleep.' And to help her laugh over her nightmares, George wrote humorously:

> Whenever you see a gombee dance
> You may safely say
> That's quite by chance.
> They seldom see themselves as others
> For gombees never meet their brothers.

The book is a playful parody of the child's kingdom, with its humanized animals and whimsical adults.

These drawings already show his considerable skill in craftsmanship which would flower later. But at the moment they were to enter a child's world and re-create an imaginary somewhat Alice in wonderland-like world. As Diana reminisced in an article which reached on the day of her father's funeral,

> We began every morning like that – my father was the most wonderful playfellow in the world. Together we would go on fascinating imaginary journeys where the counterpane became the great milky ocean and Garuda, the Divine Eagle, would fly us off to visit

> Indra on his throne in his special heaven. King Vikram dispensed justice on earth while above the clouds heavenly maidens danced for our amusement.[4]

Diana would watch her father painting,

> At tea time I went to my father's studio and played at his feet while he painted. He always gave me drawing paper and crayons and I coloured steadily or played with the worn-out brushes. The bristles of these old brushes had fallen out and what was left was so stiff that they felt like solid wood to me. I watched with admiration as my father painted. The brushes were so flexible when he handled them! He dabbled the bristles in his palette and covered the canvas with sweeping strokes of colour. 'What a man of power!' I thought to myself. He admired me too. Taking up each of my pictures he would ask me about them and tell me how much he liked the colours I had chosen and tactfully try to discover what I had tried to represent. We spent most of our day in mutually enjoying our work.[5]
>
> Today, he said, he would show me how to write secret messages with lime juice. Then we went back to our usual games in the heavenly kingdoms where kinnaras sang and we could fly freely over magical lands and milky oceans.[6]

George certainly revelled in the fact that Diana resembled him physically 'I'm glad you like Diana. If you cannot see the resemblance to me it is because you haven't seen her in the flesh. Of course she is a refined and feminised version of me, much nicer in every way.'[7] He wallows in despair when she doesn't enjoy the Kandyan dance:

> I was very disappointed to find that she did not appreciate Ukkuva's reddekki dance yesterday here in my room, but began to whimper. I put it down to her teething. She doesn't seem to like Ukkuwa, who adores her. Dhirananda says that it is because of the natural feeling of repulsion which little vadagath babies, who are pure, have towards low caste people. But I don't think that's true.[8]

Into this world entered a bit later, another doe-eyed little girl Flavia. And the trio were complete in themselves!

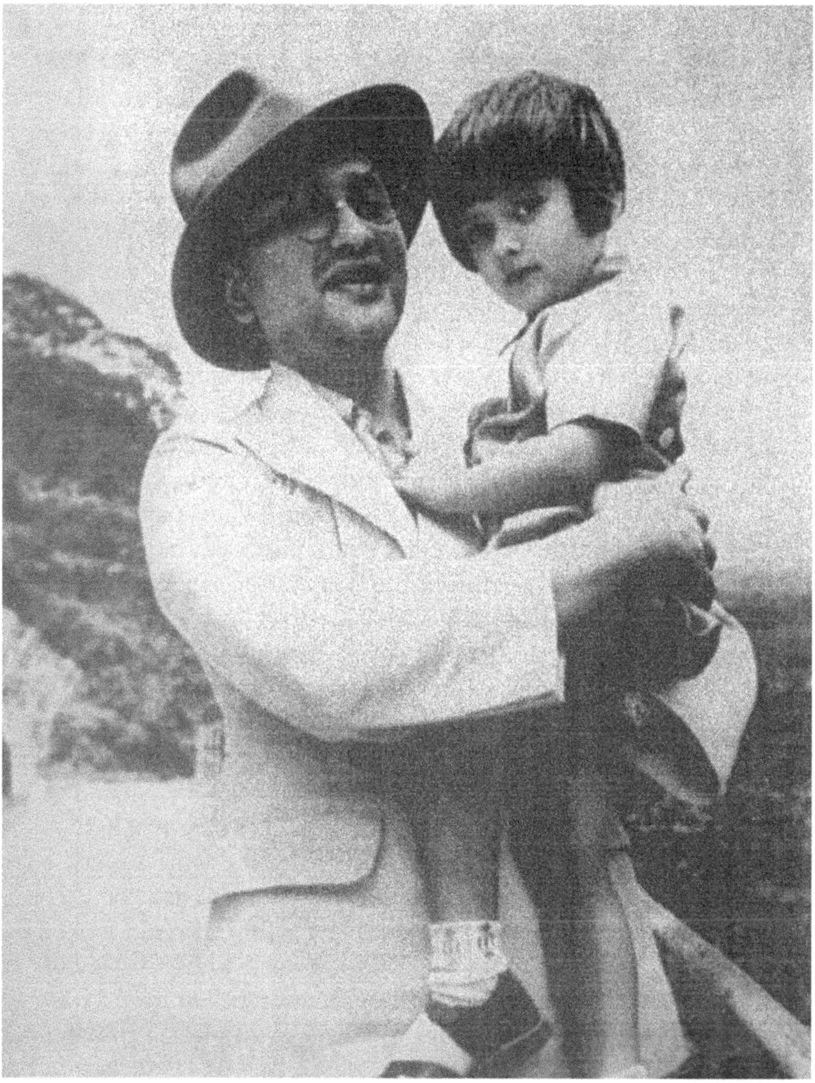

Figure 2.2 George Keyt with his daughter Diana.
Courtesy: Martin Russell Archives.

The world of kings and heroes from mythology also had its downside and these could rupture this idyllic children's world. Thus when Diana was taken to see a night performance:

> Across the water came the reedy music of the horanewa and the Hevisi drums from the Dalada Maligawa . . . After we had eaten, my father carried me on his shoulder to the Bogambara Green which was now humming with exciting activity . . . In a large tent we sat . . . The ladies sprang about and danced off the stage, and now came some figures, almost life size but moving so stiffly that I was chilled with fear. My father told that they were rukada puppets that were like dolls and that somebody we couldn't see was making them move. A king sat on the throne surrounded by Kandyan noblemen in their clothes like those they wore when walking in the perahara. They dragged in a noblewoman who carried her baby in her wooden arms. The king and his courtiers made her put her baby in a mortar hollowed out of a log and pound the infant with a pestle made out of a smaller log. The mother sang a sad song while she rhythmically pounded her baby and her other child, a little boy shouted defiantly at the king. They seized the other child but I could watch no more. I could not repress my screams of horror and my father immediately carried me out.

I found out later that this was a re-enactment of the story of Ehelapola's wife. The vengeful king forced her to kill her children because the secret of the entrance to the Kandyan Kingdom had been betrayed to the English. Ehelapola, disgusted by the King's cruelty and unfairness, had become a traitor . . . His wife and babies would pay the price of treachery . . . My father walked around the carnival and bought me some sweets. I grew calm. We stopped to talk with the rickshaw coolie who had come to enjoy the festival when my father inadvertently turned so that, as I looked over his shoulder, I could see the puppet noblewoman whose ornaments and jewels were being stripped off by the executioner. I started crying and they had to soothe me all over again. . .'[9] A child's world growing dark, however, was soon to become a reality which this episode seems to have foreshadowed.

The angst of marriage

Inexplicably, even to himself, George was unhappy and looking for something else. The orderly, polite world was beginning to stifle him. Ruth was a devout Catholic and had a rigid sense of discipline, which he found anesthetized his sensibilities. In many ways he felt he was dying a slow death. George writes to Van Geyzel, 'I'm so sick of everything. Can't you send me some snake-poison for injection.'[10]

> I'm on the one hand harassed by immediate and trivial things, and, on the other by an awareness of the inert condition, come over me as a result of the crushing I've received – the ill treatment all round, the attitude of contempt or indifference so undeserved in any case whatever my alleged faults.[11]

At this juncture his friendship with Van Geyzel was turning out to be invaluable. Unfettered by domestic worries and relationship crisis these were some of his most intense and interesting communications.

Leonard Colvin Van Geyzel was born in Colombo on 4 September 1905 to Dr. Colvin Thomasz Van Geyzel and Antoinette Aileen Beling. The youngest of three sons, he studied at Royal College in Colombo and Cambridge University in England. He was a descendant of the early Dutch settlers of Ceylon, a poet and first cousin of the artist Geoffrey Beling. He was strongly linked to the '43 Group and Lionel Wendt, whose untimely death caused him along with Harold Peiris and a group of like-minded individuals to build the Lionel Wendt Memorial Art Centre and Theatre.

Perhaps Van Geyzel's greatest contribution to the arts in Ceylon can be found in the first authoritative work on Lionel Wendt, the book *Lionel Wendt's Ceylon* published by Lincolns – Prager in 1950. Lester James Peries, the internationally acclaimed Sri Lankan film director and brother of another '43 Group member Ivan Peries, was encouraged by Lionel Wendt to write to the fortnightly paper called *Kesari*, which was put out by Lionel Wendt. According to Lester, the paper carried sections on art and the literary editor Len Van Geyzel was a superb judge of writing. Wallace Stevens, the great American poet, never published a poem without first showing it to Len. Van Geyzel's correspondence (or 'splendid sequence of letters') with the American Modernist poet Wallace Stevens (1879–1955) has been well documented. He had from 1937 to 1954 corresponded with Geyzel and over the years many items from Van Geyzel were sent to him – from a wooden Buddha to shipments of local tea. Stevens was fascinated by Ceylon, and wrote to Van Geyzel that, imaginatively and earthily, it was alive and of the sun like Florida. It seems that not only did Len introduce Ceylon to Wallace Stevens through artefacts and collectibles, he also introduced him to the work of George Keyt and

E.F.C. Ludowyk. On 24 May 1940, Wallace Stevens wrote to L.C. Van Geyzel saying:

> I was most interested in your long letter, and I cannot tell you how grateful I am for the occasional message from Ceylon. The little volume of poems reached me in perfect condition [George Keyt] appears to have an exceedingly abstract mind, at least on paper. This is a curious thing in a painter. I say appears to have instead of has because, if you will place his own poems besides the translations [of *Gita Govinda*], you will see how, in the translations he has gone for the concrete; consequentially, the abstraction in his own poems is just as likely as not to be due to some peculiarity of character instead of to a type of mind.[12]

It was no wonder that in the constant communication with Len, George was to find solace in those lonely years when he found little else to comfort him.

The poetic phase

George's own work was beginning to take shape and had moved very far from the sketches of the early days. He was now making paintings that were expressive of feelings unlike the earlier ones which periscoped external life. His inner anguish was evident in works like *Balm of Absence* (1936) where a reclining woman is lost in reverie of her loved one and in conjuring his image she finds consolation. In an even more moving work, the voluptuous, brown-skinned woman lies with her body bared dreaming of her love, unaware of her surroundings. Was this a means of healing his own consistently wounded self that could not be consoled?

For George the first step in painting was very difficult, 'Whenever I want to paint I don't feel nice and I hate to start. Once started its fine.'[13] But these ruminations fly to the wind when the much awaited canvas arrives:

> So the canvas has come thanks to you and I'm going to have it opened now and visvakarma is getting impatient in my loins and I'm on the verge of an orgasm and the apsaras crowding round me try to look lady-like and indifferent in an agony of sexual desire etc.[14]

But these were momentary triumphs as he would soon enough be plunged into despair. Between 1935 and 1937 George was unable to paint because of an emotional crisis.

> I'm only just rising again out of that wrong condition which makes painting impossible. When in this condition, the prosaic, the common, it is madness to attempt painting because one is aware of having got separated from that portion of one's being which being separated is seen and appears ridiculous. And that portion is the sublime. Then one is like poor Cervantes who scoffed at the heroic and sublime. One might as well make comic strips and be 'sensible'. . . All my bad pictures were painted when I was separated from the god in me. This is the cause of all bad pictures, no matter who the artist was, however genuine.[15]

To divert himself and also give expression to subterranean currents he turned towards poetry and wrote vociferously. The volumes of poetry, *Poems* (1936), *The Darkness Disrobed* (1937) and *Image in Absence* (1937), were all written in this period.

But George was no stranger to poetry. He had read a great deal from Shakespeare to Shelley. Indeed he writes in detail to Geyzel about Shelley, 'I loved and realised Shelley when I was a child, and the man Shelley still exists for me as much as the marvelous soul expression Shelley does. How can such an avatar diminish?'[16] Of Yeats he didn't seem to care much:

> Yeats to me is very irrelevant. To read his 'autobiographies' is like reading something in a somnolent state – just before actual sleep, you know the condition . . . When he under-rates real geniuses and when he overrates ordinary people, it's all the same. Except for the names, they may as well be the sort of colorless creatures, unreal, he dreams of in his verses.[17]

At the time of writing his poetry he was reading Paul Eluard, Baudelaire and Neruda, Mallarme as well as Poe and Dante's *La Vita Nuova* from an earlier period. But while he was also aware of medieval Sinhalese and Sanskrit writing George mentions in an interview quite tellingly that merely to read poetry was not enough. 'In reading alone there is no flesh and blood. Unless you know this, you cannot see beyond the externals of the drama. These works were meant to be performed, and then they were wonderfully stylized, with mudras, Kathakali.' He speaks of a Kathakali performance:

> Once in Kerala I was privileged to see a performance of an episode from the Mahabharata – that of Bhimsena seeking celestial flowers from the region of Kubera for Draupadi. It was an all-night performance, done at my request. It was simply marvelous. The villagers all came – they sat round about, men on one side, women on the other – all night, without a whisper. Ancient Sanskrit drama is not different.[18]

His poems carried the weight of his learning and spoke in lucid, metaphoric verses about his inner state. Thus in *Disrobing the Darkness* he writes,

> Displaying the hidden desire of limbs in solitude
> And silent mouths
> And proud hips
> I consort with none when I disrobe the darkness
> The night mistaken for itself the garment[19]

If the reverie and solitude of aloneness yet provided comfort in its silence he veered between hopefulness and despair. Thus,

> The desired image continues to subsist on absence,
> Continues to subsist in me,
> And presents a masquerade of itself,
> An assumption of itself,
> Many moods and sources of its face and voices
> in things not visible,
> The breath of feelings which hasten across my path,
> The contemplation of a shadow. . . .[20]

The terror, anguish, loneliness and also the emergence of an evocative image from the dark are portrayed in these moving verses. Unlike his paintings that assemble a conceptual frame for sensual delight George's poetry is many layered, dense and metaphoric. In these solitary years, on the cusp of a magnitudinal change, the verses reflected his groping for something that he himself could not define. As he mentions in an interview:

> My own life was confused and upset. There was a terrible tension in the world at the same time which also affected me, which seemed

> to be an extension of myself, of my own tension . . . It seemed to me that all aspects of the environment at that time reflected me – the poet – such as drought, uncertainty, constriction.[21]

His poems seek a muse yet not a muse, a fullness yet also a void, an anchor yet not an anchor. Devoid of specificity, they seemed to refer to his immediate preoccupations and seemed to travel in an unknown direction. How moving then the lines:

> The absence of a desired image makes a tortuous path
> And my feet keep journeying in a direction different
> from my travels . . .[22]

A new muse

His eyes, perhaps his soul, were wandering. He writes of 'Marcia', possibly Anil de Silva, who was a good friend:

> Marcia removed the Mallarme poems without my knowledge and admitted it afterwards. So I must get that back first. Poor old Marcia. Saw her yesterday, looking quite well and very Louise Rainerish. How I do regret her not neglecting to give this household a taste of her bad reputation in taking money from me! She is loathed so much in consequence! The one thing I was worried about and which I assumed she wouldn't do, she did. So foolish. Because she depended on me so much in other and better ways and I found her so useful sexually. Don't tell anyone.[23]

One wonders if the sexual forays George seemed to be making were more in the nature of the very imbecility he flung on his close friend, the artist Geoffrey Beling. He had known him well and the latter was in the habit of dropping in at George's place often unannounced and staying on for dinner. The very sexuality he accused Geoff of could well be true of him:

> If there is a slight mix up as well in Geoff's case, I think – I don't know these things of course – that Geoff sexually is still a child, just a little boy of 8 or 9. There's something in what you say about its being better for Geoff not to marry.[24]

But surely nothing could be truer of Keyt himself!

His real attention was obviously caught by someone else and he waxes eloquent about her:

> Real beauty is often vague except in secret and it cannot be communicated because others lack the means of seeing it. To put it crudely, beauty is something subjective. . . . My little Radha, my goddess, wishes me to stop writing now. She has moonbeams for smiles like Ashok mata. She smiles and calls out to me. So I must stop. Three of the household are away. So how can I send their love? But I send my love . . .[25]

The secrecy of this love invariably made it very attractive for the artist who painted his loved one in mystical terms. Yet it was not to remain a secret for long. One day Ruth came home and discovered him in the arms of Diana's maid Lucia and was shocked! For her their relationship was over. It could have been a flirtation or a serious romance. But she felt she could not take it anymore and wanted him to leave. In an effort to bring about a reconciliation, Lionel Wendt met him and suggested that he had a chance to go back to Ruth if he would retract. He thought for a while and said 'No' he would not go back to her. And in that 'No' perhaps lay the whirling depths of his desire to break out of the rigid, antiseptic world and engage with the earthy, rugged, reality outside. It must be noted that for George there was always an acute awareness of a world besides that of polite society and he longed both to be part of it and to engage with it in his paintings.

He wrote for instance to Geyzel, 'I'm sorry I discouraged you over the Sinhalese! Of course learn Sinhalese . . . Elu is quite different to colloquial Sinhalese – that's really the classical Elu. The misra basha is to my mind much nicer and full-blooded, with so many tributaries.'[26]

George and Ruth separated and he decided to live with Lucia – the Manike of later years, in her village and with this he renounced not just his entire household but the snug, comfortable, upper-class life he had been used to. The results of this caused a havoc to say the least. Little is known but one can imagine the effect this had on the household. Ruth it seems was devastated. And the young daughters, it was decided, would be shifted to Peggy and Harold's household and looked after by them. Yet another life was going to overtake the canvas of George's existence and shape it in myriad ways. There would be no turning back.

A family divided

The turmoil and difficulties of that shift were borne by the girls who adjusted to the humming household with its round of activities. Harold's daughters from an earlier marriage Damayanti and Indumati lived there along with Paul and Lionel who were the children of Peggy. This large household with its cook and his chauffer and the nanny was run under the benevolent care of Harold and Peggy with great care. Their memories of this place were happy ones for the children. Diana recalls:

> A rubber estate was on the side with the sleeping area and in my shared bedroom I would lie in bed watching the tops of the trees moving constantly in the mountain wind. At night they seemed to be courtiers from some palace with their endless bowing. On stormy

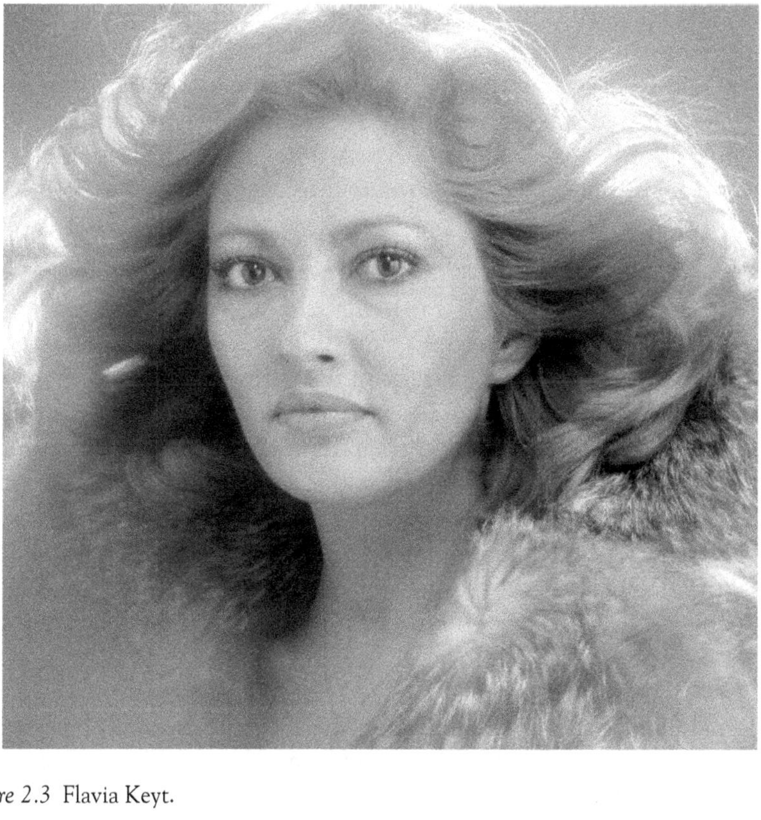

Figure 2.3 Flavia Keyt.

Courtesy: Martin Russell Archives.

> nights they would bow so low that their heads would be likely to meet the ground . . . The front of the house where the living room was, also had a huge balcony, almost a terrace, wrapping around to the entrance staircase. I used to sit with my legs dangling over the edge and watch the raincloud moving from the peak of Hunasgrirya, over the lake and up the hill. It seemed like an advancing army. The rain was streaming from the cloud and as it reached me I was deluged with the huge drips of the tropical downpour. Exhilarating thunderclaps and lightning flashes filled the air.[27]

The house itself was unusual, built by Andrew Boyd who was inspired by Le Corbusier. A friend remembers:

> We visited each other's houses to play together and when I and my sister went to Harold's house which was built high above the Kandy lake, we called it the 'glass house' because it was built in an unusual architectural style which made it appear so due to its lengths of glass wall which were very unconventional for the time. But that was typical of Harold. He was a very rich man and could afford to experiment with new styles and new ideas. All the subsequent houses he lived in were interesting.[28]

But for George, the Boyd house was an example of fake modernity. He wrote:

> But full of mystification to the Boyd type of idiot so anxious to be 'modern'. He's a typical instance of the performing-monkey mentality. See his 'modern' architecture nonsense. And what is this modern architecture to a great extent? Also fashionable bunk and a vulgarization of a vulgarization! Ideas taken from the sort of low-down vulgarization of cubism used mostly for up-to-date advertisements . . . and applied to architecture in combination with an arid skeleton-like version of Japanese architecture (the 'cubist' style, interior, which they hit on centuries and centuries ago).[29]

Nonetheless, happy days were spent here by the children playing and with their music teacher Mr Elmer de Haan, who would come up all the way to Kandy. Diana remembered squirting him with water from above. In the lower level was a studio and guest living area where the musician, photographer and cultural impresario Lionel Wendt would stay and play the Bechstein which was set up for him. There was the doll's wedding remembered vividly by Diana:

> Elaborate weddings were held for the dolls. We only had one male doll a Charlie McCarthy puppet with a movable jaw. The poor fellow married all the females in turn committing terrible acts of doll bigamy. With his articulated jaw he was the only doll able to say 'I do' in the many ceremonies held in his behalf. Once, when Lionel Wendt was staying, he was in bed with a fever so we did not send him one of our elaborate invitations. He sent us a note 'Why was I not invited to the wedding?' . . . We tried to apologise and pushed some of the wedding feast to him under the door. He said that the snacks mollified him.[30]

The head of the house was Harold Peiris who was educated at Cambridge where he had obtained an upper-second Law Degree in 1926. He was as debonair as he was erudite knowing nine languages and well read in literature, history and philosophy. He was also a Sanskritist and had translated Jayadeva's *Gita Govinda* into English along with George Keyt. A Pali scholar he had studied Buddhist writing and had an abiding interest in Buddhist philosophy. 'Yet he wore his learning lightly and never spoke or acted in a pedantic or overbearing manner', writes Damayanti Peiris his daughter.[31]

Harold was also a mass of contradictions in that as an immoderately rich person who had inherited a large amount of wealth he was by conviction a Marxist and also a very compassionate person who gave away all his wealth in terms of land. His daughter states:

> Though nominally a Christian, having had a very strict Anglo-Catholic upbringing, he would privately admit to really being an agnostic and Buddhist at heart; this may have been due to the early influence of his devoutly Buddhist paternal grandmother, Apollonia de Soysa, founder of the Gothami Vihare in Borella.[32]

Harold Peiris married twice. His first marriage in 1928 was to Leah, daughter of S.W. Dassenaike, a retired PWD engineer and a member of the Legislative Council of Ceylon, that lasted twelve years. They had two daughters, Damayanti and Indumati. After the failure of his first marriage he married Constance Alicia (Peggy) Keyt, sister of George Keyt. They married in 1940 and the marriage lasted until his death in 1981.

The two were well suited to each other where both were very extrovert and sociable, extremely devoted to promoting the arts, generous and hospitable. They kept their house open and their lavish hospitality became known in all the homes they lived in, whether in Kandy, Nuwara Eliya, Boralesgamuwa or latterly, at Alfred House in Kollupitiya.

The Gatsby years

Michael Ondatjee remembers visiting their house elsewhere and seeing George Keyt's works there.

> My mother looks out of her Colombo window thinking of divorce, my father wakes after three days of alcohol, his body hardly able to move from the stiffness in muscles he cannot remember exerting. . . . I stood like this in the long mornings of my childhood unable to bear the wait till full daylight when I could go and visit the Peiris family down the road in Boralesgamuwa; the wonderful, long days I spent there with Paul and Lionel and Aunt Peggy who would casually object to my climbing all over her bookcases in my naked and dirty feet. Bookcases I stood under again this week which were full of signed first editions of poems by Neruda and Lawrence and George Keyt. All this was here before I dreamed of getting married, having children, wanting to write.[33]

The house built by Boyd, however, was also one that carried the scars of family divisions. Harold's first wife left him and eloped with Andrew Boyd to live in England. Her children Damayanti and Indumati were left behind to be cared for by Peggy. Damayanti recalls that Indu was initially taken by the mother and then returned. The sense of rejection must have been carried deep inside by Indu. Damayanti herself was not allowed to be in contact with her mother and came across her by accident in London. Diana and Flavia also though ostensibly happy did feel the absence of their mother – a void difficult for anyone to fulfil. Later Diana and Flavia were sent to Europe for further studies.

There were two sons from the marriage, Paul and Lionel. They suffered a tragic loss when Paul, the elder son, was run over and killed in an accident while hitch-hiking in Germany. Lionel was to become a priest later and works in a community outside Colombo.

This was the flip side of the 'Great Gatsby' years of the 1920s which had carried over to the 1930s. In his novel *Running in the Family* Ondatjee writes of those heady days when the family would cavort till late in the night:

> During the whole month of August my mother would close down her dancing school and go to the races. So would my grandmother Lalla. Her figure at the races is ingrained in several people's memories: a large hat at a rakish angle that she wore with no consideration for anyone behind her, one hand on her hip, one hand on her hat, and a blue jacaranda blossom pinned to the shoulder or her dusty black dress, looking off into the drama of the one-hundred – yard stretch with the intensity of one preparing for the coming of Magi. When the races were over, groups would depart for dinner, dance till early morning, go swimming and have a breakfast at the Mount Lavinia Hotel. Then go to bed till noon when it was time for the races once more.[34]

Everyone, it seemed, remained wild and spoilt 'Love affairs rainbowed over marriages and lasted for ever – so it often seemed that marriage was the greater infidelity.'[35] But from the flaming 1920s till the war the frolicking went on uninterrupted. Then it vanished like a drunken dream and what took place instead were the gushing streams of reality. In Ondaatje's case his fun-loving parents with their chic elegance and their sartorian evenings parted ways forever, the father between his bouts of drinking married again and the mother went away to live in London. The poignant tale of drunken revelry and no-holds-barred relationships would end recoiling on its own dream.

The onset of the Second World War would overtake every possibility of regeneration in the 1940s. It was George, however, ensconced in his studio who foresaw the impending war even in the thirties.

> I feel so SICK having read about the Hitler terror in Lord Marley's book. Why can't the rest of Europe put a stop to it? Germany was always the juvenile among nation. Of course there will be a terrific war one of these days.[36]

And then again:

> The horrid superiority attitude of English I prefer to Hitlerite German attitude. After all if a fellow feels Olympian and moves

> about scorning you, you can laugh at his stupidity and not care. But its different where a low arrogant lout overburdened with his own ferocity feels inwardly humiliated and hates you ferociously for it and meddles with you and bullies you with a jeering crowd of cads and makes life hell for you and yours and everything you love and value . . . I have always loathed everything German – and I now feel that to sympathise with them in any way is to be either ignorant or ignoble. What can be more 'provincial' than the German mentality?[37]

If all this was prescient, the Boyd house saw only the British tommies wandering on the hill. Diana writes:

> British officers, exploring Kandy, would climb up the road and wander around the top of the hill. They thought they would come upon a public park. Peggy and Harold would send a servant to invite them to the house. We would see them talking with the servant in his white jacket with silver buttons and then follow him into the house. Harold and Peggy would invite them to tea and give them a good time.[38]

The war activities, however, were going to usher in a person who would be Georg Keyt's closest associate and benefactor – the Englishman Martin Russell. Their long relationship would reap a rich harvest of paintings, recollections and most of all friendship.

Notes

1 Letter to Geyzel, April 8 1933.
2 To Van Geyzel from Kandy. Possibly 1936.
3 *George Keyt: Nursery Rhymes for My Daughter Diana*, compiled by Diana Keyt, Vijitha Yapa Publications, Colombo, 2013.
4 Diana Keyt, 'The Darkening Green,' *Sunday Times*, 29 August, 1993 carried in George Keyt, *A Centennial Anthology*, The George Keyt Foundation, Colombo, 2001.
5 Keyt, op. cit., p. 159.
6 Keyt, 'The Darkening Green,' Ibid., p. 160.
7 Letter to Geyzel, April 25, 1936.
8 Ibid.
9 Keyt, 'The Darkening Green,' op. cit., p. 160.
10 Letter to Geyzel, October 10, 1933.
11 Letter to Geyzel, undated.
12 Holly Stevens (Ed), *The Letters of Wallace Stevens*, Berkeley, Los Angeles, London, University of California Press, 1996 (reprint), pp. 355–356.

13 Letter to Geyzel, November 13, 1933.
14 Ibid.
15 Letter to Geyzel from Kandy, January 10, 1934.
16 Letter to Geyzel, undated.
17 Letter to Geyzel, op. cit.
18 Interview with Keyt by Ellen Dissanayake, *Journal of South Asian Literature*, Vol. 12, Nos. 1 and 2, 1976, pp. 91–102, Michigan.
19 H.A.I. Goonetileke (Ed), *George Keyt, Collected Poems*, The George Keyt Foundation, Colombo, 1991, p. 57.
20 Ibid., p. 71.
21 Interview, Ellen Dissanayake, Ibid., pp. 91–102.
22 Keyt, op. cit., p. 71.
23 Letter to Geyzel, March 27 1938.
24 Letter to Geyzel, undated.
25 Letter to Geyzel, June 8 1937.
26 Letter to Geyzel, June 10, 1934.
27 Diana Keyt, *The Andrew Boyd House in Kandy*, publication not mentioned.
28 Shelagh Goonewardene, *A Personal View of George Keyt*, publication not mentioned.
29 Letter to Geyzel, November 30, 1933.
30 Keyt, op. cit.
31 Damayanti Peiris, 'My Father Harold,' Wijeya Newspapers Ltd., 2001.
32 Damayanti, op. cit.
33 Michael Ondaatje, *Running in the Family*, Bloomsbury Publishing, London, 2009, p. 230.
34 Ondaatje, op. cit., pp. 42–43.
35 Ondaatje, p. 47.
36 Letter to Geyzel, October 10, 1933.
37 Letter to Geyzel, November 30, 1933.
38 Diana Keyt, 'The Darkening Green,' op. cit.

3

AWAY AND BEYOND

Like the renunciation of Buddha, which he would paint with such depth and sensuality later, George left everything behind him – the ease of existence, the immense fondness for his daughters and of course the artistic environment he had grown up with. The young painter also, in many ways, turned his back on the Western milieu of his upbringing to search for more rooted and indigenous methods. He decided to live with Lucia whom he now named Pilawela Manike and they shifted to the village, at first to Ranawana near Hunangoya, then to Amunugama and finally in 1950 to Sirimalwatta where he built his own house and later built a large studio in the garden. In these rural surroundings, with their dense thicket of trees, lush vegetation and an existence of simplicity George was to live for the next two decades.

Martin Russell was to point out:

> Keyt's elopement with Manike – if elopement is the right word – from his own home, from his Roman Catholic wife and his two daughters, and effectively from a European way of life, was, in itself a momentous sad and tragic event. I am not aware any description of it has been published although it clearly inspired some of his poetry. In my book, . . . *Draupadi* and . . . *Abhisarika*, reflect the cataclysm, which produced, not ripples in a pond, but waves which reached far and wide in human and artistic consequence. Manike was the catalyst which gave rise to these developments. Sinhalese and Indian culture was the beneficiary.[1]

George had not been able to paint much between the years 1935 and 1937 but yet he had made a moving work titled *Sringara Rasa* (1936) (which is with the Victoria and Albert Museum, London) or the *Psalm of Love*, in which he brushes in a dark, voluptuous woman and a muscular male figure in passionate embrace, inseparable from each other. The plants around the couple are like a glowing halo that embalms the poetic lyricism of their entwined forms. *In Abhisarkia* (1939) we have the triumphant, sensuous and calm woman confident of her powers, enmeshed in diaphanous clothes which reveal her voluptuous form beneath. The side curtain serves to create a distancing effect almost as if a performance is being enacted and the viewer is both participant and observer. In many ways the painting is reminiscent of the Tamil theatre George is used to visit in Colombo in the late 1920s and his acquaintance with the performers. His incorporation of theatrical details and costumes and the movement of figures on the surface hark back to these early experiences.

The painting was a favourite one of George's and when it was displayed in Rotterdam in 1954 and sold to a buyer he felt the loss. He would rather have had William Archer, then Head of the Indian section of the Victoria and Albert Museum who was familiar with his work and a friend of his and who wanted to buy the work, have it rather than an unknown person and Russell made enquiries on his behalf to find the new owner. This was surely quite a triumph for the woman who would be the reigning queen in George's life in the next two decades. Another work reveals the multivalent *Maheshvara* (1938) holding his spear and sitting astride his bull, his dangling penis as large as that of the bulls'! Anxious, frightened, charged there could not have been a more intense work! The earlier statuesque calm of the figures breaks into a frenzy of movement and the frame is barely able to contain the energy.

George had made a break with academic naturalism by the early 1930s and his move towards modernism was provided an impetus by the exposure to the French art magazine Cahiers d'Art, most likely in the possession of Lionel Wendt. It has been suggested that issues 7 and 8 of 1932 and 1933 which featured the works of Cezanne, Picasso and Braque particularly had an immediate and revolutionary influence on him.[2] Matisse and Fernand Leger's works seen in other issues of Cahiers d'Art also provided the sensuous tactility to his figures, which was in accord with his temperament. In this Gauginesque move towards the brown-skinned, sensuous, 'native' form, his own contribution was the creation of a powerful female persona who was both mythological and real. The rotund, flamboyant and billowing forms evident in his earlier still life of Buddhist objects could now be used to full effect as he created his sensual and voluptuous women in their dark, looming presence rather like mother goddesses. But George's use of the calligraphic, bounding line and glowing colours, his juxtapositioning of aerial views with frontal perspectives were created from his own experience of indigenous traditions.

The strong woman

To many the woman he chose to live with was an ordinary person with no singular attribute to invite such dramatic decisions. But Manike was an exception. As a close friend, Martin Russell wrote in her obituary when she passed away on January 4, 2000:

> Manike had extensive knowledge derived from Kandyan life, local conversation and reading. On one occasion, when I asked Keyt how valleys in the Kandyan countryside had been reconstructed to create extensive flat paddy fields at diminishing levels, with a controlled supply of rain water he consulted Manike, who, without hesitation, gave a long comprehensive answer which Keyt translated for me. She described how the labour had been assembled and what tools had been used, how the sides of the valleys had been dug away, how the stone had been separated from the soil and used to partition the water levels, and the soil had been spread evenly to make fertile fields. As her words were translated, I could envisage the whole ancient process.[3]

He added, 'In a way I am pleased Manike never learned English. She was protected from much coarseness in our present civilization.'[4]

This was a period of isolation for George but it also bought him close to Kandyan village life. He changed into his sarong, grew his hair and tied it behind him and no longer sported ties and shoes. His life still consisted of painting while all the nitty-gritty of existence was borne by Manike, who cooked and washed and cleaned. She was content to be his caretaker, while George painted and read and even flirted with the village maidens.

To that, Manike turned a tolerant blind eye as morals were not so strict and monogamy was not a notion fully implemented in village life.

A Kandyan village is surrounded by green paddy fields leading to gentle hills and the 'valleys are aglow with verdant vegetation, and studded with arboreal groves in which Keyt could well have imagined his favourite Blue God (Sri Krishna) summoning the gopis on his haunting flute, while Radha peeped coyly amidst the foliage.'[5] In these primeval surroundings, it was as if Keyt's own subterranean instincts came to the fore. The emergent works would be dark, sensuous and strong, whirling him

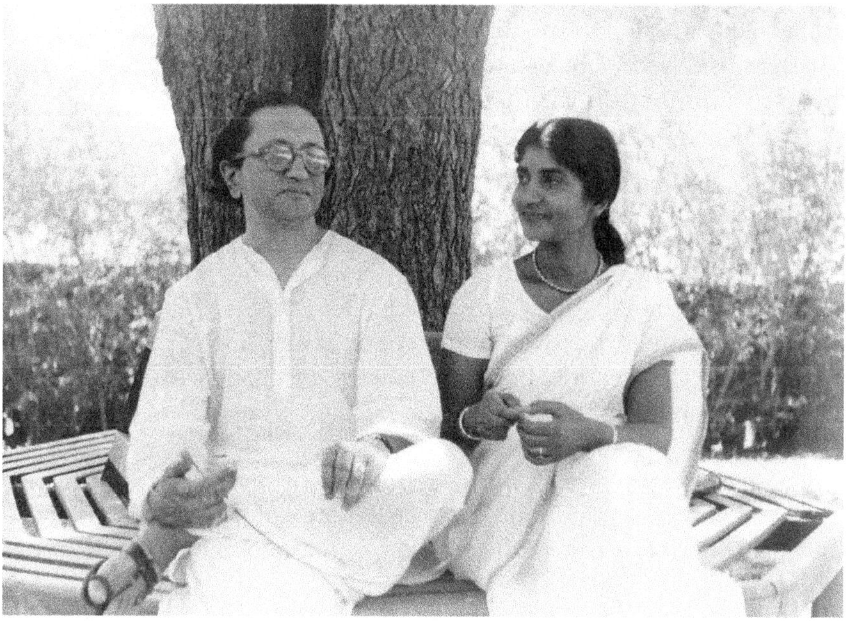

Figure 3.1 George and Manike.
Courtesy: Martin Russell Archives.

in a direction which he could not predict. It has to be said that George's strongest and most powerful paintings emerged in this period. It was as if he had surrendered to elemental forces within him. He had mostly not given in to undue cerebral activity to interfere with his art or poetry but retained an equilibrium with the animal inside him. As he stated in an interview when asked about his poetry, 'Yes, as with the painting. I got into the power of it. Once I was in the power of it, it would have its way.' Then again, 'Once the mood is upon me, I am under its power and do not have to struggle.'[6]

Keyt's *Jalaja* (1938) rises from the churning ocean and her pendulous breasts and boulder thighs could break a mountain. In another version of *Jalaja* (1938) the dancer in her strong motions creates ripples on the surface. Yet again *Jalaja* (1939) pirouettes her powerful, fleshy, dark body rotating the earth. There is a resonance of the sumptuous nudes in Renoir's *Nymphs* series (1918) with their large breasts and heavy thighs, where integrity of form replaces its dissolution by light, a pre-occupation with the Impressionists. It is as if these are set into motion by Keyt: contorted, gyrating, axial movements caught in the vortex of a storm. Borrowing from traditional Kandyan paintings the figures are shown in full, three-quarter or side face. The great aesthete Coomaraswamy speaking of these temple paintings pointed out:

> The off eye is foreshortened in three-quarter face presentation, but the near eye is drawn as if seen in front view and the same is true of profiles. Lines to indicate the eye socket are drawn above and below the lines of the eye itself. The four lines just mentioned are drawn in red, the eyebrow black. The pupil is a black spot. In large paintings the white of the eye on either side of the pupil is barred by vertical red lines, curved concentrically with the limit of the pupil.[7]

The facial expressions adapted by Keyt in his figures are thus seen as vital and in constant motion. These figures are not passive victims of destiny but the strong, dark earth goddesses who would smoulder and set him on fire.

If anything, this was Kali who roamed naked with skulls around her neck and no fair-skinned Lakshmi who in her slim, svelte form would be crowned the goddess of wealth and would be Vishnu's consort.

Jalaja to an extent reflected George's own agitated self, his frenzied world which was about to be ripped apart by cataclysmic waves. There would be a rhythmic pattern of agitation and serenity that would alternate in all his work, creating panegyrics of light and dark. The later *Nayika* series are of a calmer, more lyrical frame of mind where the turbulence seems to have settled down. The *Nayika* (1942) with her burnished skin, slanting, fish-shaped eyes and pouting lips is yet imbued with an inner strength and grace. The women strong and lissome, with their evocative gaze and graceful curve of the back, suggest miniature traditions. The emblazoned red background symbolic of passion, the condensed line from forehead to nose and the fish-shaped slanting large eyes seem to echo the traditions of Mewar, Basohli and Central India. Their connection with lush vegetation brings them into close osmotic contact with a fecund, fertile world. In *Woman with Sheaf* (1943) the soft mass of the form is moulded to the flow of the vegetation as the large soulful eyes glisten against the dark skin. In his vibrant work *Sringar* (1944) we have the woman sitting on a low stool gazing at herself in the mirror. Her dark body glistens catching the reflections of the room even as the mirror reflects the slanted, haunting eyes. The vital body of the woman electrifies the triangles and diagonals of the

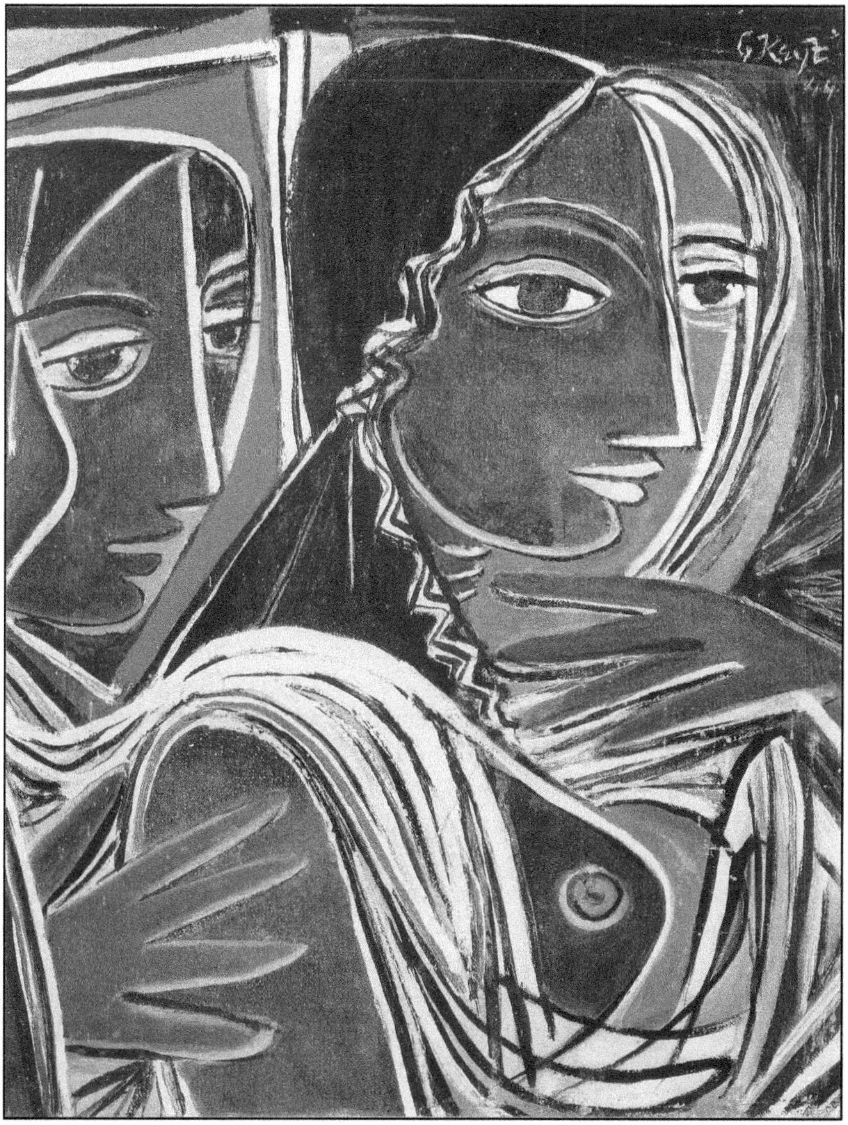

Figure 3.2 Nayika and Sakhi.

George Keyt.
Oil on canvas, 1944.
Courtesy: Martin Russell Archives.

room making everything in it come alive. 'Yes, that is an obsessive idea of mine [the mirror]'. In one of my poems a girl gazes at her reflection and asks, 'But where am I among the things that are visible.'[8] In Keyt's tribute to the ordinary woman, the everyday form is elevated to an iconic height.

The dark bold line encases the figure in strong, rigorous strokes that are unwavering. Never had his lines been more bounding, or the brush strokes more charged. The strong, primary colours glowed as his brush darted across the canvas. His compositions became infused with a vision that had been lurking in his earlier work. The shy hesitant forms give way to bold, confident figures which would dominate the stage from now onwards.

Inspired by real people they would evolve as if they had a life of their own. 'The "image" began with an actual person, then ceased to be that.'[9]

Maidens of Sigiriya

The strong and graceful feminine forms which were etched by Keyt at this juncture could have a kinship with the sensuous Sigiriya maidens. They were mostly made from their hips upwards like the ladies of Sigiriya whose torsos are swathed in clouds. These were figures of voluptuous women carrying offerings and were found at the rock fortress at Sigiriya constructed by King Kasyapa in the 5th century (AD 477–495). The guilty king had murdered his father and then constructed a rock fortress at Sigiriya where he lived for 18 years till his half-brother Moggallana returned to Ceylon from India with an army and defeated him. The account is vividly described in *Mahavamsa*, the great Pali chronicle of Ceylon. The rock paintings, it is believed, were commissioned by King Kasyapa and once formed an entire gallery enveloping the rock hill or Lion Rock. As John Still observed in 1907, 'The whole face of the hill appears to have been a gigantic picture gallery . . . The largest picture in the world perhaps.'[10] The first person to find his way into the fresco pocket and to see the paintings was Murray, an engineer from the Public Works Department. He made meticulous tracings, then copied it in pastel and published a paper in 1891. According to the cultural historian Senake Bandaranayake:

> The poems in the graffiti on the Mirror Wall . . . dating from about the sixth to the thirteenth or fourteenth century, are mostly addressed to the ladies in the paintings, who seem also to have been studied and reproduced in the eighteenth century by the Kandyan artists who painted the Dambulla murals.[11]

It was Keyt who then re-invented their forms for modernist purposes and projected the iconic woman in her diverse roles.

This parade of celestial nymphs singly or in pairs carrying offerings or flowers from their dramatic location high up on the rock hill is almost like they are dispersing flowers over humanity. The art historian Benjamin Rowland remarks, 'The divinity of these almost oppressively sensuous queens is indicated only by the clouds that veil them below the waist and by a sort of urna on the forehead, a device used to designate divine beings in India.'[12] Interestingly these forms are drawn almost freehand, with many corrections that are noticeable particularly of the hands of certain figures. The nymphs with their nubile, swelling breasts and their tiny waists almost the size of the girth of the neck are on the one hand the stuff of dreams and on the other their earthy robustness marks them out creating a bewitching duality. As Rowland points out, 'If the boldness of the drawing and the brilliance of the colours are recognizable as typically Singhalese, the actual physical types represented, with heavy-lidded eyes,

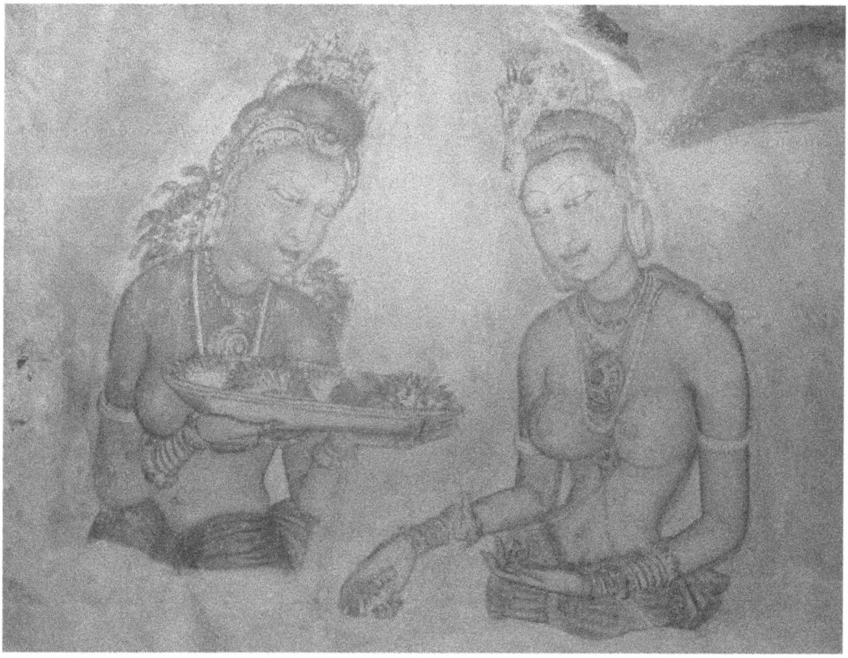

Figure 3.3 Sigiriya maidens.
Courtesy: Maseeh Rahman.

sharp aquiline noses, and full lips, may be taken as direct reflexions of actual Singhalese types.'[13] The wall paintings are contemporaneous with the fresco paintings at Ajanta Caves of the Gupta period but if the latter excel in their refined depths and their humanistic overtones that were the inspiration for the iconic Indo-Hungarian artist Amrita Sher-Gil's masterly works, the former in their robust sensuality seemed to have been a source of inspiration for George Keyt.

It was perhaps these works which came to the fore during his stay in a remote village that made Van Geyzel comment, 'Keyt had no precursors; only ancestors from a remote antiquity'.[14] But what ancestors! In their lyrical grace and their sensuous bodies no one could have found a more inspirational medium.

In many ways George felt more alone than ever. As he wrote to Geyzel:

> I feel fine in the mornings, but wilt away completely by midday, just like the vegetation around here! The greatest drawback in my life is the (now) telling effect of my exile, my complete and tomb-like isolation – which forces me into exploiting the last dregs of a never refreshed and replenished subjectivity.[15]

Vivien Leigh visit

But if he forsook the world it did not forsake him. It came to his doorstep intrigued by the famous artist who had renounced everything to paint in the 'wilderness'. Vivien Leigh the British star who had risen to meteoric fame in her role as Scarlett O'Hara in *Gone with the Wind* arrived in Ceylon for a shoot of her new film *Elephant Walk*. The film loosely based on a novel by Robert Standish concerned a tea planter, John Wiley, who arrives with his bride to his mansion Elephant Walk so called because it is built across the traditional marching route of the elephants. The bride somewhat taken aback by the haunting presence of the 'Guvnor' Wiley's father is also alienated by her husband who spends the evenings with his drinking and scrounging cronies. Nonetheless she is about to elope with one of them when a group of marauding elephants make her bond with and reunite with him again. Ironically enough, the role of the alienated husband is played by Peter Finch with whom Vivien felt a growing attraction not the least for their common Eastern background.

Vivien had been born of a young English couple stationed in Calcutta in the early part of the 20th century and had grown up in the typical colonial home accompanying her parents to watch cricket matches at the

Bengal Club, the races and polo games at the Calcutta Turf Club and the soirees and theatrical events of the resident English gentry there. She even played little Bo Peep at the Ootacamund children's theatre where the three-year-old was dressed as a Dresden shepherdess, replete with sheep crook, flowered bonnet and rosettes on her shoes and skirt. She seemed to have shown an aptitude for acting even at this early stage. When she was barely a young girl of seven she was sent away to England to be educated in the proper English manner and she never returned to the place of her birth. According to one of her biographers Anne Edwards when she reached Ceylon:

> was part of the world that she had not been in since childhood, and it evoked many memories – blurred and only dimly recalled. She had not really known what to expect, and it was far more beautiful that she imagined. Everywhere there was an abundance of nature . . . The big sea stretched blue to the horizon, the tropical jungles were emerald green, and the seashore was palm-fringed. There was the ruins at Anuradhapura, the mountains and glaciers that rose above the jungles, the sense of witchery and legend.[16]

This ecstatic reunion however soon gave way to the heat and humidity of the island and with the sense of nothing tangible to hold on to led to the surfacing of an inner turmoil in her waning relationship with Laurence Olivier and her own mental illness that began to surface in an unmanageable manner. To shoot on the sets became increasingly difficult for her and 'It took an entire day and two huge but harmless snakes to film the sequence where the reptile was wound around Vivien's neck.'[17] In the midst of her busy schedule, however, she paid a visit to George Keyt and bought a painting as did Peter Finch. '. . . and then there was Peter Finch and Vivien Leigh who came twice and took some paintings and drawings though I'm wondering whether I should on second thoughts retain the paintings . . .'[18] George laid aside his customary cynicism and wrote about her in laudatory terms:

> I don't know whether you know Vivien Leigh but I think she's really nice – so different from that junglee mylee who wanted to be painted naked and by whom I was taken in at the start – so horribly American and with that kind of 'beauty' like in 'Esquire' you know. Vivien said she's telegraphing to her husband to come

out and that he must come and see my paintings here and meet me. I hear he's a good Shakespeare actor.[19]

Years later, after Vivien Leigh had passed away, Martin attempted to trace the paintings bought by her and Peter Finch. He even wrote to Shirley Luke, secretary to Lord Olivier, inviting Lord and Lady Olivier to the George's show in London and speaking about the paintings:

After Vivien Leigh died, one of her executors did approach me to ask if I would like to buy the paintings. I did not in fact buy them, so presumably they are still somewhere in England. If you can find out the name of the firm of solicitors who dealt with Vivien Leigh's affairs, they might be able to tell us who the executors were and we could follow the matter up from there.[20]

Martin to his regret could not manage to acquire the painting.

Around this time the British writer Evelyn Waugh who was having a nervous breakdown visited George along with the director of the Museum of Modern Art, New York, Monroe Wheeler. It was the celebrated French photographer Henri Cartier-Bresson who had sent Monroe to meet George. Henri and his Javanese wife Ratna Mohini who was a dancer as well were close friends of George and he waxes eloquent about them to Russell.

I'm glad you got such a nice letter from Ratna – She is Shakti, in some ways, and is certainly loved, honoured and submitted to by her lord who is gentlest and sweetest of all the talented and industrious bipeds in the three worlds and they are certainly true friends Manike's and mine so that you can rely on them – when they heard that Monroe Wheeler (of the Museum of Modern Art New York) was coming here they sent an 'embrace' and their love, so that although I didn't care for Monroe Wheeler and preferred Evelyn Waugh, who accompanied him to see me, I was nice to the polite snob.[21]

Elsewhere he wrote to Martin, 'I told Evelyn Waugh that the only English novelist I read was Walter Scott and waited for the guffaw – but Waugh was serious and remarked "He is very good".'[22]

The visit proved to be a raconteur's delight. Evelyn later wrote about it to his wife Laura:

> I ran into him (Monroe) in Colombo and we went off together for a few days looking at ruins and calling on a most eccentric local painter who lived in a very clean house with dozens of cheerful pictures by himself – half folk-art, half Picasso. He had nothing in the house and had to send out for three cigarettes and a box of matches.[23]

Martin mentions in his account of George:

> When Evelyn Waugh was having a nervous break-down in Ceylon part of which he describes in the Ordeal of Gilbert Pinfold, he called on Keyt in his house in Sirimalwatte, and gave an entertaining account in a letter to his wife. Keyt's oral descriptions of the meeting were hilarious, but have probably not been committed to paper. Waugh was not aware he was suffering from delusions or hallucinations; Keyt noticed nothing mad about Waugh, and they had a long and valuable conversation . . .[24]

Waugh's breakdown from which he was recovering in Sri Lanka had to do with hearing voices that mocked him. As he mentions:

> As I write this I hear the odious voices of the psychologist repeating every word in my ear. As they are in Aden and I am here it is a more remarkable feat than Tanker's box. It is most putting off. You must realize that this is the reason for the rather cold tone of this letter.[25]

Then again:

> But it is a huge relief to realize that I am merely the victim of the malice of others, not mad myself as I really feared for a few days. I must stay on at this island for a week or so and then will come back and no doubt I shall be able to find some rival telepathist who will teach me how to ward these people off . . .[26]

The voices continue to conspire against him, even enter and rejoin his thoughts so that clearly work becomes impossible for him. In his novel *The*

Ordeal of Gilbert Pinfold a middle-aged writer suffering from a disorder of the nerves is advised to go on a holiday and finds the only possible one for him, the S.S. *Caliban* sailing for Ceylon. The narrative of the journey proves to be one of conspiratorial looks, whispers and adversarial events. When he finally reaches Colombo tired and sweaty and wearing the wrong clothes, he feels no exhilaration on arrival. In the hotel he meets an acquaintance who is the New York collector for art galleries and they visit a ruin on the other side of the island. 'This seemed to exhaust the artistic resources of the island.' Clearly the trip was a dismal venture and amidst the rising crescendo of hostile voices he keeps hearing Mr. Pinfold returns home as he graphically describes in his novel *The Ordeal of Gilbert Pinfold.*[27]

Encounter with Pablo Neruda

But it was the Chilean poet Pablo Neruda who provided the most incisive insights into Keyt and his work. In a review of his exhibition held jointly with Beling at the Ferguson Memorial Hall in January 1930, he wrote:

> Keyt, I think, is the living nucleus of a great painter. In all his work there is the moderation of maturity, the beautiful stability of achievement – qualities most precious in so young an artist. Magically though he places his colours, and carefully though he distributes his plastic volumes, Keyt's pictures nevertheless produce a dramatic effect, particularly in his paintings of Sinhalese people. These figures take on a strange expressive grandeur, and radiate an aura of intensely profound feeling.[28]

The poet who served as the Consul for his country had arrived in Sri Lanka in 1928 to serve with the Chilean Embassy in Colombo until the early 1930s. He lived in complete solitude in a bungalow near the sea with only a dog, a mongoose and a boy who did his work and returned to the village at night. Alone as he was he noted, 'Yet I also recall it as the most luminous, as if a lightning flash of extraordinary brightness had stopped at my window to throw light on my destiny inside and out.'[29] This solitude was only interrupted by the pianist, photographer, critic and cinematographer Lionel Wendt, a close friend of George Keyt, the 'central figure of a cultural life torn between the death rattles of the Empire and a human appraisal of the untrapped values of Ceylon'.[30] Wendt would send every week all the latest books from England by a cyclist loaded with a sack of books. The most hilarious as well as heart-wrenching of his encounters during this period was with the toilet cleaner who carried the detritus in a pail on her head every morning from a hole at the back of the house. He saw that it was a dusky Tamil woman, the most beautiful he had seen in Ceylon. Neruda manages to waylay her and to sleep with her only to find that she was like a silent statue without any expression. It was, however, the most memorable of his encounters in the country and he writes in detail about it in his memoirs. He was to leave as Consul for Singapore and Batavia in 1930.

George used to meet Neruda often and remained friendly with him even after he left. Indeed in a somewhat speculative letter he even imagined that Pablo had come to India to make his way to Ceylon to meet him.

> Do you know that Pablo Neruda had written to Boyd [Andrew] that he was coming out to see me? That is why he went to India! He has a painting of mine the nude model who posed for which – I must have told you – attempted suicide (the Kandy lake) when she left me and met her husband on the way.[31]

It seems that in January 1930 in a joint exhibition with Beling hung in the hall of a Christian organization the presence of a nude painting by Keyt led to an objection by the organization. At this juncture, Neruda who was present exclaimed, 'That's all right. They can hang them outside!' Keyt presented the poet with a painting that he was to carry with him wherever he travelled.[32] Later in 1957 he was revisited by Neruda along with the great Brazilian writer Jorge Amado and his wife Zelia who stopped in Ceylon en route to China on a peace mission. The latter was apparently a great admirer of Keyt's paintings and asked that he autograph Martin Russell's book on him and said that he would write about him as soon as he returned to Brazil after his trip to Europe. Neruda, overcome with nostalgia, found that his house was dilapidated and worm eaten and was going to be torn down soon. He wrote,

> I found none of my old friends. And yet the island knocked on the door of my heart again with its sharp sound, with its immense scintillation of light. The sea was still humming the same old tune under the palms, over against the reefs . . .[33]

Wendt had died but he looked up George Keyt and asked for a copy of the early review he had done on him.

> Neruda was anxious to have a copy of the appreciation he wrote many years ago as he said it was the first of the sort he had ever

> written and his wife too was eager. They all were in ecstasies over my picture in the University library too, particularly Amado, but I had no way of giving him good reproductions as I haven't any, of all my work or most of it.[34]

He was having a stream of visitors, among whom 'an intimate and very lovely woman friend of Picasso's also came to see me and was very happy here, also Rolfide Mare' who has known Picasso from his early days of struggle – but the latter wanted "cubist" works, so was disappointed. Mrs. Hilda Young who came to Ceylon with Richard Rumbrld and who, especially the latter, got very friendly with me, wanted another picture of mine after she returned to London (to give Richard for his birthday as he came to admire me very much) was sent on to you by me . . .'[35] Sometime in the early 1950s he was visited by the Indian photographer Sunil Janah and he recorded this in a letter to Barbara Buchanan nee Smith with the laconic remark, 'I've been visited lately by two futile Indians called Sunil Janah and his wife whose name's too barbaric (!) for me to repeat . . .'[36] The most endearing of his visitors was Edward Fitzgerald who wrote to Martin about it many years later:

> If my memory serves me right I bought it [George Keyt painting] in 1968 during a visit to Ceylon on behalf of Oxford University Press whom I represented. I believe it was a bookseller in Colombo who suggested that I visit George Keyt, whom he described as Ceylon's equivalent of Picasso . . . I visited George Keyt at his home in the jungle, and spent the morning with him. He was in great form, a very striking looking man, with a fine head of grey hair, and who oozed great charm. . . . He took me to his picture gallery which was quite near his quarters. He gave me a personal explanation of each picture, and what inspired him in each particular case. I selected the one I liked best, which he painted in 1962. The title was, he explained as 'The Confidante' or as he emphasized 'The Go Betweens'. I paid the equivalent of about twenty five pounds in local currency. . . . Looking back it was quite an experience to meet and be entertained by the great man, whose quiet simplicity and charm left one with very pleasant memories of the occasion.[37]

In those isolated conditions but with his muse firmly in place, George was to carve a place for himself in modern art. But village life also represented a continuation of a sophisticated, ancient culture which had been lost in the cities and Keyt was quick to partake of this while drawing from the resourceful inventions of the 20th-century painters in Europe and elsewhere. As Russell put it succinctly:

> The affairs of the village regulated the conversation. But this conversation was not so regulated as some would suppose. The art was the great art of Kandyan dancing. The religion was the grand, humane, intellectual, inexhaustible Buddhist faith. The history was the continuous history of 186 kings recorded by Buddhist priests in Pali chronicles. Sinhalese poetry, almost dead in the towns, still flourishes in the country. . . . Although himself a sophisticated man, he did not see in the life of the peasantry something merely picturesque and primitive. He found instead a different sophistication, deeper and older than anything he had experienced among the English-speaking townsmen of Ceylon. . . . The seclusion of Hunang-oya was essential to the work. Nor was this seclusion either purely deliberate or quite accidental; it was part of the pattern of a remarkable life.[38]

Soon a major breakthrough would take place catapulting Keyt to the pinnacle of fame.

Notes

1 Martin Russell, 'Tribute to Pilawela Manike,' *Sunday Leader*, Colombo, February 9, 2000.
2 W.G. Archer, *India and Modern Art*, Allen and Unwin, London, 1959, p. 124.
3 Martin Russell, 'Obit of Manike,' *Sunday Leader*, Colombo, February 9, 2000.
4 Russell, op. cit.
5 H.A.I. Goonetileke, *George Keyt – A Life in Art*, The George Keyt Foundation, Colombo, Sri Lanka, 1989, p. 3.
6 Interview with Keyt by Ellen Dissanayake, *Journal of South Asian Literature*, Vol. 12, Nos. 1 and 2, Michigan, 1976.
7 Ananda K. Coomaraswamy, *Mediaeval Sinhalese Art*, Pantheon Books, New York, 1956, p. 169.
8 Interview with Ellen Dissanayake, *Journal of South Asian Literature*, Michigan, 1976, p. 133.
9 Dissanayake, Ibid., p. 133.
10 John Still, *Ancient Capitals of Ceylon*, H.W. Cave, Colombo, 1907.
11 Senake Bandaranayake, 'Sigiriya, City, Palace and Royal Gardens,' in *The Cultural Triangle*, UNESCO Publishing, Paris, 2006, p. 116.
12 Benjamin Rowland, *The Art and Architecture of India*, Penguin Books, Baltimore, MD, 1967.

13 Ibid.
14 Len Van Geyzel, *George Keyt*, Marg Publications, Volume 1, Bombay, India.
15 Letter to Geyzel, March 2, 1945.
16 Anne Edwards, *Vivien Leigh, A Biography*, Taylor Trade Publishing, Lanham, 1977.
17 Ibid.
18 Letter to Barbara from Sirimalwatta, undated.
19 Ibid.
20 Letter to Shirley Luke, London, September 4, 1982.
21 Letter to Martin, October 11, 1954.
22 Letter to Martin from Sirimalwatta, undated.
23 Evelyn Waugh in a letter to Laura Waugh, February 16, 1954.
24 Martin Russell, 'George Keyt Obituary,' *The Times*, London, August 19, 1993.
25 Evelyn Waugh in letter to Laura Waugh, op. cit.
26 Ibid.
27 Evelyn Waugh, *The Ordeal of Gilbert Pinfold*, Penguin Classics, London, 1957.
28 Martin Russell, *George Keyt*, Marg Publications, Bombay, 1950.
29 Pablo Neruda, *Memoirs*, Souvenir Press, London, 2011, p. 89.
30 Neruda, op. cit., p. 93.
31 Letter to Barbara from Sirimalwatta, Gunnepana, February 11, 1957.
32 Neville Weereratne, *43 Group, A Chronicle of Fifty Years in the Art of Sri Lanka*, Lantana Publishing, Australia, 1993, p. 112.
33 Neruda, op. cit., p. 229.
34 Letter to Martin Russell, September 14, 1957.
35 Ibid.
36 Letter to Barbara, Gunnepana date mentioned in Sinhalese.
37 Letter to Martin from Edward Fitzgerald, Kent, August 2, 1993.
38 Russell, op. cit., p. 52.

4

BUDDHISM AND SENSUALITY

Surrounded as he was with the revival of Buddhist practices particularly in Kandy, where the great Temple of Tooth is still the most important place of pilgrimage, George had even as a teenager been very influenced by the religion. He would visit the Malwatte monastery where, unlike in school, he was an attentive student and learnt both Sinhala and Buddhism. The typical objects of the monastery such as its brass vessels, palm fans and ola leaf manuscripts fascinated him and he would make them the earliest subjects of his still life studies. As he wrote to Len Van Geyzel:

> This isn't exactly the Braque style of line but resembles it superficially. Its evolved from certain line formulas suggested at the time I was trying to make sort of welded together compositions from objects like the vatahapatha (Buddhist) fan, alms-bowl etc . . . But I'm going to make another – bigger – of Buddhist objects more spread out and although actually connected by unbroken line less obviously so.[1]

George would also make paintings of the monks, in all their gravity and dignity, and this included a portrait of his friend, the venerable Pinnavela Dhirananda Thero. He was also to publish poems, stories, articles and drawings in W.E. Bastian's *The Buddhist Annual in Ceylon*, the main Buddhist publication in English. This was a period of a tremendous Buddhist revival and Keyt was drawn very much to it. He was often at Buddhist temples and moved around with the monks particularly at Malwatta Vihara, which was not far from his home. It was here that he met his mentor the Venerable Pinnawela Dheerananda but when he confessed to him a longing to join the Sangha he was dissuaded by the monk. Famously, when his father was returning home from a field trip attired in his safari jacket, puttees and pith helmet, his car was held up by a large crowd at the Kandy market listening raptly to a preacher. When he dismounted he discovered that the orator was his son George, clad in white costume and holding forth on Buddhist doctrine in English![2]

It was this bent of mind, which finally culminated in the making of the magnificent murals on the life of the Buddha at the Gotami Vihara in Borella situated on the outskirts of Colombo between 1939 and 1940. It was Keyt's brother-in-law Harold Pieris, whose great grandmother Lady Apolonia de Soysa had donated the land of the Vihara to the Buddhist sect in 1900, who secured him a commission to make the murals. Keyt's work there was interrupted by his visit to India in 1939 and on his return he lived at Gotami Vihara for six months as he worked on the walls of the temple, which had been created by the architect Andrew Boyd. He took no fees for this work but only his food and the cost of paint were paid for.

Larger than life

Keyt made no sketches or preparatory drawings for the murals at the Vihara but narrated the life of the Buddha in sweeping linear strokes of burnt sienna on the dry plaster. The panels are life sized, about 75 inches, and the murals on the outer surface of the inner wall of the circumambulatory delineating the scenes after enlightenment, i.e. Buddha's final visit to his birthplace Kapilvasthu, his first sermon and the final one of his death, are the largest. Lionel Wendt on seeing these encouraged Keyt to leave the original drawings as they were but at the request of Telwatte Amarawansa, the Viharadhipathi (head of the temple complex), he filled in the outlines by applying colour and then thickening the lines. As a tribute to his patron he then painted Amarawansa as a disciple at the feet of the Buddha which could be seen as an act of reverence.

These towering images which narrated the life of Buddha had moved away considerably from the traditional friezes at Kandyan temples and elsewhere in Ceylon. While these invited intimacy the ones in the temples were narrow friezes of less than one foot tall. The Jataka (stories of the historical Buddha's past lives) or the *solosmasthana* (images of sixteen Buddhist pilgrimage centres), the *sat-sati* (the seven weeks after the Buddha attains enlightenment) or the *suvisi-vivarana* (the account of the historical Buddha receiving the prophecy of his future Buddhahood from 24 Buddhas of the past), which are a necessity in the Kandyan period temple, were not included by Keyt in Borella. Degaldoruwa for instance, which was not far from Keyt's home when he was growing up, has a continuous narrative on the wall in which highly stylized figures operate on a flat plane which is bright red. Keyt's works, on the other hand, made a powerful sensory impact where the figures loom large in the foreground causing the red to recede into the background so that their engagements with the viewer become vital. He also uses green and white to balance the overwhelming reds, browns and yellows of the composition and blue marks of the water bodies, celestial orbs and draped folds of cloth. Grey and black are used for hair, garments and the alms bowl. The original line drawings remain dominant and it is believed that after he had filled it in with colour he had strengthened the lines. Yet unlike the density of the Kandyan wall paintings, here fewer coats of paint were applied and the overall effect remains modernist where the process of painting is emphasized. Keyt's work, however, was akin to the wall paintings in that he adopted an earthy palette and avoided using obviously artificial hues so that pinks and blues of his canvas paintings are not evident here.

It was in his use of space and the treatment of narrative that he differed considerably from the traditional mode. While relaying a method of continuous narration, these looming figures, unlike the ordered figures of Kandy temples, spill over from the frame. They are not punctuated by foliage buildings or objects as in the traditional friezes but connected by decorative patterns of drapery and floral designs that overflow from one scene to the next.

The Buddha unfolds

The sensual, sustained drama of Buddha's life which unfolded in this Vihara and is revealed to the unprepared visitor on entering the relatively simple structure could not be more powerful. Each episode from Maya's dream to the renunciation of his wife and child and the final sermon is a tableaux vivant which replaces the proscenium and curtains with a platform on which the persona of the drama unfold. The tableau while remaining complete with gesture and costume does not however freeze but collapses into the next dramatic moment seamlessly and effortlessly, thereby providing the effect of theatre and motion picture simultaneously. The notion of fixity in the moment and yet endless movement makes the moment as it were timeless while shifting and transforming. In mobilizing the fixity of the easel painting frame which would urge towards modernism, however, the dramatis personae also change their forms and it is this which will eventually become the hallmark of Keyt's contemporaneity and the pioneering effort he made for South Asian post-colonial identity.

In the final attack on Buddha by Mara, he is, unlike in the traditional forms, not shown in the *Bhumi sparsha* mode but in the *dhyani mudra* or the meditative mode. The scholar Sonal Khullar points out:

> Any of these iconographic details would have affirmed Keyt's allegiance to a Sinhalese textual and pictorial tradition and signaled the distinctiveness of Lankan Buddhism. The cumulative effect of these dislocating visual gestures is to point to a new national art that does not aspire to the preservation of a canon and reproduction of 'tradition' as it was construed by Coomaraswamy among others but rather to the 'freedom' stemming from sensual pleasure and embodied encounter. Keyt expects that his dynamic revisions of this religious event, unlike the 'fixed images' and 'frozen imagery' of the past will free the modern sensorium and open it up to the contingencies of an 'uncertain' 'changeable' postcolonial future.[3]

Underlying these developments is a third text – that of Buddhism itself – which with its orthodox Thervada practices which rigidly adhere to the structure would be opened out towards a new national modern. According to Sonal Khullar,

> The cycle of paintings on the newly whitewashed, blank walls of Gotami Vihara come to anxiously transact what it means for the citizen-self to be modern (and national), for the nation to modernize (even secularize) and for its art to be modernist (and nationalist). At the same time, Keyt's humanized and secularized depiction of the life of the Buddha expands the nationalist and traditionalist claims of his project towards the global modern. Thus the Gotami murals aspire to a double location in the nascent national (Buddhist) polity and in the sphere of global (secular) modernity.[4]

We must note that Keyt had in his growing years witnessed the tide of politics turning in favour of Buddhist nationalism during and after the First World War. Even earlier, the British had under the Kandyan convention of 1815 pledged to protect Buddhism following which the Buddhist Sangha continued to enjoy a great deal of prestige and power. By the beginning of the 20th century the Buddhists attacked the colonial system with increasing vigour and this was subsequently given impetus by the manner in which the British forces put down the riots of 1916. The agitation gained further momentum by this and universal adult franchise was granted, the earliest in the subcontinent, to Ceylon in 1931 and the administration of the island passed into the hands of the predominantly Ceylonese and Buddhist group. Keyt therefore grew up at a time when 15 years of agitation were beginning to bear fruit and was naturally drawn to the Buddhist faith and for five or six years of his life closely drawn to Buddhist activities. His syncretic vision however was open to secular and humanistic expansions and drew from all religions. In any case, he was born a Christian, aspired towards becoming a Buddhist monk and considered himself a Hindu in his predilections. In later years it is believed that George converted to Islam in order to marry his last wife Kusum.

Towards a secular form

The significant changes made in the depiction of Buddha's eventful life by Keyt would make a departure from the stylized traditional depictions in the temples and monasteries that existed in Ceylon. Degaldoruwa for instance has the narrative style in boustrophedon sequence within narrow friezes and is highly stylized inviting ritual obeisance. Unlike the panels Keyt's figures are not read like a scroll or viewed as a visual liturgy as in the traditional narrative.

There are many ways by which the viewer is drawn into a relationship with Buddha's narrative. In Keyt's delineation the figures are naturalistically shown and reflect the forms and features of the local population. Buddha himself is not seen as a being apart but as someone who is part of the general legion and there is no auratic circle separating him from others. In his first sermon his direct frontal gaze makes the viewer feel that he is being personally addressed. In the scene of Buddha's birth the viewer is given an insider's point of view where full visual access is given to the queen's figure unlike the archaic images where the event is concealed by the curtain. The infant Buddha is cradled in the lap of a male figure and the intimate tactile quality of this is echoed in the physical, loving relationship between Prince Siddhartha and Yashodhara in their marriage scene and subsequent acts of intimacy. As Khullar points out,

> The relatively small space of the temple and the large, brimming images on its walls (with the viewer's body comparable to the size of the figures in the narrative and thereby spatially implicated in

it) generate an experience that is more somatic and interactive than that offered by older Kandyan painting.[5]

Indeed the gods are barely distinguishable from humans and the humanizing of gods extends to devices like the deliberate curve of Queen Mahamaya's buttocks or Prince Siddhartha's rolls of baby fat in his birth scene. Khullar observes,

> In contrast to the relatively rigid or fixed figures of Kandyan friezes, Keyt's smooth lines and curvilinear forms produce a fluid rhythm to the panels that suggests movement and spontaneity. Fleshy, curvy bodies, which flow into each other with no sharp

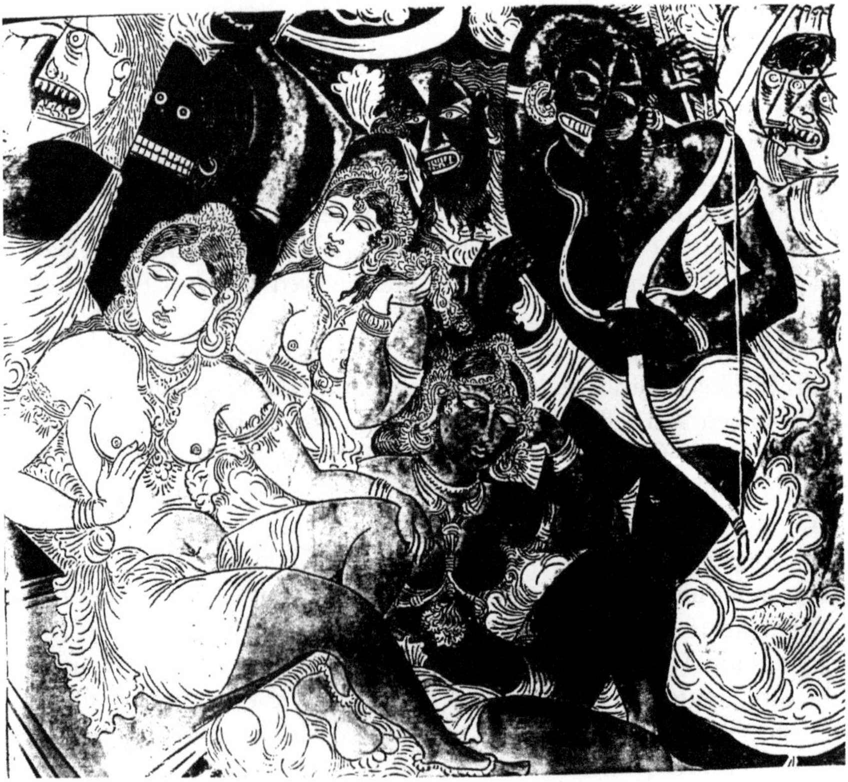

Figure 4.1 Defeat of Mara and his daughters.

George Keyt.
Gotami Vihara mural.
Courtesy: Martin Russell Archive.

> edges or objects to impede their languorous rhythm, dominate the field of vision conveying a deep sensuality to these images.[6]

In many ways Keyt considered himself rooted in tradition but segued it with contemporaneity. As he stated, 'I have (naturally) always been Asiatic: what someone called "spiritual voluptuousness".'[7] He was considerably influenced by the thinker and aesthete Ananda K. Coomaraswamy who had written extensively on the artistic traditions of Ceylon, particularly in his path-breaking tome, *Mediaeval Sinhalese Art*, written in 1908 and considered a classic to this day. If Coomaraswamy's vision was seen as idealized and non-historical it carried within it germs of sound knowledge and vitality about cultures which he saw disappearing before his eyes. According to the art historian Senake Bandaranayake,

> Of course, Coomaraswamy was not unaware of some of the oppressive aspects of Asian or European feudalism, but he nevertheless upheld that social system vis-à-vis the conditions prevailing in industrial-capitalist society. In his strong opposition to the latter he argued away any misgivings he might have had about the former. . . . Pursuing his idealist notions about traditional societies, he scarcely follows up the brief insights into feudal oppression . . .[8]

Yet, despite this his development and refinement of traditional Sri Lankan and Indian art and culture are incontestable and it was this which greatly influenced George Keyt. He also had valuable insights into the possibilities of developing arts and crafts for the future. As Bandaranayake points out,

> Coomaraswamy made an important contribution to the national struggles of this region when – at the height of colonial rule and hegemony – he helped the people of South Asia to appreciate the vitality and importance of their traditional cultures and historical civilizations. He carried the technical and scientific level of these studies to a standard comparable with that achieved anywhere else. He put forward the important view that the art and culture of the past could be meaningfully transmitted and interpreted to serve the needs of the present, even though – partly due to his misinterpretation of the relationship between traditional culture and society – this aspect of his work has received scant consideration.[9]

About the guild system which produced art in traditional societies, for instance, Coomaraswamy stated,

> The community cannot afford to dispense with the intellectual and imaginative forces, the educational and ethical factors which go with the existence of skilled craftsmen and small workshops. It must, therefore, protect these in their proper sphere. This can be done only by restoring the entire control of production to the actual workers, as in the old guild systems; or by the endowment of craftsmanship as in Ceylon, in the feudal manner, but substituting for the king or overlord the democratic community as patron.[10]

In Keyt's works the traditional elements are never absent but carried forward as with his Borella murals.

Mara's tale

It is when Mara and his army confront Buddha in the final stage that we find the disruptions in these works reach their climax. Unlike the conventional depictions of Mara with multiple arms seated on his mount, the elephant Girimekhala, there is no identifiable Mara figure and the vast army is simplified in Keyt's murals to ten demonic figures.

As Khullar points out, 'While it is difficult to visually correlate Keyt's demons with specific sins, the simplified composition, formal abstraction and individuated physical characteristics of the figure indicates a doctrinal shift towards the modern account of the narrative.'[11]

Interestingly in the Borella murals good and evil are not separated from each other and the attack of Mara and his group is in intimate contact with the Buddha. Unlike the paintings at Dambulla, Degaludorwa and other temples where the evil god Mara and his entourage are separated from Buddha, here they even touch the godly figure. Good and evil are hence seen as intertwined and intermixed much in the manner of the dramatic delineation of Mahisha and the goddess in the paintings of the Indian modernist artist Tyeb Mehta. Indeed the depiction of evil shadows Buddha's life journey at many points much as it forms a concurrent layer of existence where good is always shadowed by evil. Hence it becomes a factor to contend with at all points and at each juncture good in the form of Buddha triumphs over it and continues his journey. The extreme calm on his face when encountered by the evil Mara in various situations of his life is to point to the direction in which violence could be overtaken and transcended.

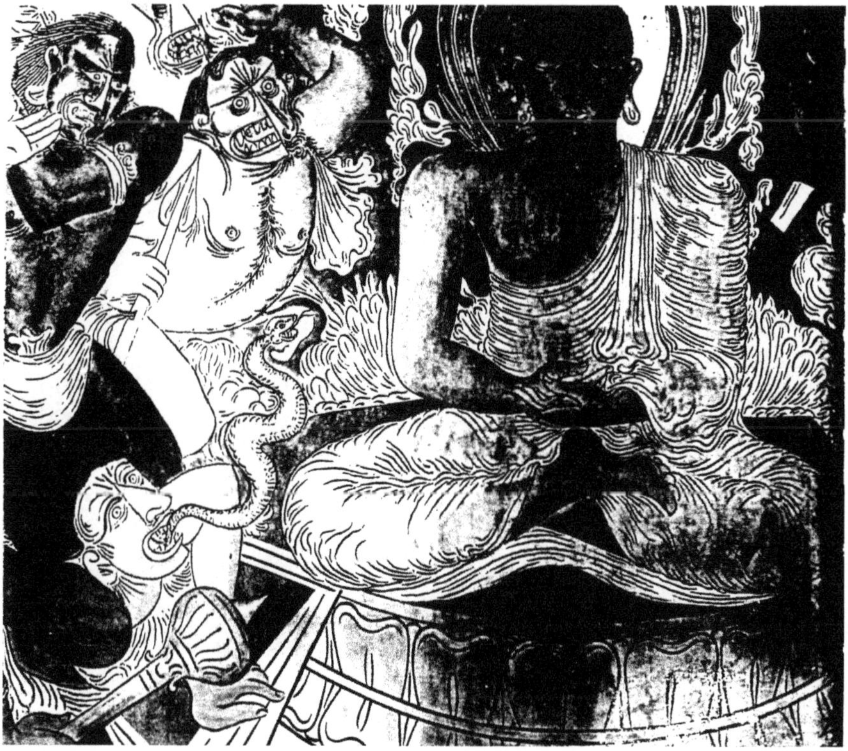

Figure 4.2 Mara's demonic army surrounding the Buddha.

George Keyt.
Gotami Vihara mural.
Courtesy: Martin Russell Archive.

Many similarities can be drawn in his depiction of Mara and the armies and the works by Picasso like the *Dreams and Lies of Franco* that led to his masterly *Guernica.* In the dislocations of Mara's devilish visage and the deployment of wild hair, fuming, frothing mouths with a serpent emanating from one of them and glaring eyes he is recalling the suite of paintings which were created by Picasso during the time of the Spanish Civil War. These sinister forms surrounding the serene Buddha are about the same size as him and highlight the proximity of evil. Yet the demons are differentiated by the sharp, angular edges of their faces, which disintegrate as one moves from the left to the right of the frame. The ones closest to the Buddha assume more abstracted, cubist forms than some of the others that have human torsos and legs and the splitting and doubling of the

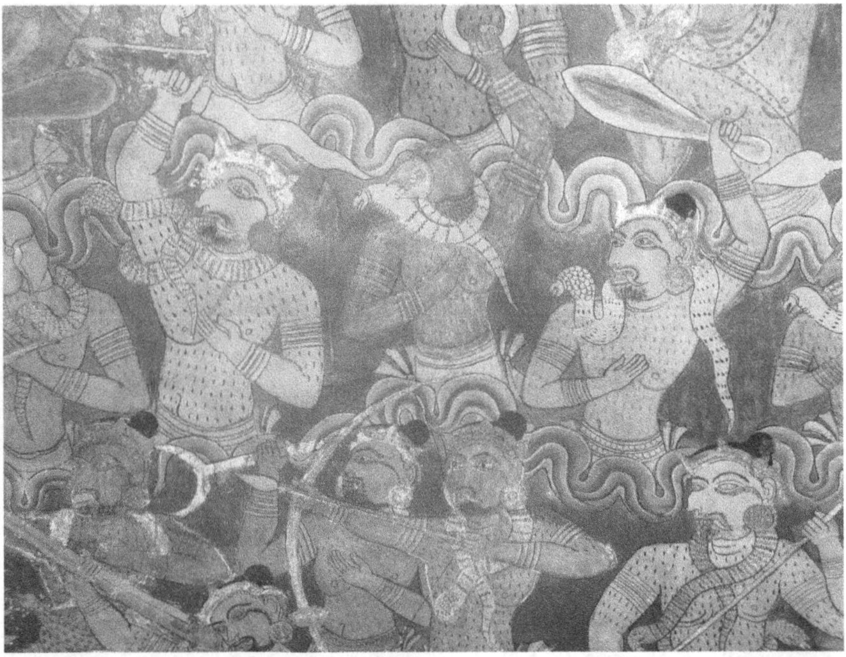

Figure 4.3 Forces of Mara.

Dambulla Caves.
Courtesy: Maseeh Rahman.

figure suggest a duality and an internal struggle between good and evil within the same form.

These depictions of Mara draw from Picasso's depiction of evil in his suite of etchings made in January 1937, four months before he began sketching for the *Guernica*. In converting humans into polyp-like monsters Picasso vividly depicted Franco living a lie rather than the truth, following a dream rather than life. He is caricatured in various forms representing manifestations of evil and evoking undiluted disgust. In one powerful work, Franco is shown as an arrogant *maja* wearing a mantilla and comb and carrying a fan embellished with an image of the Virgin in one hand and a sword in the other! In these powerful images Picasso provokes horror and revulsion for evil which was spreading its destructive energy. The Goan artist F.N. Souza expressed his postwar angst based in London in works like *Six Gentlemen of Our Times* (1955) where the grotesques faces had gnashing mouths and soulless eyes placed on the forehead revealing the petrification of violence. The nexus between the well-heeled and the powerful is forcefully bought out in these works which express his disillusionment with humanity. George Keyt on the other hand experimented with structures as he shifted the fuming armies of Mara into close-ups and full tubular forms.

Keyt had witnessed the struggle against colonial rule during his visit to India in 1939 and was aware of the ravages of the raging Second World War. These had provoked from him a series of powerful works drawing from the Mahabharat, the Indian epic poem about civil and cosmic war. This was a period when he made works like *Draupadi* (1938), *Yama and Savitri* (1938) and *Bhima and Jarasandha* (1943). The Mara scenes at Borella emerged from his personal and political turmoil of this period expressing a mood of conflict and angst about the emergence of evil.

The finale of the murals is also a definitive move towards modernist images that seek to align with the present. The three daughters of Mara are supposed to tempt him in the seven weeks after he attains enlightenment and these are influenced by the maidens drawn obviously from the Sigiriya style. The fact that these are juxtaposed against the Cubist images of Mara's army concludes the whole gamut of the national which emerges in these works.

> The murals performance of nationhood emerges most clearly in this last panel where Keyt makes visual allusions to the Lankan past and to the European present so that the classical Sigiriya maidens assume the form of the daughters of Mara and Picasso's beasts of war assume the form of the armies of Mara.[12]

With its oscillations from the past the narrative now acquires a dramatic shift towards modernity and by amplification with an emergent national identity.

The strong woman

Interestingly, Yashodhara is not the fair-skinned damsel who is deemed queen and with whom Gotama consorts. This would reflect Keyt's own predilections towards the dark-skinned Manike, his personal muse with whom he had entered into a passionate relationship and would soon set up home. But it also reflected the move away from the fair-skinned, white woman towards a dark skin type which would be emblematic of the modernity of South Asia.

The consort of Buddha becomes the role model for a darker hued non-Western figure who would signal a break from the Western form of fair-skinned portraiture. She is always shown frontally and the full stretch of her form is carefully delineated to signal the move towards the 'other', the alternative, the alluring but also powerful symbol of womanhood. She is non-fair, non-Western, fully frontal and non-seductive but her allure lies in her significant presence. In the move towards an alternative modernity Keyt is also asserting the woman in the fullness of her personality. For the iconic Indo-Hungarian artist Amrita Sher-Gil the early signs of wanting to be a part of the 'other' were visible in many ways in her work of the mid-1930s where Gaugin became the signpost to move towards a sensuous, darker hued, non-Western figure. In her self-portrait made around this time, *Self Portrait* (1932), she as a woman in gay abandon who with her brazen smile also questions the conventional portrait of the woman. In its nascent stage these early signs of moving away from the conventional depiction of the figure is marked by the smile which could be read as a critique of the coy feminine figure she had learnt to depict as part of her training. Significantly enough around this time, in her Hungarian visit from Paris, Amrita had made the *Gypsy Girl from Zebegeny* (1932) where we see an earthy woman in red and black surrounded by the greens around her in abandon and free of conventional ties. Keyt not unaware of Gaugin's work also moves in the same direction albeit his own predilections. It was this multi-layered move by George Keyt which makes this a significant moment in his work and the art of the island. In the binaries that emerged in these murals he would tilt towards an emergent modernism in art as well as nod to tradition, to tableaux and free flowing, mimetic and modernist and fair and dark figures. In these uneasy combinations which yet made a composite narrative, we have the triumphant moment which would henceforth beckon modernity and internationalism.

If all this was to fructify in the form of the dark, sensuous figure of Yashodhara it was also a merging of identities which became analogous with the Tamil goddess Kannagi known as the Buddhist goddess Pattini worshipped by both communities to this day. In this shared heritage which is common to both Tamils and Buddhists in Sri Lanka we have one of the many syncretic practices which are prevalent in Sri Lanka. Pattini-Kannagi, the fearless protagonist of the South Indian Tamil epic Silappadikaram, is the strong woman who remains chaste and loyal to Kovalan, despite his unfaithfulness and betrayal. But she is also the woman who can vent fury when outraged by her widowhood and tears out her left breast and sets alight an entire city in her determination to redress injustice. Pattini is the only female deity who is accorded a place of honour within the Sinhala Buddhist (Thervada) pantheon. She is considered one of the four guardian deities of Sri Lanka, a protector of Buddhism, and a Bodhisattva aspiring to attain enlightenment. It was this synoptic vision which crossed boundaries in the Borella murals and was the face of modernism the country was struggling towards post-Independence.

There were many thresholds that Keyt crossed in the Borella works which left the conventional pilgrim puzzled and somewhat disconcerted. The very immediacy and immersion in the paintings was overwhelming for the viewer/worshipper.

With the dark-skinned wife of Buddha he was also epistemic and hence emblematic of the 'other'. It may be noted that Yashodhara remains a shadowy figure in Buddhist texts who but reveals herself at the time of marriage, on the birth of their son Rahul and also when Buddha returns to Kapilvastu, and she urges her son to claim his inheritance and hence join the Buddhist sect. According to the pioneering scholar of Pali and Buddhist studies Dharmanand Kosambi (1876–1947) whose son D.D. Kosambi is well known as an eminent historian, Yashodhara according to the Buddhist text *Lalita – vistara* mentions that she was a strong woman with a mind of her own. It mentions that she did not cover her head with the end of the sari when she went to her martial home, which invited criticism, and that she made a strong reply to this rebuke. She spoke boldly when she married Prince Siddharth and said that she would be his life companion through bad and good times.

It becomes evident also in Keyt's mural that Yashodhara though of lissome figure is fully clothed as against Maya the mother. Her gravity and dignity are unmatched in *Bodhisattva: A Play* written in 1945.[13] There are no passionate depictions here of the god with his consort so agilely shown in Tibetan thangkas. The iconographic depiction where the god image and the goddess, the male and female body, inextricably wound together in an erotic posture leading to a vortex of emanating energy is abstained from here. The erotic charge of the goddess, in fact, associated with Tibetan Buddhism could be read here as the woman with unbounding intellectual and sensual powers.

Keyt's liberal Buddhism here signalled the birth of a nation and its formative identity. And what indeed was Buddha walking away from when he renounced his wife and child? The tableaux in the Borella murals where he leaves his family is the most moving of all. It shows him not looking at his wife and child – the child that had just been born. The historical Buddha is little known and there have been only a few accounts, but in the narrativized Buddha writers like Vilas Sarang paint a very poignant moment.

> To take his leave! No, he could not take leave of his dear wife, of his loving parents – no, no, cross that *dear*, cross that *loving* – just wife, parents, of his servants – and of the little one that had come into his world just that day, his son – a son . . . a son . . . his son . . .
>
> Was there a flutter in his heart? No, it was an illusion. Like everything else. . . . And he had not seen his son yet! What was his son? What was his face like? . . .
>
> Siddharth walked into the room silently. He had no intention of waking his wife. All he wanted to do was to have a look at his son. The first look – and the last one.
>
> He stood by the bedside. A breeze was blowing from the window beside Bimba's bed. Just at that moment, the oil lamp beside the bed was extinguished by a sudden gust. There was still light enough to have a dim look at things but Siddharth saw that Bimba had held her hand protectively over her child's head, and it was impossible for Siddharth to see his son.
>
> It might take a long while before Bimba moved her hand. Siddharth could not wait that long.
>
> He turned back. Disappointed? Let down? No, no. More like stone.[14]

And he rides away on his favourite horse Kanthak into the vast unknown.

And that poignant moment is resonated in Keyt's mural at Borella. Keyt's Buddhism was an experiment with modernity, sensuous, desirable, open-ended and forever in the process of transformation. But to arrive at that liminal state the past with all its secure anchors and its rooted reality had to be given up.

All the more creditable then that Keyt's singularly visionary approach on the secularization of Buddhism in the island remained a testimony to his humanistic leanings despite the growing imperialistic spread. When he first did the works, its overflowing sensuous mode made the monks worry that there wouldn't be *dana* from the donors. But today it is probably the second most visited monument after the Sigiriya caves and remains a famous iconic site.

Notes

1 Letter to Geyzel, October 10, 1933.
2 Tissa Devandra, *The Lives of Keyt*, Observer Pictorial, Sri Lanka, 1991, p. 19.
3 Sonal Khullar, Department of Art History, Berkeley University, 'The Life of the Buddha and the art of the nation: postcolonial modernity in George Keyt's Life of the Buddha at Gotami Vihara,' 2004, pp. 32–33.
4 Ibid., p. 4.
5 Ibid., p. 25.
6 Ibid., p. 26.
7 Letter to Geyzel, November 30, 1933.
8 Senake Bandaranayake, *Ananda Coomaraswamy and Approaches to the Study of Traditional Sri Lankan Art and Society*, Paroksa, Coomaraswamy Centenary Seminar Papers, Lalit Kala Akademi, New Delhi, 1984, p. 33.
9 Ibid., p. 35.
10 Ananda K. Coomaraswamy, *Mediaeval Sinhalese Art*, Pantheon Books, New York, 1956, p. viii.
11 Khullar, op. cit., p. 32.
12 Ibid., p. 30.
13 Meera Kosambi (Ed), *Dharmanand Kosambi. The Essential Writings*, Permanent Black, New Delhi, 2010, pp. 358–408.
14 Vilas Sarang, *The Dhamma Man*, Penguin Books, 2011, pp. 71–73.

5

THE '43 GROUP AND MODERNISM UNFOLDS

George retreated to his forest residence after completing the Borella murals. It was here that he composed some of his most vivid and sensuous paintings. In many ways we can see in the bold delineation, the distortion of form and the bisection and dissection of faces the influence of Picasso. Keyt had seen and read a great deal of Western art by this time and also through Wendt had seen issues of Cahier d'Art. His understanding of Picasso can be assessed from portions of his letters to friends. As he writes,

> So funny the application of Cubism to architecture! As Picasso said, as if Michelangelo should be invited to dinner by some admirer and shown a renascence sideboard suggested by his statue of Moses. But of course it doesn't follow that to be influenced by certain kinds of pictures and sculpture is to produce vulgarized versions of the genuine thing. . . . If the creative talent is there no vulgarization will result. See Raphael and Braque. Most of Braque is almost identical with Picasso, who influenced him so much. But yet no vulgarization. Juan Gris I know nothing of and I didn't like the only thing I saw of his – reproduced in Gertrude Stein's book.[1]

The distortions of form, the dissection of space and even the compositions could be considered influenced by Picasso but equally it was subsumed by his own sensibility. Added to this was an innate ability not just for draughtsmanship but also a deep and grave understanding of the depth and grandeur of his own tradition.

As he moved to its village not far away and lived and painted there in the splendour of isolation George was to draw upon the dignity and civilization of the people which was embedded in their own culture. He etched the figures in darkness and made them luminous. Their early eloquence and sensual presence matched only their articulation as formal entities.

Many of his works evoked the sublime love of the god Krishna with the cowherdess Radha. Indeed in 1940 he collaborated with Harold Pieris, his brother-in-law, and a Sanskrit scholar from Oxford, on the translation of the Hindu love epic, *Gita Govinda* written by Jayadeva in Bengal in the 12th century. The drawings which accompanied these verses spoke of the ecstatic godliness of love, its unbearable lyrical grace and of its sublime fulfilment.

In his earlier works such as *Sri Krishna and the Gopis* (1936) we have the blue god in his yellow robe dancing with women of different hues and expressions, merging and separating from them in a whirl of movement. As Martin Russell pointed out, the experimentation with division of forms began much earlier with works such as *Two Women* (1933). According to him:

> In Sri Krishna and the Gopis we see an important application of the scheme which first appears . . . in the picture *Two Women* for representing two heads as one or one head as two, by merging the full-face and profile aspects. Keyt has used this scheme – one might almost say he has established a convention for using this scheme – to depict the tantric relationship of Radha and Krishna (the female counterpart of God being an aspect of God) . . . In India the idea is vastly older. The *Ardhanarisvara, Siva and Parvati* represented as one person, is found in very early Mathura sculpture.[2]

Despite his isolation in the village his work had attracted attention and exhibitions held. In 1936 his paintings along with that of Justin Daraniyagala had been held at the Colombo Art Gallery where each artist had contributed 45 paintings and Keyt had sold eleven. Geoff Beling had already shown thrice with Keyt and reviewed it for *Ceylon Daily News*,

> Various are the influences in his paintings – Sinhalese, Tamil, Indian, Sittara, modern. Various are the feelings aroused. Through abstract form, decorative form, and representational form the pictures range; but it is the strong, bold sense of rhythm and design that unifies them, and is the key to their understanding.[3]

The '43 Group forms

In viewing the burgeoning forms in George's work, it was Lionel Wendt who drew him out for the formation of the '43 Group in Colombo. In essence it was George's friendship and support from Lionel which was to provide the main impetus for his growth in these early years. Wendt (1900–1944) of Sri Lankan and Dutch descent had tried his hand at painting but had found photography to be his medium instead. In many of his photographs of local life such as the fishermen or his domestic help not only did he use modernist techniques, such as photo montage, solarization, and copper toning, but his works also challenged the colonialist's gaze of the 'native', reclaimed through his reconfiguration of his people. He came from a privileged family, and had travelled to England at the age of 19 to become a lawyer and receive training as a concert pianist. When Wendt returned to Sri Lanka in 1924 he took up photography and in 1930 organized a landmark photo exhibition. Five years later he co-founded the Photographic Society of Ceylon. Wendt was, however, a man of many talents and apart from excelling in photography, he was a brilliant pianist and an aesthete who gathered around him people of diverse skills from dancers and writers to musicians and painters. Lionel's soirees at his home at Guildford Crescent in Colombo were well known.

In the authoritative work on him, *Lionel Wendt's Ceylon*, the introduction to which was written by L.C. Van Geyzel with a technical note by Bernard G. Thornley, the quintessential Wendt appears to be a man of considerable inner means,

> Lionel Wendt's capacity for work was endless. It came from some inexhaustible source of energy that seemed to inform his whole personality, and which, alas made him ignore the symptoms of the disease which finally proved fatal because he knew that doctors would have ordered him to bed. It was not unusual to come upon him in some crowded place squinting into a view-finder, wide brimmed hat thrust back, glasses pushed up on a profoundly sweating forehead and having to be constantly wiped – somehow a characteristic gesture – quite unmindful of curious passers-by. In his studio he was inaccessible. It must not be assumed however that he worked in isolation. He was, in fact, largely responsible for organizing groups devoted to music, painting and photography which have gone on doing good work, and although he was indifferent to his own reputation he was quick to defend other artists.

> One recalls with delight many such explosive attacks which must have caused incautious critics considerable discomfiture.[4]

One of Lionel's main concerns was to break the caste barrier where the lower castes were looked down upon. According to Lionel Peiris, George Keyt's nephew,

> Wendt supported local dance, especially Kandyan dance and helped to preserve and develop it. . . . The ruling class looked down upon dancers because they were of a low caste. One of them spoke disparagingly to Surumba [brilliant Kandyan dancer] Wendt slapped him and said 'How dare you. This man is far superior. Apologise at once![5]

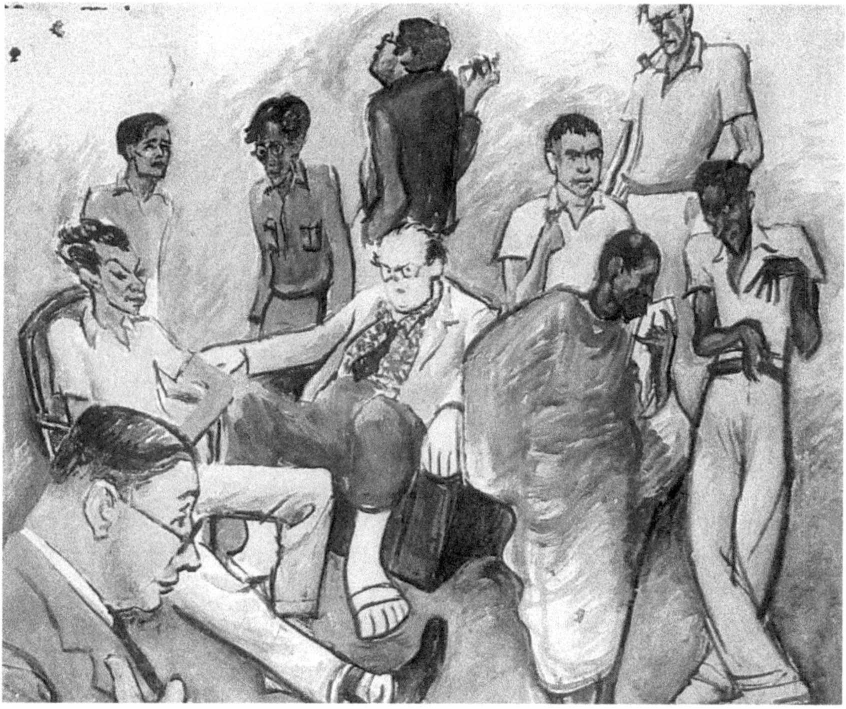

Figure 5.1 The '43 Group.

G. Beling.
Oil on canvas.
Courtesy: Martin Russell Archives.

In 1952 in the Souvenir catalogue of the International Exhibition of Paintings, Van Geyzel wrote a piece titled 'Contemporary Painting in Ceylon'. In it he notes that:

> It was Winzer who introduced the first exhibition by George Keyt and Geoffrey Beling which Lionel Wendt had organized and which Pablo Neruda the famous Chilean poet who was at that time Chilean Consul, hailed in the press as an event of real importance. After Winzer went away it was Lionel Wendt who was the chief impresario of vital movements in painting, and it was he who was largely responsible for founding the '43 Group in the war years.[6]

By 1943 Keyt's work was ripe for a more public exposure. And perhaps this was true of other artists as well, so if the '43 Group had not been formed it would have had to be invented. According to the art writer and artist Nevile Weeraratne:

> It blossomed as though it had to be – its growth till that moment had been somewhat invisible. But minds were at work in men and women everywhere – but let me confine myself to the art world of that time, where an intellectual resurgence had already begun but had as yet no legitimate expression. Justin Daraniyagala, Harry Pieris, George Keyt and Geoff Beling (themselves important artists and a source of inspiration and encouragement), Lionel Wendt, Arthur van Langenberg, Harry Wendt, Harold Pieris, Mrs. Forbes, Lyn Ludowyk and many more were intellectually alive.[7]

Cultural climate

The vibrant cultural atmosphere of the period which supported the '43 Group was evident in the activities of people like Saratchandra and Irangini, Lester Peries, C.F.C. Ludowyk and Len Van Geyzel, to name a few.

Evelyn Frederick Charles Ludowyk (1906–85) is considered a 'cult figure in English studies' as at the age of thirty, he was the first Sri Lankan to be appointed to the position of Professor of English at the Ceylon University College (later the University of Ceylon), the only university in the island at the time. Acclaimed both in Sri Lanka, for being an inspiring teacher and producer of plays, and abroad as a scholar of Shakespeare studies (his book *Understanding Shakespeare* along with his editions of six plays was published by the Cambridge University Press) he was a historian as well, for his authorship of *The Story of Ceylon* and his *Modern History of Ceylon*.

Ludowyk's name was widely associated with English Theatre, which was as important as his teaching of English. It was he who introduced the works of Euripides, Moliere, S.L. Hsiung, Shudraka, Shakespeare, Brecht, Pirandello and Eugene O'Neil to Sri Lankan audiences. He also had a brief but significant connection with Sinhala theatre, and his production of Gogol's *Marriage* in Sinhala was an important landmark in the development of the Sinhala theatre.

In 1956 Lyn Ludowyk left Sri Lanka for England but his deep concern for Sri Lanka and his students never flagged and he kept in touch with many of them even after he settled in Suffolk.

And then there is Irangani Serasinghe (1927–), the legendary stage, screen and television actress. Since her debut in *Rekava*, Serasinghe (nee Meedeniya) has become recognized for playing heroic figures in various films and television serials. Irangini entered the University of Ceylon in 1947 and immersed herself in the Ceylon theatre scene while there under the guidance of Professor Ludowyk and also became a proficient dancer with lessons from Chitrasena. Irangini first hit the stage in Prof. Cuthbert Amarasinghe's production of *The Second Mrs. Tanqueray* in 1948.

A disturbing incident occurred when she was performing in another production. It seems that she was acting in a play about a man who had very high ideals in the university. But when he became a politician he began compromising on those ideals against the advice of his wife. He met a soothsayer who said that the 'light would go out' on September 26th and strangely enough he gets shot on that day. According to Irangani,

> Fate had it that Dr. S.W.D.R. Bandarnaike was killed on 26th of September ! [1959] It was such a shattering shock to us. . . . The play was shown purely for entertainment and after hearing this line we had the CID on us! They were wondering how we knew this would really happen on the 26th of September! Poor Christine [Spittle] has just chosen a date that came to her mind. We were questioned by the CID and later released. The Burghers of this country were treated like aliens at one time. They were made to feel so bad that they had, in fact, to leave the country. But when you think back they have given so much to this country.[8]

Lester James Peries, the legendary film-maker, cast her in his debut feature film *Rekava* as the mother of its protagonist. The film has since achieved an iconic status in Sri Lanka. In 1960 she married Winston Serasinghe who had appeared in *Rekava* and some other productions with her. Since then, Irangani Serasinghe achieved fame as an actress appearing in many of Peries's early works. Then followed the little screen which made her a household name in Sri Lanka both widely respected and much loved.

Something of a rebel Irangani recalls that in her college days she would do things that good Sinhala girls were not supposed to.

> All the girls used to wince and were terribly shy to pass the canteen because of the comments and whistles from the boys. We didn't care two hoots and just to show off we even started smoking in front of them. I really disliked cigarettes but we did all the things that we were not supposed to do. We rode bicycles when good Sinhala girls were not supposed to ride . . .[9]

Irangani is also known as an indefatigable environmentalist and the founder of the 'Rek Rekaganno', the voluntary service organization which takes the message of conservation and the importance of nature to grass roots in Sri Lanka.

Ediriweera Sarachchandra's (1914–96) contribution to theatre in Sri Lanka, and his single-handed creation of modern Sinhala drama, made him 'a legend in his own lifetime'. Referred to as the *Renaissance Man* of 20th-century Sri Lanka, he was born to a family with mixed religious beliefs where his mother was Christian and his father Buddhist. Through his mother's family he was exposed to Western music, the English language and even played the organ in his local church. In 1939 he married his first wife Aileen Beleth and went to Santiniketan with her where he studied music and Indian philosophy.

Having being influenced by Indian cultural nationalism he discarded his Westernized name and adopted a new name after the famed Bengali novelist Sarat Chandra Chatterjee. After he finished his studies at Santiniketan he went on to do a master's at the University of London in Western Philosophy and by 1949 had earned a PhD from the same university for his thesis 'The Buddhist Psychology of Perception'. In 1944 Sarachchandra took up an appointment as a lecturer in Pali at the University of Ceylon and once again in 1952. That same year he published 'The Folk Drama of Ceylon', a seminal work on the subject of indigenous drama.

As a teacher and scholar Sarachchandra made a huge impact in literary criticism and critical thinking. However, in the field of drama he gave 'explosive new direction' to 'Sinhala theatre' and his creative career was at its peak with his production of *Maname* (1956) and *Sinhabahu* (1962). Ediriweera Sarachchandra pioneered an indigenous theatre tradition which gave birth to a form of 'Stylized Theatre' adopted as the *modern indigenous theatre* of Ceylon. The period 1933–54 was a time during which Sri Lankan theatre-goers were in need of an 'intellectual theatre'. The prevalent theatre traditions in Ceylon failed to attract the English-educated bourgeoisie and Sarachchandra's frustration with the theatre productions of the University College led him to develop a study of folk drama in Sri Lanka. He was influenced by a variety of folk theatre devices as well as the folk drama of India, Japan, China and Ceylon when creating his stylized method of drama. He also carried out research in remote villages, where the folk theatre was a lively activity.

Sarachchandra produced his first stylist play *Maname* in 1956 to widespread acclaim. *Maname* is generally considered the first real Sinhala drama, signalling the transition from the *Nadagam* or folk drama to the modern theatrical drama format. It was praised especially for drawing influence from the traditional *nadagam* play style. He continued as a playwright, developing his play *Sinhabahu* in 1961, which is widely considered his best work. Most of his plays were adaptations from Buddhist *Jatakas* or Sinhala folklore giving his work instant and lasting popularity with the population that identified with their roots.

Closely associated with the others and with the '43 Group was Arthur van Langenberg. Langenberg's fame was derived from the work he did as a stage producer but it was not the only thing he involved himself in. His 'day job' as Secretary of the Port Commission meant that he had a large public to serve and Harold Peiris recalls that he was a man who worked unceasingly for the people he loved. He was extremely fond of young people and loved working with them. He taught English to students who could not speak the language and once a week he would go up to Kandy to teach English in three large schools there. He was also interested in architecture and is said to have shared his sister Trixie's ingenuity in building and rebuilding. Likewise he has been depicted as a 'wonderful pianist' and 'could draw and paint extremely well'. Undoubtedly, these talents would have proved useful to him as a stage producer. He was also a highly gifted calligraphist and Harold Peiris felt that for that alone Arthur van Langenberg's letters were worth preserving.

Circle of friends

There is a hilarious account of the three friends – Ian Goonetileke, George Claessen and Van Langenberg – around the '43 Group. As Goonetileke recollects:

> The high tide of our friendship centred round the decision in 1946 to float *Jataka* a firm which would publish the creative work of '43 Group artists. Arthur's interest in such a quixotic venture, doomed to extinction from the start, was typical of his selfless generosity and idealism. Realising that George and I were hooked on this indiscretion he put in his five hundred rupees with an aplomb which melted our sombre anxieties into dazzling hues of a resplendent *Skira*-like future! The brilliant little Foreword he contributed to the first and only book – a slender sheaf of Claessen drawings was a model of the kind, and provided a glimpse, all too rare, of his precious gift of breaking through to a true appreciation of a work of art. That this sort of merchandise was not popular provender was swiftly and predictably established, but not before it provided a spring-board for George's final self-exilement to frigid climes. Arthur and I saw him off one blustery chilly evening in 1949 to his lonely berth. It was the end of a bohemian triumvirate in which Arthur was both Alladin and the genie.[10]

Arthur apparently became a household name in Ceylon when he was cast in the role of a Portuguese captain in Lester James Peries's 1960 film *Sandesaya*. Unfortunately though good at training actors and teaching elocution, he was not considered a good actor. But as the projection of a popular image of what a Portuguese captain should be like in 17th-century occupied Ceylon, he was an instant success with the mass audience.

Lester James Peries (1919–) the iconic film-maker was the brother of the painter Ivan Peries and also present at the inaugural meeting of the '43 Group which took place at Lionel's house on Guildford Crescent. Lester is an internationally acclaimed Sri Lankan film director, screenwriter, and film producer. An active filmmaker since 1949, Peries has been involved in over 28 films, including shorts and documentaries for many of which he has received critical acclaim. The credit also goes to him for making films which had to do with Sri Lanka, 'All our early films were made in South India and had nothing to do with the sensibility of Sri Lanka.'[11]

At the age of 11 Lester was given an 8 mm Kodak projector by his father as a gift. He attended St. Peter's College in Colombo as a teenager before dropping out to pursue a career in journalism at the age of 17. He found his first work with the *Daily News* writing for the blue pages. In 1939 he joined *The Times of Ceylon* working under the Indian editor Frank Moraes. He also reviewed books on Radio Ceylon for a short period. In 1947 Peries travelled to England on his mother's advice to join his brother Ivan who was there on an art scholarship. Moraes suggested writing a column from the country to be published in *The Times*, which became 'Letter on the Arts from England'. In 1964, Lester married Sumitra Gunawardene, who is also a distinguished directress now. Peries's films often deal with Sri Lankan family life in rural settings and conflicted characters.

In 1956, Lester made his entry into national cinema with the globally acclaimed *Rekava*, which was a story based on village life. With this he revolutionized Sri Lankan cinema, giving it a unique identity. Afterwards he made many award-winning films such as *Gamperaliya* in 1964 based on Martin Wickramasinghe's famous novel *Delowak Athara* in 1966; *Golu Hadawatha* in 1968 based on the novel by Karunasena Jayalath; *Nidhanaya* in 1970; *Yuganthaya* in 1983 and many more.

It is believed that the Indian star the late Raj Kapoor highly impressed by the movie *Rekhava* had recommended to Sri Lankan producer K. Gunaratnam to utilize the talents of this consummate cinematographer in his future productions. In consequence Gunaratnam offered the direction of his film *Sandeshaya* to Lester who did an excellent job bringing the film to the pinnacle of its international acclaim.

Sitting in Lester's ambient sitting room and speaking to him was an enlightening experience. He was 93 at the time of our meeting (Colombo, July 2012) and fully aware of the times and his memory was intact. His wife Sumitra would occasionally interject to fill in the blanks.

> I was an outsider, the only outsider who was permitted to attend the first meeting. This was convened by Harry Peiris, my brother [Ivan Peries] and three others and the central figure of the '43 Group was Lionel Wendt. Lionel was not a painter, he was a photographer but he knew as much about painting, literature, music and he was clearly meant to be musician. Even in the first

> exhibition there was a lot of controversy . . . people who criticized, laughed or didn't agree with the transition from a realistic painting to this. It was Lionel shepherding this group and getting them together was a feat by itself.

The friendship between Lester and Lionel Wendt couldn't have been closer. He remembers the last week before Lionel passed away in 1944 because he met him and presented him with the book *Appointment at Samarra* by John O'hara, which he wanted to read. A week later he heard that Lionel had died. 'He was someone collecting the flock, not wanting them to fight or be envious of each other. To die at 44 seems far too early. How much he could have done', he said wistfully.[12]

At the behest primarily of Lionel Wendt the '43 Group was formed where Wendt was the main organizer and the artist Harry Pieris was the secretary. Its common aim was to break the shackles of sterile academic naturalism

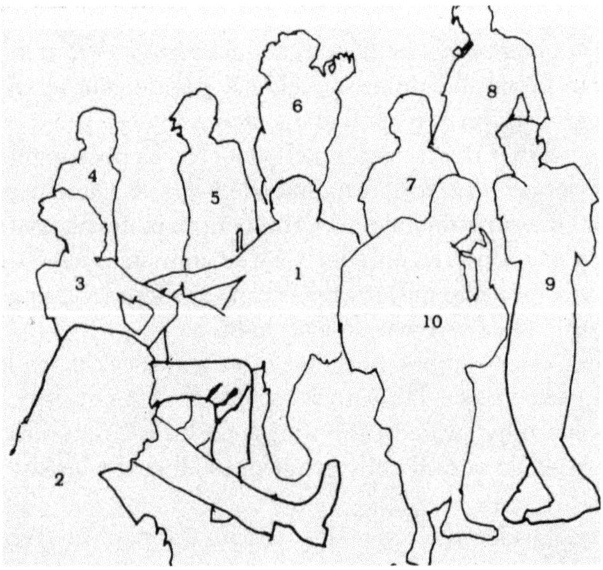

Figure 5.2 Key to the '43 Group.

A.C. Collette.
Watercolour.
1. Lionel Wendt seated in the centre, 2. G. Beling, 3. Harry Pieris, 4. Richard Gabriel, 5. Ivan Peries, 6. George Keyt, 7. George Claessen, 8. A.C. Collette, 9. Justin Daraniyala, 10. L.T.P. Manjusri.
Courtesy: Martin Russell Archive.

and forge a group of artists who were independent and were committed to modernist art. The Group had as its members George Keyt, L T P Manjusri, Justin Daraniyagala, Richard Gabriel, W J G Beling, Ivan Peries, Harry Pieris, George Claessen and Aubrey Collette. The bondedness of a common quest made it at the same time inclusive, thereby having a caricaturist like Collette or even a Buddhist monk like Manjusri. The Sapumal Foundation in Colombo, which is housed in the Harry Peiris residence in Colombo, showcases the works of the '43 Group. This ambient old house was left by Harry after his death for the housing of the collection, many of the works being from the Lionel Wendt collection which had been sold to build the Wendt centre. According to L.S.D. Pieris, the persipicacious chairman of the Foundation, 'The most important objective of the trustees is the conservation and preservation of the collection; the upkeep of the

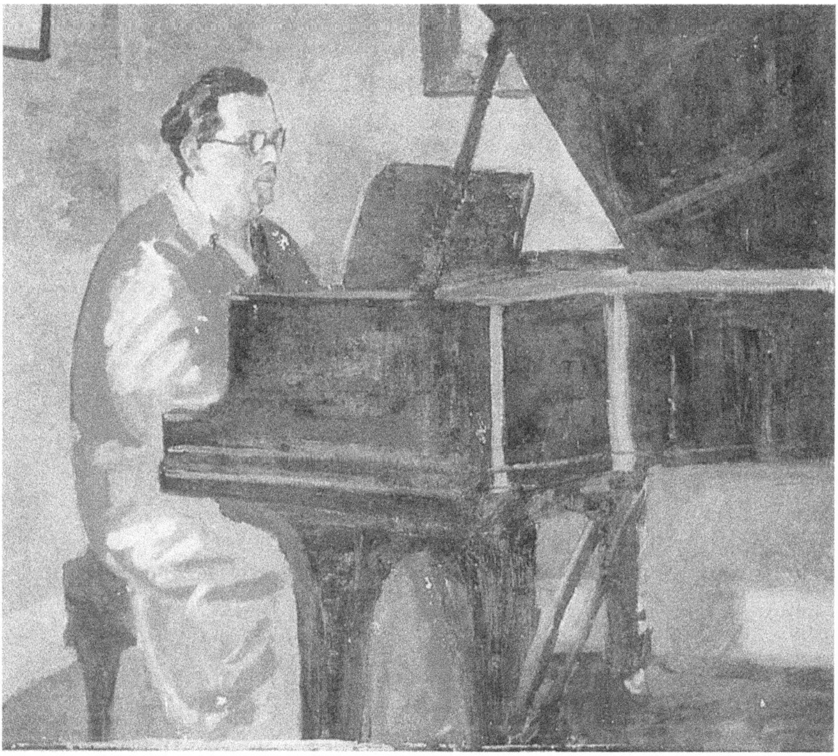

Figure 5.3 Portrait of Lionel Wendt.

A.C. Collette.
Watercolour on paper.
Courtesy: Martin Russell Archive.

old house – over one hundred years old – as well as the maintenance of the garden; and retaining the ambience of the art centre.' It is here that we see the famous drawing of the Group made by Aubrey Collette. Indeed Collette's sketch of the Group reveals its inner dynamics and immortalizes it for history. The watercolour on paper had Wendt at the centre, his large feet firmly placed on the floor. Next to him sits Harry Pieris spread out in an easy fashion. The orange-robed Manjusri gazes thoughtfully out of the picture. A detached George Keyt smoking a cigarette looks far removed from the group. As Gabriel pointed out, 'Keyt also was aloof. In that Colette cartoon you can see Keyt looking at his picture while the others were together and Daraniyagala at the edge still stands tall.'[13]

Their heterogeneous role in modernity also symbolizes the forms of free-flowing hybrid modernism which was beginning to take shape in the art of the subcontinent. They had no manifesto and their group meetings were often works of great camaraderie. Their common aim was to make a break with the Victorian academism taught in art schools, which was considered redundant to contemporary expression. It was felt that modern art had to be forged for Ceylon and indeed for the subcontinent which while aligning with international styles was rooted in the indigenous aesthetics of the country. That their modernism in a sense was a grappling for identity, after centuries of colonial rule, was understood and this search warranted a form of expression which relayed the life of the common folk.

The artists

Lionel Wendt (1900–44) present at the meeting was not himself an artist but a connoisseur of art and it was at his initiative that the Group had come about. The secretary Harry Peiris (1904–88) had been sent abroad to study painting when he was 19 and had entered the Royal College of Art in South Kensington when Sir William Rothenstein was principal. Eventually he was persuaded to go to Paris, the Mecca of art at the time, and he worked for six years there under Robert Falk. It was here that Harry associated with Matisse and his family and apart from having the benefit of the artist's views on his work and art he also cast some pieces of sculpture in the Matisse foundry. Harry was to leave for Santiniketan where he worked under Rabindranath Tagore and Nandalal Bose. When he returned to Sri Lanka in 1938 he had made works which were influenced by the Bengal landscapes as well as the cave paintings of Ajanta. Harry had by now developed into a skilled portraitist, but in both landscapes and portraits there was an architectural construction evident

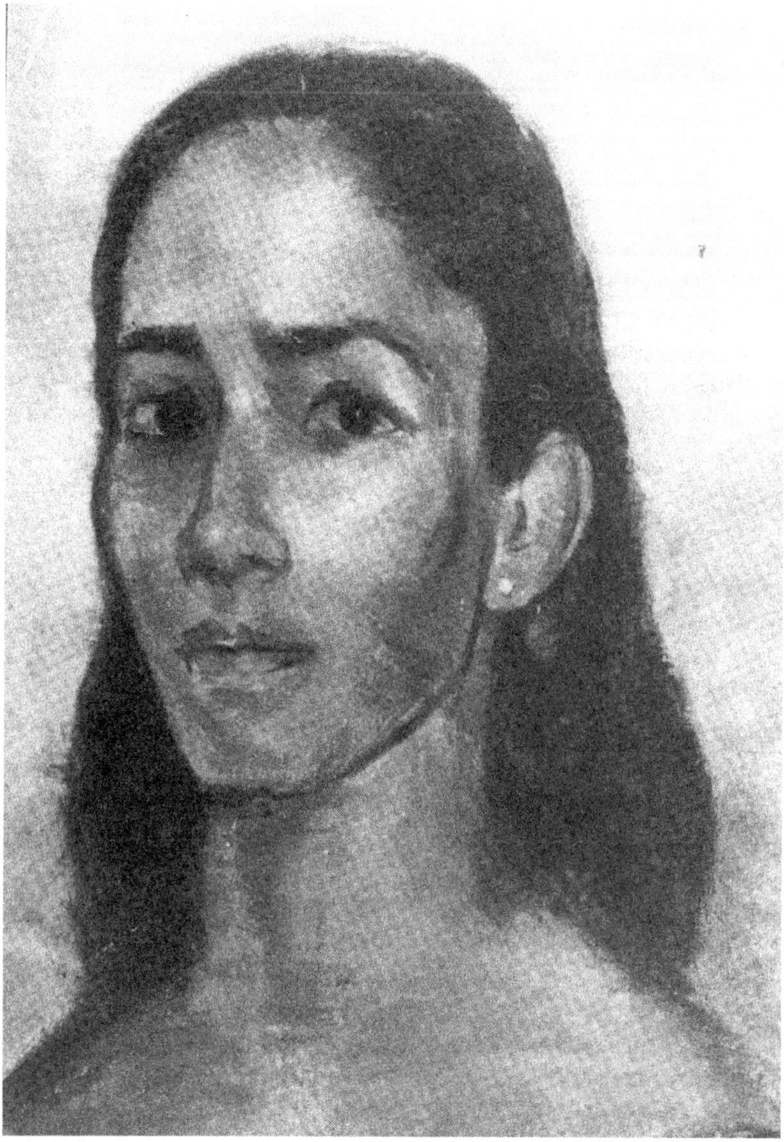

Figure 5.4 Portrait of Niloufer.

Harry Pieris.
Oil on canvas, 1967.
Courtesy: Martin Russell Archive.

which became the hallmark of his work. In time to come he was not only the secretary of the group but also a teacher who had trained many artists including Ivan Peiris and Richard Gabriel.

Present at the group meeting was Ivan Peries (1921–88), the brother of the famed film-maker, as mentioned earlier, Lester James Peries. It was Ivan in many ways who had also helped Wendt bring about the Group by meeting artists individually and speaking to them about the need to break away from academic art and move towards their own individual articulations. In his own work we see silent, elegant figures by the sea or in the fields, grave and introspective. Their elongated forms in the early years were reminiscent of El Greco in their simplicity and elegance and not surprisingly a work of his which was bought by Wendt in 1941 was titled *Homage to El Greco*. Ivan was to base himself in London from 1953 onwards and his works like *The Wave* (1955), *The Return* (1956) and *The Arrival* (1959–60) drew attention for their grave, meditative calm. Despite the fact that the subject of his work is derived from water and bathing which are familiar activities in Sri Lanka, these do not relay dynamic activity but seem frozen in an undefined time suspended in a quiet but not restful community. *The Arrival*, for instance, is an allegorical painting with its marriage of myth and reality and evokes sensuousness with its forefronting of three nymphs in a lotus pond with a frog and a fish. The blue horseman in the distance seems like a mythical figure signifying the presence of male valour and dignity and a sense of liberal freedom. In this vast panorama of infinite stillness we have layers of meaning emerging which engage with both Sri Lanka's past and present.

These paintings, which became darker in tone, speak of cultural dislocation marked by a period of intensity in the painter's life. Following completion of *The Arrival*, Ivan was sectioned for temporary insanity; the painting had taken him 'two years to plan, six months to execute, working 20 hours a day'. He collapsed and spent six months in Friern Barnet, where he was kept under sedation. These somehow lent his later work an even greater gravity and solemnity. Looking through Ivan's process in these works, according to Ashley Halpe, 'gives one a richer sense of the complexity of cultural being in a post colonial context and helps to define the heroism of the artist's triumph over disjuncture and psychic disturbance'.[14] Senake Bandaranayake summed up Peries's work as

> the product of a purely painterly meditation on the painter's indigenous experience. His mature work displays that fine control over feeling and technique that is present in all his work.

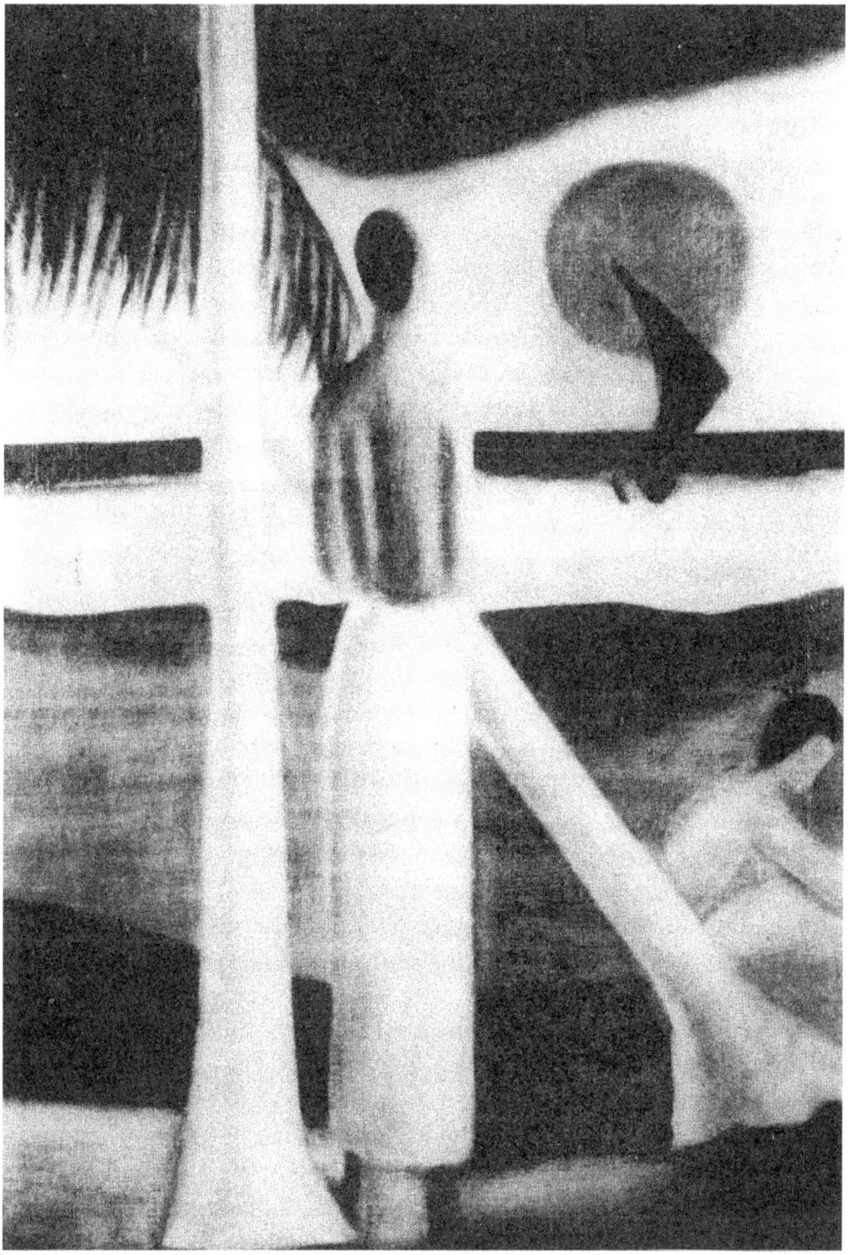

Figure 5.5 The Wave.

Ivan Peries.
Oil on canvas, 1955.
Courtesy: Martin Russell Archive.

> Influences have already been completely absorbed and digested; they are operative as far as the entire convention of landscape within which the picture exists. Now in his full maturity, yet sufficiently removed in time to have absorbed and digested his experience, Peries has completely mastered his vision and his material.[15]

Perhaps the only artist in the Group who had an inheritance of art was Geoff Beling (1907–92). His father had been an artist and influenced him greatly since the beginning. William Wright Beling's earliest sketches are dated to 1891 and are mostly pen and ink studies of sea and sky, rocks, ships and small sailing craft. In 1894 he joined the Customs Department and until his death served at the Revenue Collecting Department. This seems to have been a fruitful period of his career as the harbour of Colombo provided him with many opportunities for making seascapes. Later he developed into an unrivalled landscapist whose works were not only the first of their kind but reflected the land and its undulating stretches.

His son Geoff was also a protégée of Winzer like George Keyt and their talent had been spotted very early. Geoff's landscapes were spatial arrangements of masses which were partially abstracted to convey geometric forms. His still life compositions had a greater complexity and depth and had a quality of being seen from an overview revealing their essential characteristics. But it was with his portraits that he excelled culling the personality of the subject with a few brilliant strokes. In his *Portrait of Lionel Wendt* for instance, seated in a flaming red dressing gown in front of his Grand piano he was to reveal the intensity of his musical talent and the humanistic overtones that characterized his life and work. Beling, however, was to renounce painting altogether in favour of a missionary work but he also guided the course of art education in the country from the time that he took over from Winzer in 1932 as Chief Inspector of Art.

The abstract artist in the Group was George Claessen (1909–99). His works have large swathes of glowing colour, which create a rippling textured surface effect and a serene upliftment from mundane matters. It was when he shifted to Melbourne that he began to make abstract works that were primarily experiments in dazzling colour harmonies and juxtapositions. Claessen once again shifted and was domiciled in London since 1949 and it was here that the lyricism of his works and their calm, serene majesty began to draw attention. According to his daughter Esmeralda Claessen based in London, 'My father was self-educated. He matriculated but couldn't go to university because he didn't have enough money. But he was very well-read.'[16] Apart from art, there were many other facets to his personality,

> He was a mystic. He loved mineralogy and for him five was a lucky number. It had to be five of everything. His reclusive nature kept him isolated so that when he turned 90 he didn't want the High Commissioner to come and facilitate him. But he was an abstractionist at a time when in UK it was non-existent.[17]

His solo show held in London in 1962 received accolades and Conroy Maddox writing in the *Arts Review* noted that Claessen's

> abstract expressionist approach . . . bears on Monet's last period at Giverny (and) are plastic blossomings of a rocket-like launching in free space of the brush itself. Beautifully toned colours are applied in distinct areas, with each colour tending to sound one note in a total chord of repeated, contrasting or complementary colours. The result is a surface that becomes a unity, a vibrant and dramatic unity, yet remains infinitely varied . . .[18] (Arts Review, London, 16–30 June 1962)

Claessen's early skills were founded primarily on the strength of his drawings and the bold and sincere delineation of figures, animals and plants continued alongside his abstract paintings. What is more, he explored all forms of descriptive expression and graphic craftsmanship in oils, water colours, pastels, gouaches, drawings in pencil, ink, crayon and chalk, woodcut prints, etchings and dry point. When his purely abstract paintings surfaced in Australia they were to progressively develop into works of a gem-like effulgence which critics considered to stem from a deep religious conviction.

The youngest artist Richard Gabriel (1924–2016) who joined the Group was initiated into it as a student. He showed his work to Ivan Peiris who suggested he train with Harry and the latter asked him to complete his studies and then come to him. In the meantime there was the *World War Effort* exhibition. We met the late 87-year-old artist in his home in Melbourne where, despite his age, he was surrounded by paintings and spoke animatedly about his years with the '43 Group. According to Richard,

> Then Colombo was bombed by the Japanese. There were a few bombs and there were planes on Easter Sunday. The war was at its height and there was a commander who was in-charge – the

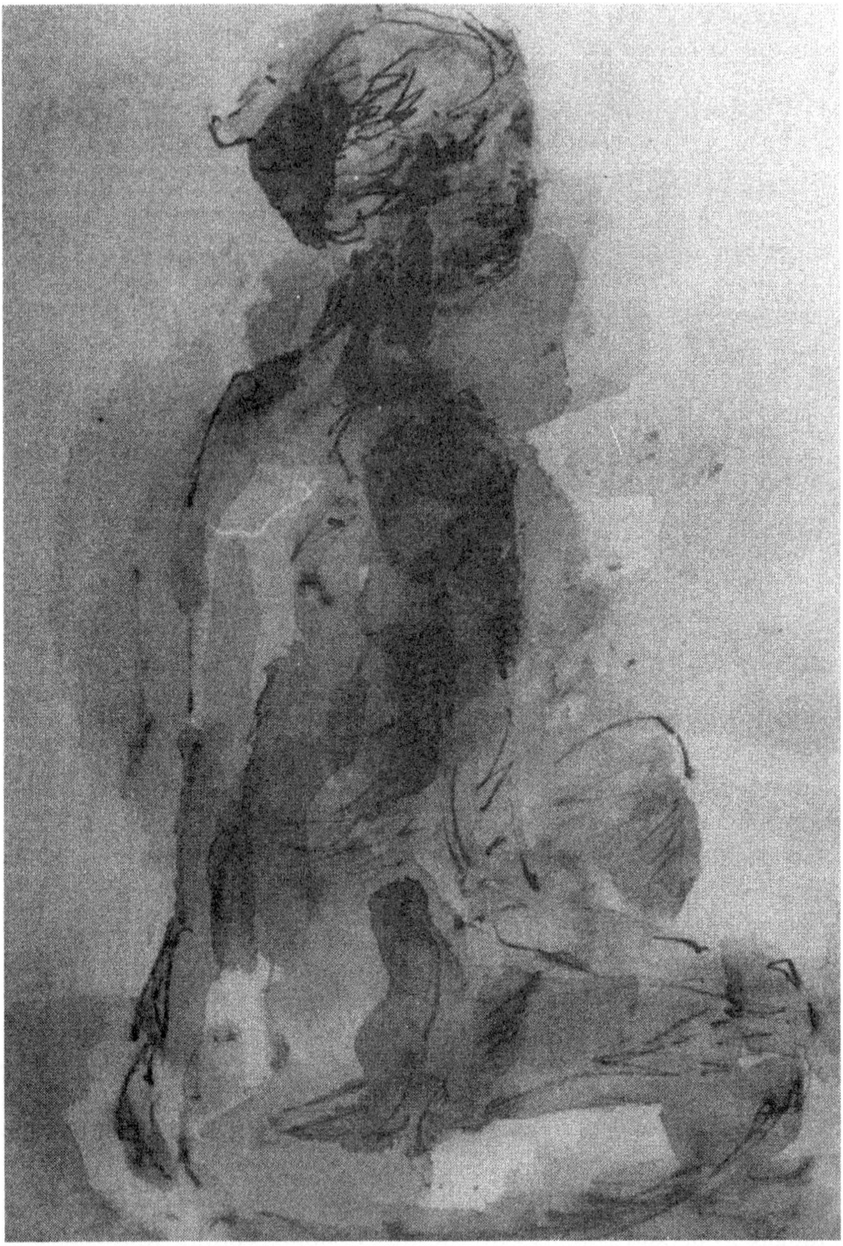

Figure 5.6 Seated nude.

George Claessen.
Oil on canvas, 1975.
Courtesy: Martin Russell Archive.

> whole country was under him and all the big schools were commandeered for their soldiers. We had holidays for three months which was very useful . . .[19]

With his old canvases and brushes, Gabriel made one oil and three pastels and won a prize. The very next day he was called by Harry to train under him. The pictures were with Ivan after the exhibition and Lionel Wendt on seeing them suggested that he be included in the Group. 'I was 18 and in in shorts. . . .' So Ivan said 'You'd better come to the first meeting and I tried to back out'. Ivan added, 'When Lionel Wendt chooses you, you can't say no. That was the first time I met Lionel Wendt – he was huge. He was always with braces because his tummy was so big but very active . . . Of course I attended the meetings but didn't utter a word'.[20] Gabriel also joined St. Joseph's College as an art master in 1944. His lack of means made him all the more inventive and this came out sometimes in humorous incidents. As he recounts, 'Father Peter Finlay called me to teach art and I was in shorts and I went and met him. I said, "Father I don't have a pair of longs, how can I teach students in this." "You can borrow" [he said] I borrowed Lester's but he was too short. So I had to keep my ass in this way [towards the wall] I don't know if the student's noticed.'[21] Perhaps this also made him observe the life of ordinary folk and he made many vibrant works of them going about their work. His best paintings were to come with the ordinary folk in the fields or with animals such as the painting *Fishermen with Boats* or *Fighting Bulls* (which was bought by the *Musee Petit Palais* during the exhibition of the Group there in January 1953) where the assured drawing and strong colours marked them out. While his visual language is largely engaged with lives of the ordinary workers in Sri Lanka and the strength and dignity of their bearing, the simplicity and grace of his works convey this with remarkable agility. As the art theorist John Berger pointed out, 'the serious imagination of Richard Gabriel' expressed with considerable skill, 'a superb drawing of some fighting bulls has the mysterious talent of the folk artist'.[22]

Gabriel's religious faith influenced many of his works where the pitch of agony and suffering of Christ and the Madonna would be evident. His book of etchings titled simply *The Cross* and dedicated to death consisted of the 14 stations of the Cross, each painted in sepia. The series concludes with the fifteenth, which is of the Risen Christ and is in colour. As Neville Weereratne states,

> The Stations of the Cross are not sentimental illustrations of the event as told in the Gospels or as elaborated in pious legend. They

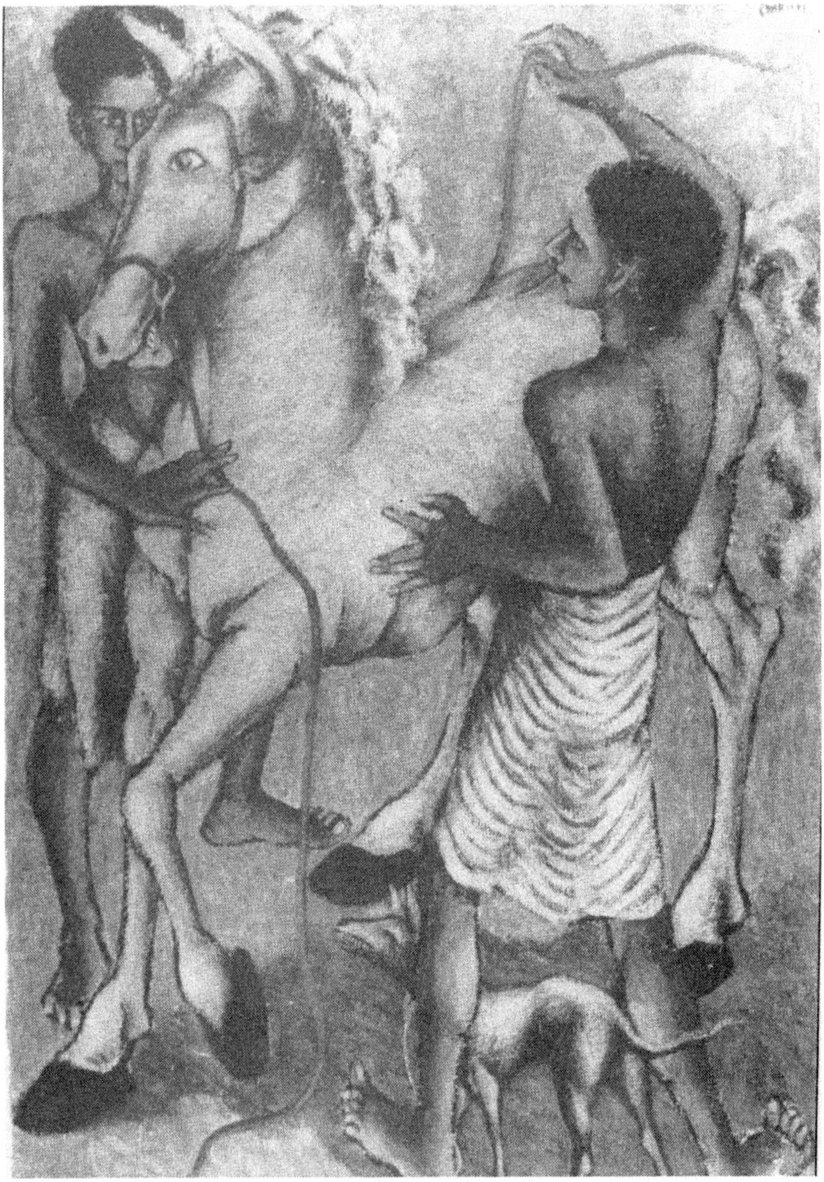

Figure 5.7 Blue horse.

Richard Gabriel.
Oil on canvas.
Courtesy: Martin Russell Archive.

> have a suppressed anger. The etchings are about pain, hurt and anguish. With the violence done to Christ, representing humanity, have come the odours of death and decay.[23]

But Richard had from the earliest times been inspired by the figure of Christ and he had sculpted from the bark of a fallen tree one for the local church. He remembered,

> I retired early at 35 and then I got some work to carve a statue out of wood at my wife's ancestral home. Close to where Justin [Daraniyagala] lived there was a tree and they said it was sandalwood – Sri Lankan sandalwood because Indian sandalwood is different, better, they use this for medicine. So I asked my wife's father and he cut it and brought it in a cart and I carved a figure for one of the church's headquarters. It came out very well.[24]

A monk member

An unusual member of the Group was the Buddhist monk Manjusri Thero (1902–82). His chequered career began at the age of 13 when he joined the Buddhist order in the belief that he would learn to fly! He stayed on in the order and his primary interest seems to have been ancient temple paintings of which he began making copies. Later he left for Santiniketan where his encounter with Nandalal Bose drew him towards art and he returned to Sri Lanka to make copies of Buddhist temple murals. Manjusri returned to Santiniketan with these and found that these were exhibited along with Rabindranath Tagore's poems! Soon after he was also to travel to Tibet to study Tibetan iconography which influenced his work. He returned in 1937 to his own work as well as the task of copying temple murals in the belief that the impending war would leave little untouched. It was at this time that he actually discovered a 2nd century BC fresco fragment at Karambagala in the Yala jungles, which had never been seen before. When George Keyt made the Borella Buddhist murals between 1939 and 1940 he had embellished the borders with fine calligraphic work. His association with Harry Pieris led to him being invited to join the '43 Group. Manjusri was inculcated into the Group from the time of its inception and actively participated in its shows. But by the time of the third show held in 1945, as a homage to Lionel Wendt who had passed away in 1944, Manjusri had left the Group. Perhaps the reason for this was an inherent clash with the Buddhist order where the freedom to

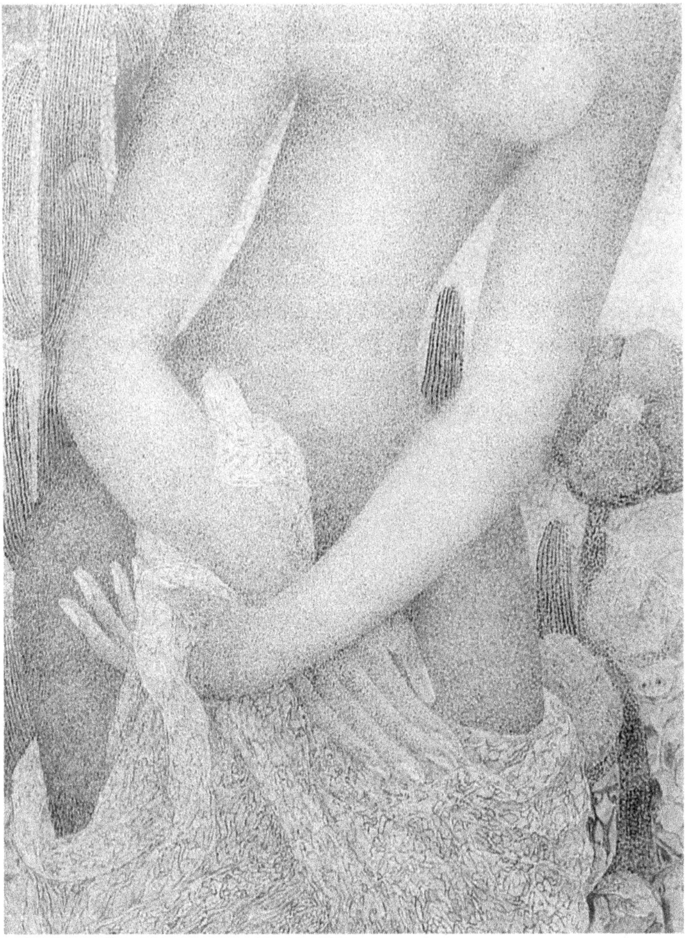

Figure 5.8 Female figure.

L.T.P. Manjusri.
Watercolour on paper.
Courtesy: Martin Russell Archive.

express could not cross boundaries and an artist like Manjusri whose work sought to transcend given realities. As Neville Weereratne points out,

> Seeing no contradiction in this, he executed some delightfully Freudian paintings. He remained quite unabashed at some aspects of these whimsical images and justified them also as being the product of his own experience and of the psychological state

> I which he found himself . . . Manjusri's sources were private, very personal: and conditioned by his milieu – the monastery, the ritual, the discipline and the morality of his chosen vocation – and moulded by his own maverick personality.[25]

In any case for most critics it was the underlying sexual content of the work which became a breach with the Buddhist order. Lester James Peries recalls his presence at the first meeting vividly,

> Manjusri in robes and he was very keen to join . . . they were not too sure whether he should come in because as it is in Colombo in 1943 getting this monk would have created a great deal of controversy. A Buddhist monk is expected to make temple murals. But not the kind of work Manjusri was painting because he was very vocal. He said there was a lot of sex in his paintings. I don't know there were certain hidden symbolical thinks in his work that would have probably lent to that kind of interpretation. So there was talk about it and Lionel Wendt said, 'Anyway let's see if we can get them all together'.[26]

Manjusri had an exhibition in London in 1948 of mural copies and original paintings which was inaugurated by Sir Herbert Reed and from there to Austria where he had exhibitions in Vienna and elsewhere. On his way back from Europe Sarachchandra who was on the same ship wrote a play on him which became very popular. This was on Manjusri's life as the novel *Malagiya Aththo* (published in English as *The Dead* in 1959) and it became part of the university syllabus.[27]

On his return Manjusri was to renounce his monk order and took to painting as a full-time vocation. He married in 1955 and subsequently had two daughters and a son and the latter Kusana was to take to painting following his father's footsteps. The three children took to art in one way or the other like making paintings for the Parliament building which were conceived by Manjusri. The original tracings made by him of temple paintings with all the colours meticulously noted proved to be invaluable because the children remade them and apart from bringing them an income retained a sense of the original works now in a state of disrepair.[28]

It is not surprising that Justin Daraniyagala (1903–67) was always posed against George Keyt for the two were not only contemporaries but did remarkable work which spearheaded the modernist moves of the 1940s. Justin's own training had taken place at both London and Paris after which he returned to Ceylon to paint, making a mark on the modernist horizon. His dark, burnished bodies with their frontal gaze looked out of the canvas and remained impacted in the mind. His heavy impasto with paint thickly piled on resulted often in glowing encrusted images. It was the entire frame, however, with its skilful blending of form, colour and composition that made his works both unique and artistic. Justin's preoccupation was entirely painterly and had to do with finishing the paintings to the edges and also visualizing the hidden side of the form which could not be seen. Yet the paintings spoke eloquently of the ordinary folk, their impoverished circumstances, the vulnerability of women and the dignity and gravity of their existence. Perhaps it was these that made his works excel and he needed no other external aid, nor did he archive tradition, and yet his works were unique in their modernist overtones. As the noted art critic John Berger pointed out:

> Like the Indonesian Affandi, he is an expressionist . . . But often as in his magnificent canvas of *A Dog* (which should be bought straight away by The Tate along with an Affandi), he is able to use the licence of expressionism to emphasise and condense associations, fears and hopes that have a far wider validity.[29]

The author and patron of the National Portrait Gallery, Christopher Ondaatje, mentions that in Paris Justin had met and painted the author Anais Nin (1903–77).

> It was in those early days in Paris and before she met Henry Miller that she posed, amongst others, for Matisse, Picasso and Justin Daraniyagala. He must have cut a strange incongruous figure in the bohemian Paris of the 1920s – far different from the boisterous self-confident Picasso and the ever quiet, romantic Mastisse. Whatever the relationship, perhaps only a fleeting artist and model experience, Daraniyagala's *Blue Nude* painting which survived his Paris days and remained in his possession for his entire life, is the only known portrait of the young Anais Nin in existence today.[30]

It is a little known fact that not only had Justin obtained a law degree at Cambridge but also a 'blue' for boxing in the Bantam weight class. According to his nephew Arjun Daraniyagala he was also deeply involved with gemology. 'He studied the Blue Sapphire in great depth and the

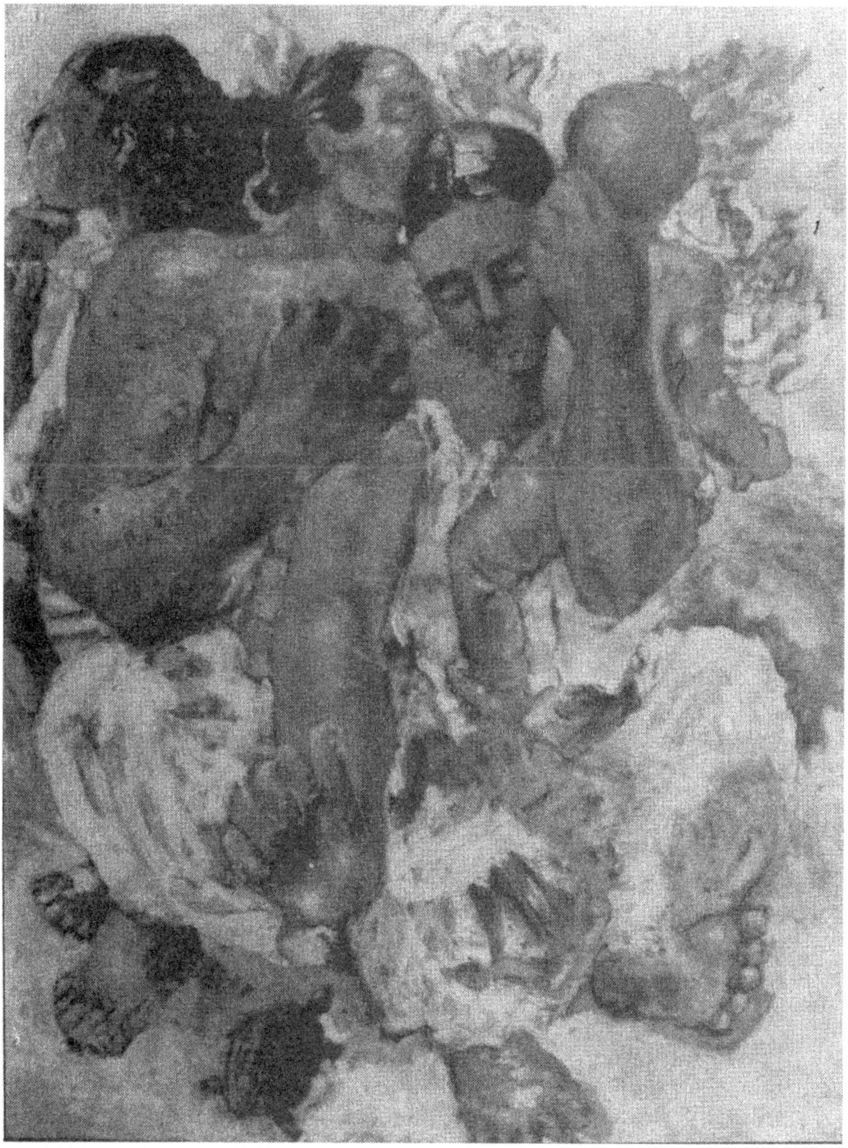

Figure 5.9 Three figures, baby and tortoise.

Justin Daraniyagala.
Oil on canvas.
Courtesy: Martin Russell Archive.

distortion of light influenced his paintings . . . He was always asking people to find him a meteorite.'[31] 'A gallery was planned for his works in the 70s but could not come about because of government policies of acquiring land.'[32] It seems that when he died because of complications arising from tuberculosis the villagers of Paysala insisted that they be allowed to express their feeling of respect for him by digging his grave and lowering the body into his final resting place.

He lived in the family coconut plantation where he had a studio and seldom met people. Justin never signed his paintings or dated them. In fact after years he would take out his paintings and make a correction. It goes without saying that he did not seek any publicity or buyers for his works for he felt that they were not for commercial purposes.

The angularities, disruptions and the camaraderie with the Group were caught ably by Aubrey Collette (1920–92), which not only reached the core of their ability to survive but also marked Collette out as a brilliant caricaturist. As his pen turned towards politicians, writers, artists he could seize the essential characteristic of the person and then with wit and sardonic humour draw upon his weaknesses but never maliciously. As Neville Weereratne remarked,

> His draughtsmanship was impeccable and that gave him the ability to distort without losing the essential features of his subject. He could exaggerate, cut up, dissect and even put a person together back to front while retaining the undeniable likeness of his victim.[33]

He contributed regularly to various dailies in Sri Lanka but was also known for his *1954 Faces* – a remarkable collection of 73 pastel studies of people. A little-known fact about Collette was that he was a fine painter as well and in these he immortalized the ordinary people and their daily existence. According to Ivan Peries, his oil paintings had

> immense verve. His metallic colours, harsh and uncompromising lines are to some extent modified by luminous colour and quite delicate yet robust handling. The social comment is always there and gives greater value to the work of art without in any way detracting from the formal qualities on which the permanence of any work must depend.[34]

Apart from the core group there were several other artists who were associated with it as members and exhibited with it. Among these were

Ralph Claessen, a sculptor, Ranjit Fernando who apart from being a painter helped to organize their exhibitions abroad, Ashley Halpe, Neville Weereratne, Sybil Keyt married to Neville Weereratne, Bevis Bawa, the brother of Geoffrey Bawa and others.

It was the British officer Martin Russell who was the most consistent chronicler of the Group and who patronized their works, especially that of George Keyt. Russell, a friend of Lionel Wendts, was based in Ceylon during this period and first saw Keyt's work at the former's house, No.18 Guildford Crescent, earlier in the same year. As he writes,

> I was introduced with some trepidation by Mr. and Mrs. James Naidoo, who had obtained with difficulty, permission to bring me. It was a Sunday morning, and we drank that powerful golden fluid, the excellent arrack of Ceylon. The pictures Wendt was then hanging in his sitting room were *Yama and Savitri*, his two *Nayikas*, *Woman with Sheaf*, *Nara Narayana* . . .[35]

On a subsequent Sunday Wendt brought out his entire collection, a great majority of them by Keyt, and Russell was profoundly excited by what he saw though, 'but at that time the local significance and the Kandyan and Indian overtones of Keyt's work were largely beyond me'.[36] It was at the first exhibition of the '43 Group which opened in the rooms of the Photographic Society at Darley Road on 20 November 1943 that he was told of its poetic quality by George Claessen. Russell who saw the truth of this was to go on to buy the entire collection of Keyt's works on display. He met Keyt at the end of the exhibition when he came from Kandy and the rest is history. 'Something of a legend had gathered about him in Colombo on account of his long seclusion in the Kandyan hills.'[37]

George's isolated existence in the village had one uninterrupted visitor who was Martin Russell who increasingly began to appreciate his work and the principal thought behind them. And it was this endearing relationship between George and Martin which was to bear the greatest rewards in the following years.

The founder and the main inspiration for the '43 Group, Lionel Wendt, however, died soon after it was formed – at the age of 44 on 19 December 1944. To many it seemed that this would also spell the death of the Group. Instead the artists marked the event with their third exhibition and dedicated it to Wendt. The exhibition took place in March 1945 appropriately enough at the Photographic Society's rooms at Darley Road. Two paintings were dedicated to Wendt – Justin Daraniyagala's *The*

Memoriam and Ivan Peries's *Homage to Lionel Wendt*. In all its 16 exhibitions from 1943 to 1967 George Keyt continued to exhibit and achieve recognition. The enthusiasm and energy of the Group in the forties, however, remained at once an important phenomenon of modernism in the subcontinent and a platform by means of which each artist developed his own individual talent.

Notes

1 Letter to Len Van Geyzel, October 10, 1933.
2 Martin Russell, *George Keyt*, Marg Publications, Bombay, 1950, p. 45.
3 Ibid., p. 47.
4 Len Van Geyzel and B.G. Thornley, *Lionel Wendt's Ceylon*, Lincolns – Prager, London, 1950, pp. 13–14.
5 Interview with the author, Colombo, July 2012.
6 Len Van Geyzel, 'Contemporary Painting in Ceylon', *Souvenir Catalogue. International Exhibition of Paintings*, Colombo Exhibition, February 1952, Art Gallery, Green Path, pp. 27–38.
7 Neville Weereratne, *43 Group: A Chronicle of Fifty Years in the Art of Sri Lanka*, Lantana, Melbourne, 1993, p. 29.
8 Irangani Serasinghe in Irangani as told to Kumardesilva, Samarnayake Publishers, Sri Lanka, 2013, p. 83.
9 Ibid., p. 53.
10 Ian Goonetileke, 'Ian Goonetileke', in Neville Weereratne (ed.), *Arthur van Langenberg*, Lionel Wendt Memorial Trust, Colombo, 1970, Chapter VI.
11 Interview with Lester Peries, Colombo, July 2012.
12 Interview with Lester Peries, Colombo, 2012.
13 Interview with Richard Gabriel, Melbourne, 2011.
14 'Potent Icons, All Mysterious', Prof. Ashley Halpe, *Sri Lanka Sunday Times* (www.sundaytimes.lk/970330/plus2.html).
15 'Ivan Peries, The 43 Group', Prof. Senake Bandaranayake, *Art Sri Lanka* (www.artsrilanka.org).
16 Conversation with Esmeralda Claessen, London, April 2013.
17 Claessen, op. cit.
18 Arts Review, London, June 16–30, 1962.
19 Interview with Richard Gabriel, Melbourne, November 2011.
20 Ibid.
21 Ibid.
22 John Berger in New Statesman and Nation, January 23, 1954.
23 Neville Weereratne, *The Art of Richard Gabriel*, Moosajees, Colombo, 1999, p. 66.
24 Interview with Gabriel, op. cit.
25 Weereratne, op. cit., p. 125.
26 Interview with Lester Peries, op. cit.
27 Interview with Kusana Manjusri by Deborah Philip, Sri Lanka, 2013.
28 Ibid.
29 John Berger, *New Statesman*, London, date not available.
30 Christopher Ondaatje in *Justin Daraniyagala*, 1902–1967, Colombo, 2011, p. 8.
31 Interview with Arjun Daraniyagala, Colombo, July 2012.
32 Ibid.

33 Neville Weereratne, *43 Group: A Chronicle of Fifty Years in the Art of Sri Lanka*, Lantana, Melbourne, 1993, p. 69.
34 Ibid., p. 72.
35 Russell, op. cit., p. 53.
36 Ibid.
37 Ibid.

6

THE INDIAN ENCOUNTER

A few years later George visited India which proved to be a defining moment in more ways than one. He had made a trip there for the first time in 1939 with his sister Peggy and Harold Peiris and had been astounded by the splendour of architecture and art which met his eye. He visited the temples of Madura, Srirangam as well as Chidambaram. He had seen the Kathakali performance at the Kerala Kala Mandala especially arranged for him and visited the birthplace of Shankaracharya and the Golden Rock at Trichinopoly among other things.

The eroticism and sensuality of ancient Indian art amazed and delighted him. According to Russell,

> In ancient India . . . the idea of human love . . . was justly celebrated in poetry, painting and above all, in the wonderfully free tradition of Hindu religious sculpture. Shyness, diffidence, delicacy of feeling were known as they are today, natural accompaniments to the love of human beings, but guilt and shame had not intruded where they do not belong. As late as the eighteenth century, and even into the early part of nineteenth, the prestige that love had in ancient India seems to have withstood the false new notions, as some of the paintings of the period prove, particularly when they tell of the life of Sri Krishna. Today, however, Puritanism infests India; but the art of Keyt stands for the truer, fuller view.[1]

Indeed so entranced was George by India that he claimed to be of Rajput descent. According to his nephew Lionel, 'Uncle George visited India with my parents and that brought him into another world. He even went to the extent of claiming that his name "Keyt" was really "Kirti" of Rajput descent.'[2]

Bhima and Jarasandha

But even more important was the work which resulted after he had witnessed the fervent fight for freedom from colonial rule in India. The powerful drawing *The Rejection of Siva* made in 1942 draws upon the fact that the British refused to make India free. Profoundly moved by the struggle against fascism in India and elsewhere a painting like *Bhima and Jarasandha* emerged which showed the last moments of the fight between Bhima and the *rakshas* Jarasandha (whose body could come together after being torn asunder) where Krishna hidden behind a bush makes a sign to Bhima to tear him into two and place the sections apart. Thus the body could get fragmented without being conjoined and the invincible *rakshas* got defeated. In the catapulting of Jarasandha who had kept 95 kings in captivity the triumph of the struggling people of India for freedom from colonial rule is suggested. In this magnificent work we witness the tensile motions of the body as it moves into a vortex of action against evil and in their fierce interlocking we sense the eternal conflict between two opposing forces. Russell pointed out,

> The magnificent drawing entitled The *Rejection of Siva* . . . was done in 1942, like many others as a protest at the refusal of the British authorities to make India free. It had also a personal significance to the artist. At that time of world conflict, Keyt's emotions were deeply engaged by the struggle against imperialism in India and Fascism abroad, and these feelings found an outlet in the work *Bhima and Jarasandha*, (1943), a painting of extreme dramatic intensity which depicts the last moments of the famous struggle when Krishna (who is seen with Arjuna) makes a sign to Bhima to tear his opponent in two.[3]

At the end of 1946 on an invitation by the cultural doyen Mulk Raj Anand and his partner, the famed Sri Lankan art impresario Anil de Silva, George visited Bombay and that was to bring about an avalanche of changes. To invite him Mulk made his way down the winding hill roads of Kandy and then deep into the woods of Amunugama.

> In this Elysian atmosphere, I found George Keyt living like a child of nature. He was wearing a dhoti. The torso was bare whitish brown. The dark hair on his head was parted in the middle, the ringlets curling under the ears. The face was made vivid by the

> blue grey eyes. He did pranam, Indian style. I embraced him from the warmth of my Punjabi temperament, to quell any Brahmanism that there may be in him. And we took to each other from the very moment of our meeting.[4]

The veteran modernist had some misgivings about George's Buddhist inclinations fearing that he veered towards the rigid and the hierarchical. But George's views soon put him at ease,

> Certain gestures of the Buddhist monks in devotion seemed to me to evoke calm. That may be the reason why I did these groups. But, for me, the feeling emotion for mood becomes religion. Not fetish! I am against all fixed images. In this sense, religious figuration and artistic expression are always different. In Sigiriya and Ajanta, the Buddhist images are formalist, while the pleasure-giving princesses, with their heavy breasts, oval faces and blandishments, are free.[5]

When he was invited to India, George readily agreed and came to India in 1946. The two were to travel together in the Krishna country – Mathura, Kurukshetra and inner Rajasthan. Mulk was to realize that Keyt was

> the answer to my prayers that Asia might produce an artist, who, whatever he takes from Europe and America, returns to the native country and recaptures the pagan pleasures of the Mura and their ghotul, of the dance on the banks of the Jamuna, of the elemental drama of seduction that is enacted by the Gaddis in the valleys below the Daula Dhar. It is a sacred moment for me, as in all my peregrination is our own vast continent, I have not come across such sincere enactments of the heart-throbs of our memory . . .[6]

Bombay exhibition

A large exhibition of his works was mounted in early 1947 at the Convocation Hall, Bombay University. At this exhibition held in March 1947, 64 paintings were shown which spanned his entire oeuvre. As George wrote to Barbara Buchanan years later,

> Regarding the big and far-reaching-in-effect exhibition in Bombay in 1947, the first of my shows in Bharat, it was in the large

> hall of the University of Bombay known as the 'Convocation hall', and like the rest of the imposing building, all in pure Victorian Gothic, which I liked very much. As Martin will tell you, it made a tremendous impact on artists and public alike. Unfortunately I have no very much of value on me and my work, lost the catalogue which was very fine and big and with excellent colour reproductions and a short biography and a sort of excellent running commentary alongside the list of pictures . . .[7]

Of this show, Rudolf von Leyden, the inveterate critic of *The Times of India*, wrote,

> The exhibition of painting by George Keyt of Ceylon brings to Bombay for the first time contemporary art of a self-willed and unusual kind which in many ways resembles that of Picasso and other western modernists. Opinions will divide and controversies will rage; so I think it best to declare myself right now for George Keyt though not with unqualified praise. The best period (1943–44) is inspired by immediate contact with life, with the people and the country of Ceylon. Colours begin to glow, forms blossom with fertility, pictures organize into fascinating patterns. In *Kacha and Devyani* an amorous couple are composed into a pattern of bright red and green, of round bulging and angular geometrical shapes and emphasized by calligraphic lines. Each element brings out the qualities of the other and joins into harmonies of a most seductive kind. . . . The greatest merit in George Keyt's painting is his courage, his inquisitive spirit and his originality, which asserts itself in truly oriental creations. If he speaks the language of Picasso, he does so in a rich and meaningful idiom of his own.

It might be noted that the paintings were very much in demand by Bombay's art-conscious viewers. They could not be sold, however, as the Indian customs authorities had waived off a duty of 60 per cent on the value of the work, provided every picture left the country at the end of the exhibition. George was bombarded with a demand to make copies and he ended up making a number of similar versions of the same painting!

George writes,

> Full committee meeting at which Mrs. Feroze Wadia (the big art patron and society woman here, just returned from America) and

> Hartwell and Hawkins and Lila Shiveshwarkar, Kekoo Gandhi and Manu Thakur and Langhammer (German savant) and Dr. Schlesinger (Viennese) and of course Mulk Raj and Mistry and Anil and another, a foreigner, attended and decided on further postponement of the show to February – just as well because, in addition to the actual reason – impossibility of having loans, screens etc – there will be time for me to turn out some more work in the way of coloured drawings etc. (none of the pictures can be sold of the stuff from Ceylon as one of the strings to the collectors bow happens to be the fact that all the pictures will be returned to Ceylon in 3 months to ensure which purpose an officer will be present when the unpacking is done – and he will stamp every picture).[8]

He was by his own confession also making works which were copies of his own. As he wrote to Martin,

> You are right about my 'basing' new paintings on old – only one could be *casually* called a copy. But then I have to consider 1) the need in my direction, and 2) the need in the direction of others, the former being the wherewithal to live here. I'm stuck here in Bombay. I came as a guest and suddenly found I had to pay for my lodging and food. My time has been taken up, and is taken up, in all sorts of ways; and I nevertheless find I like being in Indian here, and that where Priti [Manike] is concerned it is pure heaven.[9]

Ironically enough some of the original works were destroyed or damaged in a fire in a warehouse in Bombay.[10] This was Keyt's first solo exhibition and acted as a springboard for a series of important exhibitions he was to have in Sri Lanka and abroad.

Leyden was to observe later in the same year,

> We noticed then his 'style' which consists in the taking apart of natural form, forming it to his will and resetting it in even more willful compositions (did someone whisper: Picasso?). On the whole, this process leads to satisfying results (I am speaking for myself) and I yield to the fascination of *Singara* and *Abhisarna.* This fascination derives from pleasing colours and from the consistent play on contrasting form elements: the round and curving against the straight and angular. That the subject of the picture is a girl and her reflection in a mirror will take you some time

> to discover. But why not use your imagination for once in an art exhibition. I can find fault in Keyt's inconsequent mixing of materialistic elements with imagined or constructed ones of half assimilated forms such as the hands.
>
> The *Gita Govinda* drawings are easier to comprehend. They run in the tradition of Indian art with their honest joy of voluptuous form and movement. His line is mellow and melodious and avoids the obviously pretty. The Cubist *Landscape of Colaba* seems somehow superfluous because it does not tell us anything new, neither about the subject nor about Keyt. His other work quite definitely does.[11]

The review summed up Keyt's work of this period but some were not entirely happy with it. The description of Keyt as an oriental Picasso was taken up by *The Times of Ceylon*, which emphasized in a lead article that Keyt was just Keyt.[12]

The exhibition came at a critical juncture for George and it provided him with a wider exposure than he had ever got before. At the centre of this of course were Mulk Raj Anand and Anil de Silva who were at the apex of many events of this period. Their regular soirees at home had many artists, writers and film-makers present and George was warmly welcomed into the fold by them. Mulk also had been at the helm of the Progressive Artists' Group exhibitions in Bombay and inaugurated their first show in 1949. Progressive Artists like F.N. Souza and M.F. Husain seem to have derived from George Keyt's work and it is likely that they also met him.

Mulk Raj Anand and modernism

Mulk was the modernist par excellence and could be seen to have given a forceful thrust to its development in the subcontinent. He was from a relatively humble home in Patiala where his father Lalchand came from an artisanal background and his mother Ishwar Kaur from a peasant family. He graduated from Khalsa College and then ran away from home on borrowed money. After obtaining his doctoral degree in philosophy from the University of London in 1929 he claimed that he wanted to become a writer. It can be noted that it was in 1927 that George had decided to become a full-fledged artist. Mulk was to associate with different writers who formed the peak of 20th-century modernism in literature like T.S. Eliot and Leonard Woolf. By 1934 Mulk along with Sajjad Zahir and others had formed the *Progressive Writers' Association* and attended its first meeting in Lucknow under the presidentship of Munshi Premchand. As the art historian Geeta Kapur points out, 'A kind of vanguardism that was developed by the life circles of Europe and more decidedly by socialism, became Mulk's credo. Once he returned to India for good in 1945, he virtually made this political/cultural vanguardism the vocation of his life.'[13]

Mulk's support for the '43 Group and the Progressive Artists' Group which formed in Bombay in 1947 proved to be invaluable. The Progressive Artists' Group which comprised of F.N. Souza, M.F. Husain, S.H. Raza, K.H. Ara, S.K. Bakre, H.A. Gade were relatively unknown and struggling to survive at the time but were later to become leading figures in their field. It is to their credit that despite the extreme poverty of means at their disposal they were striving to arrive at a language in art which was significant to their times. The artists rejected outright what they considered the revivalistic approach of the Bengal School, even as they opposed the academic styles taught at the schools of art set up by the British. With a strong thrust towards modernism, the artists took historical reality into account and found a means of assimilating it into the present. In doing so they stepped into the difficult terrain of Indian art where folk art, the miniature schools, the Company style and an eclectic mixture of Western naturalism existed alongside, and from this medley of schools they were to create their own mode of expression. Inadvertently, in coming together they also symbolized the transcendence of the divisions created by religion, regions and caste.

Their aims seem to be similar to that of the '43 Group and Mulk promoted it with the zeal of a missionary. According to the art historian Geeta Kapur,

> In the field of Indian visual arts, Mulk Raj Anand's seminal contributions to the definition of Indian modernity range, to my mind, from the late 1940s to the late 60s: from the inception of Marg to his chairmanship of the Lalit Kala Akademi during 1966–72. By instituting in 1968 the First Triennale India, an international exhibition conceived on an ambitious scale . . . he put a seal as it were, on his lifelong commitment to modernism/internationalism.[14]

A crucial event which was important for George was the publication of the art and culture magazine *Marg* which had been founded by Mulk and Minette de Silva, Anil's sister, in 1946. Minette was one of the earliest woman architects in the subcontinent and was an associate of the

Royal Institute of British Architects. She was in close contact with the international greats of modern architecture like Le Corbusier, Walter Gropius, Richard Neutra, Siegfried Gideion and others. The magazine which became an important cultural force in the 1950s had in its very first few issues featured George and the '43 Group. In the second issue of the magazine there was an essay on Lionel Wendt by Geyzel and sketches by George along with notes on the paintings *Rasa Lila* and *Prema*. In the next issue Geyzel wrote an article on George accompanied by his line drawings. Most of the issues featured Keyt's drawings and paintings and one of them, a panel of cavorting dancers and musicians, in fact became an emblem for the magazine itself! A later issue had an essay with reproductions of three contemporaries: George Keyt, Akbar Padamsee and Chintomani Kar. A volume of *Marg* featured Ceylon with its incredible heritage of art! George wrote to Martin, 'I've done quite a lot of work for *Marg* and I must prepare you for a treat (as they say here) in the second issue, which will be very good indeed – the first issue had many unavoidable faults.'[15]

Apart from his own inclinations it was Anil de Silva in many ways who inspired Mulk to feature George and the '43 Group in Marg, which was beginning to get forefronted as the primary cultural voice of the period. Anil Marcia de Silva was a journalist, biographer, art historian and founder member of the *Indian People's Theatre Association* and a close associate of the Communist Party of India. She had come to Mumbai where her sister Minette was studying at the J.J. School of Architecture and when *Marg* was started she worked there as assistant editor for three years before leaving for Paris. Anil whose free and liberal lifestyle was to mark her out as an exceptionally bold and strong woman did invite considerable censure in her own country where the conservative norms did not inscribe such a space for women. Yet she came from a family where her mother Agnes Nell was active in the campaign for universal suffrage which was won as early as 1931 in Sri Lanka. Her father was George E. de Silva, who was president of Ceylon National Congress and Minister for Health. But she was reviled in her country both for her political stand and for her free and independent life as a woman. As the cultural critic Neloufer de Mel points out:

> In the attacks on her journalism, particularly when it was critical of Sri Lankan culture, on her political affiliations with her father's activism in the Ceylon labour movement, and on her choice of personal life-style are the dictates of a certain nationalist construction of 'respectability' as it came to be typified for bourgeois

> Sri Lankan men and women. It signified, in particular, how a woman should behave in keeping with her class and caste status, and beyond that, how a Sri Lankan woman should conduct herself in the face of the challenges wrought by western influence.[16]

In Bombay, outside the confines of the narrow restrictions of her own society Anil came into her own. She was photographed by Henri Cartier-Bresson, sketched by the nuclear physicist Homi Bhabha and co-habited with Mulk Raj Anand. She was at the helm of social events and cut quite a society figure. In the words of the social historian Kumari Jayawardene,

> Anil was charismatic. If she entered a room she would lighten up the whole place, she had a fabulous aura and she was teeming with kindness and warmth . . . She ran many salons in Paris. One was for an American crowd which had comes as refugees from McCarthyism in the 50s. The other was all the Indian artists – Raza, Padamsee, Souza, Paritosh . . .[17]

Anil left for Paris in 1950 where she married her French husband Phillipe de Vigier, member of the Communist Party. According to accounts, she 'continued to dress in exquisite saris, literally wearing her difference on her sleeve, and had a salon where South Asian students found encouragement and excellent food.'[18] She also had, in her role as the purveyor of South Asian modernity, *soirees* where artists like Francis Newton Souza, Akbar Padamsee and Paritosh Sen would be seen. It was in many ways coming full circle for Anil for finally,

> she was not defensive about her Asian identity, indeed she was proud of it; and her interest in Asian art history, deepened through exposure to the treasures at the Musee Guimet and her study at the Louvre, heightened her sense of pride in it. She was able to adopt an overarching 'Asian' identity in which class and culture mattered, but not caste or ethnic origin.[19]

Cultural awakening

George's Indian experience was to lead to a wider expansion of knowledge and art as well as lived experience. He had come at a time when India was on the cusp of Independence and apart from the fervent activity of a nation to find its feet there was a great cultural resurgence. The 1950s was an effervescent period in Mumbai, a time of discovery and experimentation in several fields. There were the Progressive Artists' Group and the Progressive Writers Group with men like Sardar Jafri and Mulk Raj Anand and their bold new directions. In theatre, there was the Indian Peoples' Theatre Association which made an impact with memorable plays like Ali Sardar Jafri's *Yeh Kiska Khoon* and Balraj Sahni's *Jadu ki Kursi* evoking nationalist sentiment. These were heady days for Mumbai cinema and unforgettable films like *Devdas* and *Achyut Kanya* trod new paths where romantic love or love for a low caste woman were lauded. It was a virtual renaissance and this was heightened by the congregation of a number of creative people like Mulk Raj Anand, Balraj Sahni, Ebrahim Alkazi and Homi Bhabha who provided encouragement and support to the artists.

This reverberating atmosphere did not leave George untouched and fascinated he was to stay on for a longer time. The teeming cultural life of Bombay kept him busy.

> I was interrupted by Lila and had to go with her and Priti to see the Indian Ballet based on Nehru's *Discovery of India* – Done by my friends Sachin Shankar, Shanti Bhardan, Sharma and the rest. I had put Jayana into this troupe – a lot of the girls, who got so friendly with us on our previous visits to Borivli, went in for an innovation in one of their costumes, based on the Kandyan style of wearing the sari (which they learnt from Priti, whom they love very much). . . . The Director of the Indian National Theatre met me after the show and with great humility and namaskar asked to be forgiven for any shortcomings in stage management as everything had to be done at such short notice. Sachin and the other men and women were so delighted to meet us behind the stage that some of them came rushing to do us namaskar half-nude! The ballet was wonderful both in dance and music. Ravi Shankar, who composed and directed the music, had a hard time getting at me, surrounded as I was by the troupe. He wanted to know whether his stuff was really O.K. as he too was so rushed that he hadn't enough time to revise the various *matras* etc. Ravi Shankar is one of the foremost musicians here. He usually plays on the sitara. The fusion of both folk and classical music (North Indian) was very well done.[20]

He also found time to travel:

> Since I met you I made a point of going to Dahanu – lovely hotel there by the sea – and went inland six miles to see the Wakli peasantry [the Warli tribe] who ware too ravishing for words – recalling early Mauryan sculpture. They talk a dialect of Marathi: I also went on a trip to the celebrated rock temple of Elephanta – one at sea from here. You've heard of this.[21]

And then again on 19 April 1947 he writes:

> I was away at Kamshet and have only just returned. It is 81 miles from here – the shortest journey I have so far done – and is a lovely hill station, though vast among sudden mountains, scattered about on the never ending plains (!)All Marathi country, i.e. the peasantry etc. Too lovely. I stayed there for 6 days in the country house of Dr. Desai which was placed at my disposal. The great Marathi historian, his brother, was there with his women, and they were kindness itself. I took a party with me – Bhupendranath Mukherji the great Sarode player, Shanka Chowdury the painter [Shanko Chowdhury] Captain Nag his wife and their 2 exquisite daughters Bani and Kalyani; and of course my Priti [Manike] Chandbhai Muchala also came as our great philosopher and friend. He was in consequence a bit of a nuisance, always addressing me as 'Maharaja Sahaab' and Priti as 'Maharani Shaab' so that it became commonly accepted that we actually *were* that sort of thing.
>
> My chief object in going was to see the famous cave temples of Karla, Bhaja, and Bedsa (Buddhist = the last 2nd century B.C. and the others Gupta) The trip, although it involved walk over 40 miles altogether was absolutely worth it, even apart from the temples – and Bhupen brought his sarode and we not only had all the Bengali music we wanted – the singing was done by the Nag girls and by Shankha too, and heavens what a repertory they had, classical, Vaishnava, folk etc. etc., even the lovely Baul songs – but we also had first rate Marathi music, as one of the Desai women in the historian's household was a superb singer.[22]

His style had undergone a subtle change and had imbibed some elements of Indian art. For one thing he had begun painting in tempera introduced to him initially by Leela Shiveshwarkar because oil colours were not easily available. He wrote:

> I've just finished a biggish picture for Sharouk Sabavala in pure tempera colour and he and Roshan are thrilled with it (on the chief wall of the best and specially done up living room of their quarters at the Taj) and am resting awhile before I attempt some large drawings based on sculpture (Ramayana) for the show. You see, certain pictures which certain people like and *want* cannot be sold as all these things have to go back. Sharouk wanted a thing done on the basis of the *Journey* and Hartwell wants my *Reverie* in tempera (after seeing Shahrouk's picture at the Taj). My dear friend Lila Shiveshwarkar was of very great help initiating me into the mysteries of tempera colour and I painted the picture in her house.[23]

He goes on to add that Martin would certainly have the pictures he wanted and also mentioned the price which seems astoundingly low:

> You may pay me Rs. 2,700 for the lot, the large and truly *vasan-vant* rabari picture included. I need money here. I have to pay Rs. 300 a month for staying here at Jassim house, and my goings and comings and every other extra costs money.[24]

The Indian moment

The art historian Geeta Kapur writes,

> In India, Mulk's preference among the 'modernist' pioneers on the scene in the 1930s and 40s included Rabindranath Tagore, Amrita Sher-Gil, and the Ceylonese painter George Keyt . . . George Keyt's rendering of a boldly modernist language to revisit the voluptuous and lyrical motifs of our subcontinental culture made a deep impact when he showed his work in Bombay in 1947 – Mulk, enchanted with his work, often used his drawings in *Marg* to emblematize and reinvent, as it were, the past through a contemporary sensibility and fresh formal structures.[25]

The sensuous beauty of India with its rich traditions allowed George a sense of serene calm. He remained in the country during this visit until 1949,

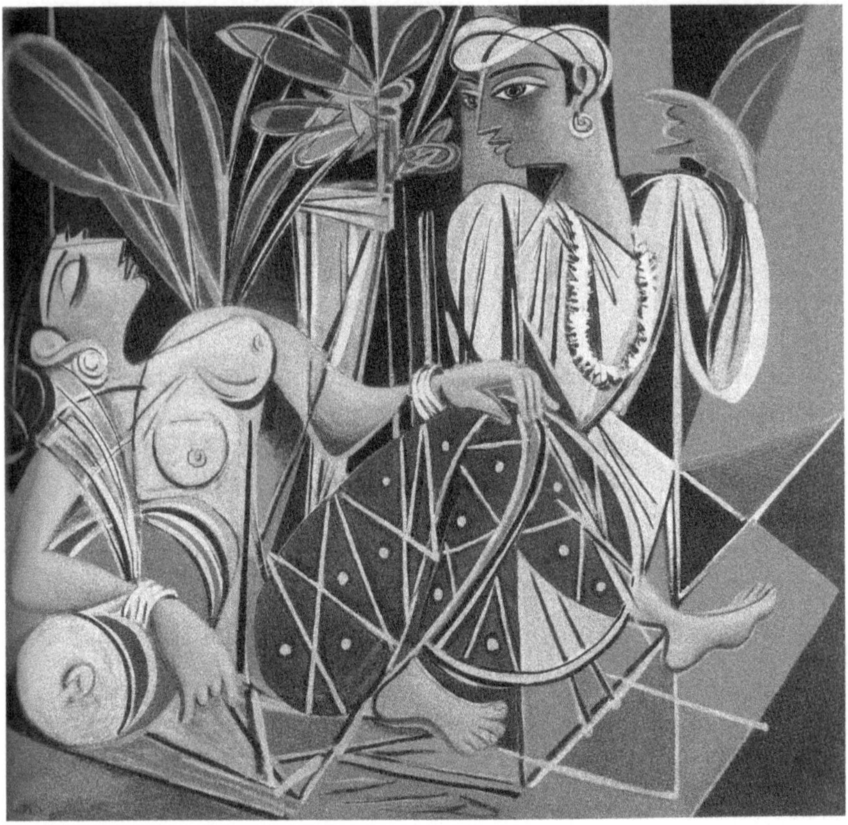

Figure 6.1 Lalita Ragini.

George Keyt.
Oil on canvas, 1951.
Courtesy: Martin Russell Archive.

getting to know the land and its people to which in spirit he belonged. His springing line, luminous colours and rhythmical forms came to life as it were and can be evidenced in paintings like *Girl Singing* (1947) with oil and tempera on masonite board. The animated form of the woman in verdant green playing the sitar imbues the surface with lyrical delight. Indeed George was one of the earliest artists to translate Indian musical modes known as ragas and raginis in modern terms.

Ragamala paintings were created in most schools of India starting in the 16th and 17th centuries where each raga personified by a colour, mood, a verse describing a story of a hero and heroine also elucidates the season and the time of day and night in which a particular raga is to be sung. The six principal ragas present in the Ragamala are Bhairava, Dipika, Sri, Malkaunsa, Megha and Hindola, and these are meant to be sung during the six seasons of the year – summer, monsoon, autumn, early winter, winter and spring. The paintings depict not just the ragas, but also their wives (*raginis*), their numerous sons (*ragaputra*) and daughters (*ragaputri*). George's penchant for the curved and sensual form allowed him to explore the feminine version of the raga and he rendered these with his inimitable flair and élan. Thus when he made *Lalit Ragini* (1951) he had the woman lying supine in all her voluptuous strength while her consort gazes at her with love and admiration. The vegetation in glowing golden form and the blazing red hark back to the sensual tradition of Basohli miniatures, yet it could also be an ordinary couple engaged in the language of love in the present. By formatting a medieval exercise in his painterly vocabulary George was to make the rich tradition of musical modes available for the contemporary mind.

Not only did he paint ragas but his whole style could be compared with that of an elaborate rendition of one. As Ellen Dissanayake points out, his paintings had less to do with narrative but it was the mood which became paramount.

> On his canvas are placed the structural and expressive lines that embody or 'prefigure' the basic artistic meaning of that theme. These lines, usually placed surely and boldly, themselves contain their ultimate working-out, and suggest what can and cannot be subsequently done, just as the notes of a raga 'determine' what is and is not later allowed. . . . Adding colour and more lines . . . can be likened to adding melody, variety, vibrancy; still under the influence of the original feeling, further embellishments or decorative details are added . . . to enhance and complete the mood.[26]

Finally George remained true to his own intentions of modernizing art in the subcontinent. A full article on him in Marg by Len Van Geyzel explained his intent. (This issue, the second, also had many of his paintings reproduced and longish captions for each by Mulk.)

> With George Keyt art in Ceylon became adult. For the first time the picture space glowed with its own vitality . . . The most powerful influence on Keyt's work at that time came from modern French painting for here was a school of painters which had

> broken with representationalism . . . although the influence of Picasso is obvious enough, Keyt's painting is in essence Asiatic . . . Compare for instance, two series of his paintings in which the subject matter is related. First, the many versions of embracing figures he was doing the early 'thirties, with the Radha-Krishna series that came a little later. The former are too often merely experimental, individual, eccentric, whereas the latter, with their mythological reference, achieve a wonderful intensity of form, that slow voluptuous line and smouldering colour. It is as though the artist provided with a subject ready to hand, so to speak, was free to concentrate on the purely aesthetic problem. When one looks at the Radha-Krishna series, at *The Lord's Departure*, *The Gajaga Vannama*, *The Maheswara* one is conscious of being in the presence of art that is typical, hieratic, that does not depend for its effect on singularity or originality . . .[27]

By 1950, Martin Russell had come out with a well-illustrated, handsome volume on him, published by *Marg*, which remains to this day the most comprehensive account of his work. These were heady days for George and ones which he would look back upon with a great deal of yearning.

Notes

1 Martin Russell, *George Keyt*, Marg Publications, Bombay, 1950, p. 45.
2 Interview with Lionel Peiris, Colombo, July 2012.
3 Russell, op. cit., p. 51.
4 Conversations by Mulk Raj Anand, George Keyt, A Felicitation Volume, Colombo, 1977.
5 Ibid.
6 Ibid.
7 Letter from Sirimalwatta to Barbara, August 14, 1982.
8 Letter to Martin, Bombay, January 14, 1947.
9 Letter to Martin from Bombay, April 19, 1947.
10 H.A.I. Goonetileke, *George Keyt, A Life in Art*, George Keyt Foundation, Colombo, 1989, p. 350.
11 Rudolf von Leyden, *Times of India*, December 1947.
12 Mentioned by Martin Russell, op. cit., p. 55.
13 Geeta Kapur, *Partisan Modernity, Mulk Raj Anand*, edited by Annapurna Garimella, Marg Publications, Mumbai, June 2005, p. 36.
14 Ibid., p. 40.
15 Letter to Martin from Bombay, February 21, 1947.
16 Neloufer de Mel, *Women and the Nation's Narrative*, Rowman and Littlefield, Lanham, MD, 2001, p. 103.
17 Interview with Kumari Jayawardena, Colombo, July 2012.
18 de Mel, op. cit., p. 150.

19 Neloufer, op. cit., p. 151.
20 Letter to Martin from Bombay, April 20, 1947.
21 Letter to Martin, Bombay, January 14, 1947.
22 Letter to Martin, Bombay, April 19, 1947.
23 Ibid.
24 Letter to Martin, Bombay, February 21, 1947.
25 Kapur, op. cit., p. 38.
26 Ellen Dissanayake, 'The Art of George Keyt and the Indian Raga', *Catalogue of the Exhibition of Recent Paintings and Drawings by George Keyt*, The Lionel Wendt Art Centre, December 1972.
27 L.C. Van Geyzel, *The Paintings of George Keyt*, Marg, Vol. 1, No. 3, October 1946, p. 41.

7

THE SAGA OF MANIKE

There was a great deal that India had to offer and George savoured it to its fullest. But the country that he experienced was a newly Independent one and it had all the fervour and zeal of a nation struggling to find its feet.

Those passionate times were to change drastically later but the climate of those days was to set the tone for the course of culture and provided the basis for much that was to follow. For George his stay in Bombay was not entirely one of unmitigated pleasure. He stayed on in the cosmopolitan city where he had made friends and where Martin Russell had stationed himself to write a book on him. But there was another important reason why he was there.

By early 1949, Manike had had a bad nervous breakdown in Bombay leaving George in utter despair. Martin writes about it in graphic detail to his mother from his room at the Taj Mahal hotel.

He mentions,

> A horrible calamity had occurred. Manike has had a complete nervous breakdown. George, who loves her beyond anything and is a deeply emotional man is in anguish. He has come to stay with me in the Taj Mahal Hotel and sleeps in my room. We know all Manike's troubles, her unusual sensibility, her separation from Ceylon, her inability to speak English, the way George has neglected and insulted [her]. These alone and my own hatred of Bombay were enough to give her a breakdown. Besides which she was treated for an intestinal complaint . . . with Mepecrine, which produces an unstable condition in a small proportion of users. She had 15 tablets. It is probable that Mepecrine precipitated the general collapse. George and I are also under great strain so it is a difficult time. I have no desire so great as that of leaving Bombay and I certainly shall not be able for a considerable time.[1]

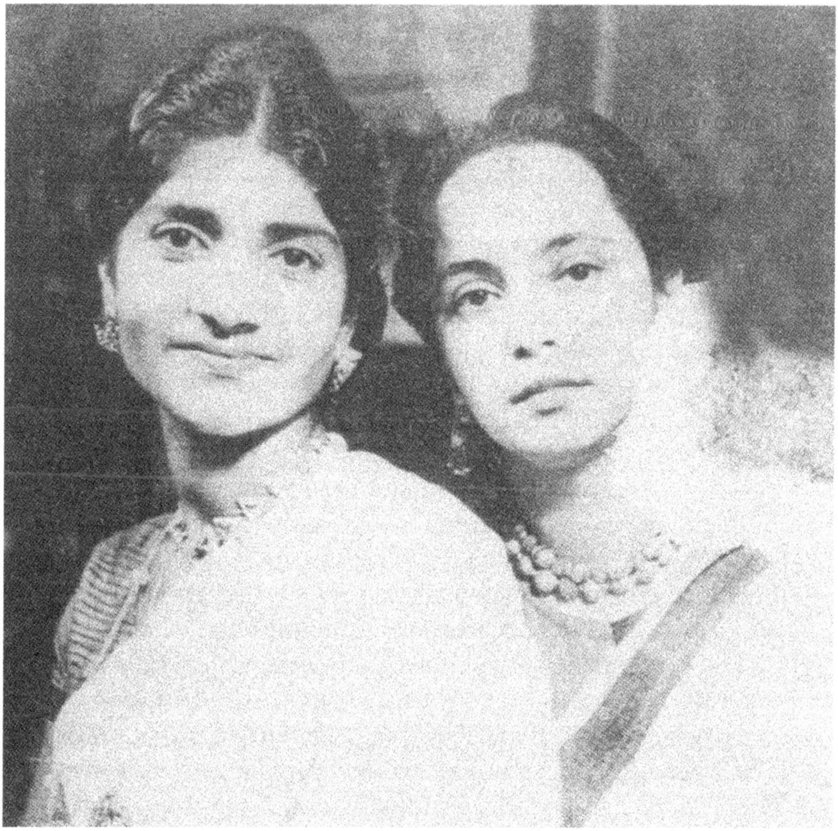

Figure 7.1 Manike and Anil de Silva.

Courtesy: Martin Russell Archive.

He continued in the letter to describe Manike's alarming behaviour,

> . . . The first two nights of Manike's collapse were exhausting and unnerving. Their flat is on the fourth floor and Manike attempted with considerable strength to wash the place up and throw herself out of the window and from the veranda. At one moment she managed to lock herself in the bathroom and we could hear her opening the window which we had fortunately bolted. I managed to break open the door by rushing against it with my shoulder. Manike spent most of the night sitting up on a sofa with me. She behaved best with me. Having had

experience of this sort of thing with Ivan I'm not alarmed by lunatics and get on well with them, at least when they are violent! We had a nurse who became terrified and was chased by the patient . . . There are no mental homes in Bombay, but there is a lunatic asylum at Thana a few miles out, which has a bad reputation for being a grim place and having all the insane uncared for . . . We were too unnerved by morning to keep Manike in the flat and the doctor arranged for her to go to Northcote Nursing Home next to my hotel. This nursing home won't accept mental patients because they disturb the others, especially the heart patients, but they agreed to accept Manike because they were told it was a Mepacrine case which would soon clear up. At first it was alright. They gave us an experienced day nurse and she succeeded in undressing Manike and putting on a night dress. But with each injection she became more violent, and the night nurse and night staff were utterly inexperienced in handling such a difficult case. I stayed at the nursing home and it became a night of unspeakable horror. She became more and more violent and she screamed without limit. The whole of the nursing home and half the hotel were woken up. The inexperienced nurses struggled to give each injection. In the course of that day and night she had six different sedatives at two hour intervals without producing anything but increasing violence. . . . At two in the morning the doctor insisted we should remove Manike immediately. Mulk Raj Anand agreed to accept her (he has a ground floor flat) and George, Shanko Chaudhuri and I removed her without difficulty in my car. How relieved she was to go! She was by no means unconscious, but unbalanced and terrified. Next day our foolish doctor arranged for her to go to St. Georges', where he said there were mental wards. With great difficulty the day nurse, Narendra Sharma, Mulk's servant Mary and I managed to take her only to find there were no mental wards. They had been closed the year before. The resident doctor refused such a violent patient. So we removed her back to Cuffe Parade. In the evening Mulk refused to have her any longer and we removed her back to the 4th floor flat, where we have the cooperation of the owner, an old Parsee lady called Mrs. Lala. During the day we had the carpenter alter the locks and bolts appropriately. So we felt safer. Except for Mulk, who is in a difficult position already with his landlord, all our friends have been wonderful and have voluntarily helped to nurse Manike night and day.[2]

Yearning for Sri Lanka

Martin's mother advised that she be taken back to Ceylon and he agreed.

> On the first night of the collapse it was my main idea. She was restless to sleep and George too exhausted to help so I sat up with her all night on a settee. She said she wanted to go to Lanka and to soothe her I repeated the names of all the Ceylon towns and villages I could remember. This incantation had some effect but she was much too ill to travel. She became violent, noisy and refused food and drink . . . In the Bombay heat such a refusal is dangerous. Enormous black marks developed round her body, on her face and forehead. She was too restless and her veins too small to receive intravenous fluid, but she was given large doses of glucose intramuscularly. When her condition got really bad we got a surgeon who fed her food through the nose . . .[3]

Eventually Manike was taken to Pune to the Yeravada Mental Hospital where she, despite the ordeal, seems to have made a recovery.

> Now she is much better and I think best for her to make a complete recovery as George means to live in India. If she went to Ceylon to recuperate she might break down on returning. George and Manike are inseparable and their mutual devotion is something extremely beautiful.[4]

George and Martin went back to Ceylon to get her younger sister Sapumali and the sister's son to make Manike feel more comfortable, although Sapumali had varicose veins and the infant had whooping cough. In the hotel George and Sapumali lived as husband and wife with the tacit approval of Manike. According to Martin:

> and such an event in no way distresses Manike – in fact she is much more comfortable mentally now she knows George is properly looked after in the Manike way – his hair is oiled, his feet washed, his plate piled ridiculously high, and at night his gentleman needs fulfilled with soft responses! How civilized the Kandyans are! I marvel at it.[5]

Meeting Barbara

Perhaps it was around this time that George struck up a friendship with Barbara Buchanan nee Smith. An attractive and warm person Barbara was of Anglo-Indian descent. Her considerable charm may have been heightened for George by the fact that she was single and sought his friendship. Barbara was based at the Oxford University Press in Bombay when under its chief R.E. Hawkins it had gained fame for its introduction and publications of Verrier Elwin's books on the art and life of central Indian tribes like the Muria and their Ghotuls. Barbara Smith as she was then known worked there editing and producing books for them. It is possible that George first met her when he approached them for the publication of his poems, but there is no mention of this in any of his letters. At any rate he would meet her frequently while in Bombay.

Barbara was perhaps friend, lover, confidante when George was undergoing difficulties with his relationship with Manike and settling down to his new life in the village. He wrote to her frequently from there and the letters had an undercurrent of passion and genuine fondness. In one of his letters there is an overt ink sketch of a man and woman in sexual embrace. This letter was written from Gunnepana dated 'Masa 1806' (according to the Ceylonese calendar) and ends with 'Yes I imagined you crying like hell when we left and I didn't know what the deuce to do about it blast it as I was far up in the sky in a silly tube that looked like snapping any moment. Come soon and stay here forever and ever. lots of love, George.' Another letter from Gunnepana dated 14 February 1951 begins with an ink sketch of a minotaur ravishing a girl from behind. It ends with 'Please write and tell me about yourself, O you who are naked under your skirt. love, George.' In a letter written on 15 April 1953, addressing her as 'Dearest my Barbara, Namaste', George writes on an even more intimate note,

> Your sweet letter. You write so much from your heart and the full network of your feelings issuing therefrom that I'm affected right down to the seat of all pleasure and never 'satiated' desire. You are among the very few *real* people I know, and in addition a *woman*. Allow me to burn deep and offer flowers and cause an orgasm before the smiling *yoni* of your karma. Allow me therefore to present my throbbing *lingam* (42 beats to the minute, nothing more) smeared with wild honey, ghi, long, pepper, rakta karavira and the thirty four varieties of the lesser fleas pulsating in masses beneath a layer of capsicum juice; yes, before the deep-bearded smile of the radiant *yoni* of your karma.

He urges her to come to Sri Lanka: 'Anyway, I must beg of you to come here whether or not Martin turns up. We want you very much. That is next month . . .' A few days later on 17 April on his birthday he writes,

> This day, the 17th, is my birthday my dearest Barbara, and I write because you sent your love and good wishes . . . I also write to tell you how surprised I am to find that I have survived till today, at least physically, although a few people like you, in your great kindness recognize me as having survived in other ways too. I say this because you little know what battering I've been through and what ferocious and consistently maintained efforts at not only spiritual but even material mutilation have been directed towards me. Feebly at first – as you know, I was always a misfit in my crowd – then a little more vigorous since about the time I was 19 or 20 when I definitely threw up all the bogus make believe I was expected to go through with, propped up against a background not my own. But terribly intensified about 1938 and onwards with the shipwreck of my marriage and my flight into the heart of Kandyan 'native' life . . . What I actually want you to do is to come here next month . . . Please come my dearest Barbara. I need you badly.

Barbara and Martin were both to come to the village and stay nearby shortly after. According to one account,

> Keyt held Russell in thrall and he became a great friend, patron and frequent visitor to Keyt and Manike's simple cottage at Sirimalwatta. With kindred souls Barbara Buchanan, C.A.W. Abeywardena and a few others they 'tired the sun with talking' of life and art, of cabbages and kings.[6]

The note of intimacy continues even when Barbara leaves for London, much to his disappointment, marries a Scottish civil engineer John Buchanan and lives there for the rest of her life. He frequently urges Martin to get together with Barbara in London even though both are married to different partners. Perhaps this reflected his own fondness for her which in many ways was a yearning for the 'other'. In the last years of his life after a long silence, Barbara was to emerge and get in touch with both Martin and George. Subsequently she became actively involved with promoting and presenting his art internationally.

A relapse

Meanwhile on Manike's recovery there is talk of her going back to Ceylon but George wanted to live in India. Yet many doubted if without George she wouldn't have another breakdown. As Martin pointed out,

> life in Ceylon has its difficulties. Being a village girl she is not accepted . . . tho' as a true Buddhist with an authentic culture of her own she is as a person worth ten of declasse' Anglicized people who despise her. In the village itself – Annugama – there are occasional caste trouble. The Annugama family – Menike Annugama and their sweet daughters would mix in any way with the dance and drummers who are for us one of the main attractions of Annugama. When George attended the marriage of the dancer Jayanand, the Annugmans were terribly distressed at the disgrace of their caste and poor Beeta, the eldest daughter wept for days! This sort of thing is very painful for poor Manike and she is really better off in Bombay where the New Stage dancers . . . They love her very much and can manage conversation in Hindi.[7]

The relief however was short-lived as Manike had another relapse! No sooner had she joined George at the New Stage bungalow in Mumbai along with her sister, she was to start feeling demented.

> The strain of life there without modern (or ancient) conveniences, with rudimentary household arrangements and peculiar Indian *laisser faire* was too much for her. Narendra Sharma came up one night to tell me about her. I phoned the psychiatrist and got a room at the nursing home and arranged more shock treatment for the following day . . .[8]

There followed a description of the electric shocks she received,

> I was present when the electric shock was given . . . In order to avoid having to strap her to the bed whilst she was conscious, four or five nurses are present to hold her down as soon as the shock starts; one feels her heart; the house surgeons put the gag in her mouth and the electrodes to her head; Lalkaka [the psychiatrist] operates the switches of his machine, a sort of big portable typewriter, another gives artificial respiration. The shock to the spectator is almost as severe as the patient. George has to be present

> in order to seek her cooperation. The convulsions and muffled strangulated cries are unnerving. But beneficial![9]

But when she recovered she would be normal,

> Manike is spreading a good deal of culture at the nursing home, lending the doctors books about Renoir and Picasso. She paints herself. The psychiatrist was puzzled to death by her paintings, the more so as George and I assured him they were entirely normal.[10]

Martin found the treatment given to Manike very un-Freudian, 'It is strange that she should be benefitted by such perfectly physical methods of treatment! It is wholly un-Freudian. I believe the cure will make her recover completely'. On seeing Manike receive yet more electric shocks George found it difficult.

> The convulsion filled him with horror – as they would have Papa, if he had had to see you so treated. It was difficult for him not to be present, as Manike wanted it. While the shocks were being given – two a week – she was perfectly sane. She had no idea what was being done to her, tho' she sensed George's anxiety and her hands used to go quite cold during the preparations. To support George I used to go and was given the role of turning the switch. This made it easier for the psychiatrist to manage the electrodes, which are applied to the head. Another doctor held Manike's jaw to prevent dislocation Then there are four nurses to hold her limbs. When the psychiatrist said 'On' I turned the switch. A tremendous spasm followed the eyes open and rolling wildly with strangulated cries and screams from the throat. The breathing stops as the spasm continues – for about 20 or 30 seconds . . . Then the spasm develops into the violent shaking, the nurses struggling to hold Manike on the bed. As this phase becomes acute the whole bed – a loose iron bed – starts rattling, mounting to a climax. . . . Eventually the convulsion dies away. Manike used to remain unconscious for half an hour or more, and wake as from a deep sleep, with no recollections of having had any unpleasant experience . . . After the electric convulsion was concluded, we decided (against the psychiatrist's view) to leave her in the nursing home for three weeks. . . . Then on the 5th day after the last shock she was profoundly depressed again and unable to come out with us – but perfectly rational. . . . We have

> not however allowed the psychiatrist to resume the shocks. So long as she remains rational we have hopes that the depression will clear naturally which really would be the end of the illness.[11]

By the next month Manike is back in Ceylon but not exactly the same person.

> Manike seems to have recovered completely but she is not exactly the same person as before. When I first knew her, five years ago she never sat at table with us or spoke, but served the food and then sat on the floor in the kitchen. When I saw her again in Bombay, she was willing to sit and eat with us, but always deferentially, in the manner of the Hindu wife of old. But the enormous attention she received during her insanity has changed all that. When doctors, nurses, psychiatrists, radiographers, heart specialists, bacteriologists crowded round the bed like the attendants on a Maharani she at last realized she was after all a valued person in her own right! Throughout her illness George spent the day with her – an inconceivably trying experience. This devotion has really made an impression. Manike is a self-confident and happy person more than before. And certainly our lives have been enriched by our extraordinary experiences. Of all these certainly the most terrible but also the one I treasure most highly was seeing a person so close to me go suddenly without warning mad in front of my eyes.[12]

And with these words which could stir an echo in most people the Manike fits ended and she was never to get them again.

Notes

1 Letter to mother from Bombay, April 3, 1949.
2 Ibid.
3 Letter to mother from Maiden's Hotel, Delhi, May 20, 1949.
4 Ibid.
5 Ibid.
6 Tissa Devendra, *The Lives of Keyt*, Observer Pictorial, Colombo, 1991.
7 Letter to mother, Maiden's Hotel, Delhi, May 20, 1949.
8 Letter to mother, Taj Mahal Hotel, June 12, 1949.
9 Ibid.
10 Letter to mother from Bombay, June 17, 1949.
11 Letter to mother from Taj Mahal Hotel, Bombay August 5, 1949.
12 Letter to mother, from Kandy, September 1, 1949.

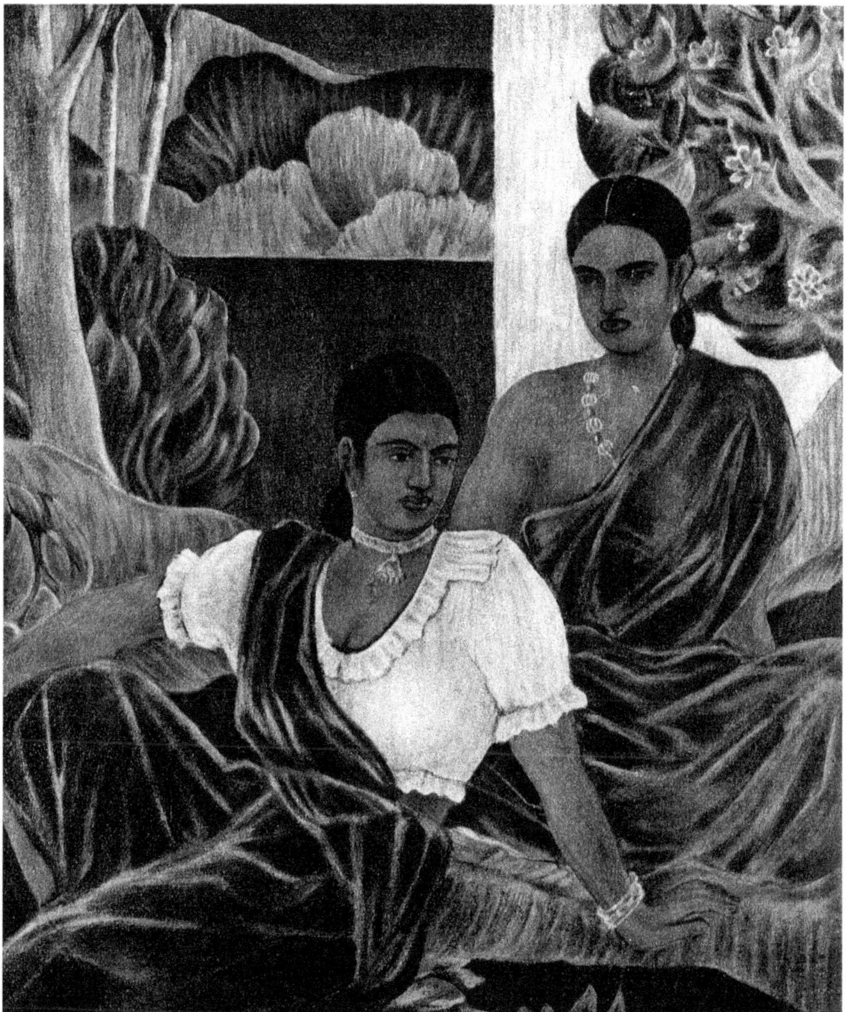

Plate I Kandyan Portrait. Oil on canvas, 1927. 76.2 × 93.98 cm

Courtesy: Martin Russell Archives.

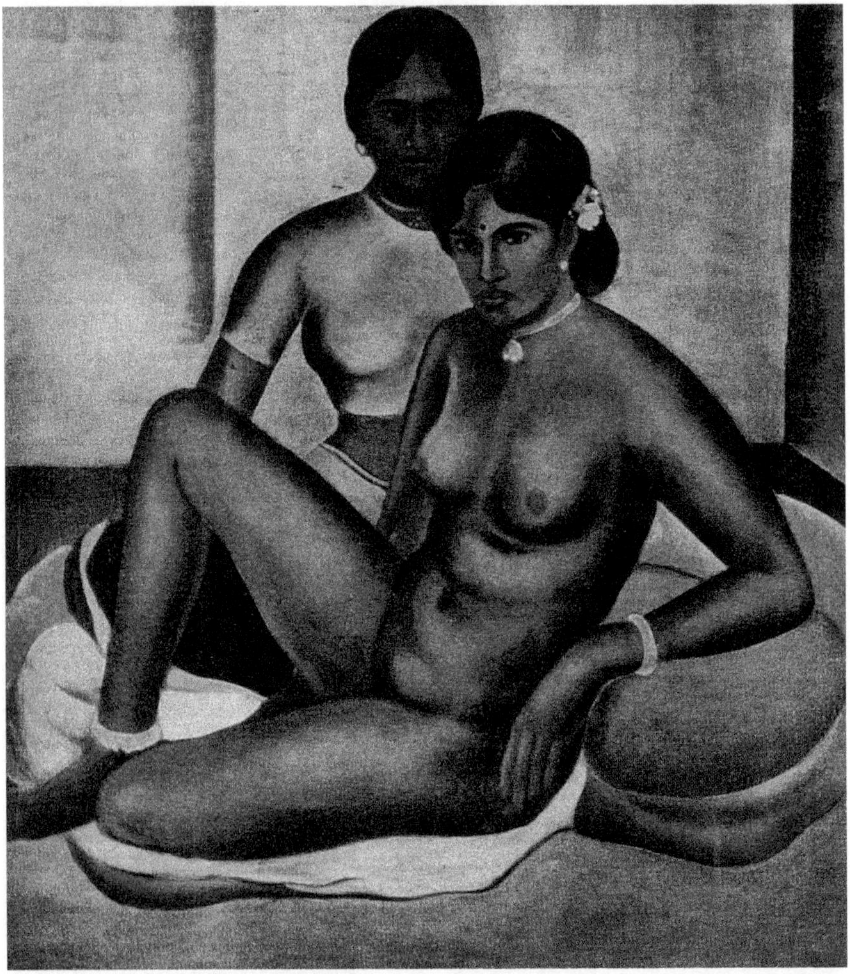

Plate II Portrait of Govindamma. Oil on canvas, 1928. 86.36 × 93.98 cm

Courtesy: Martin Russell Archives.

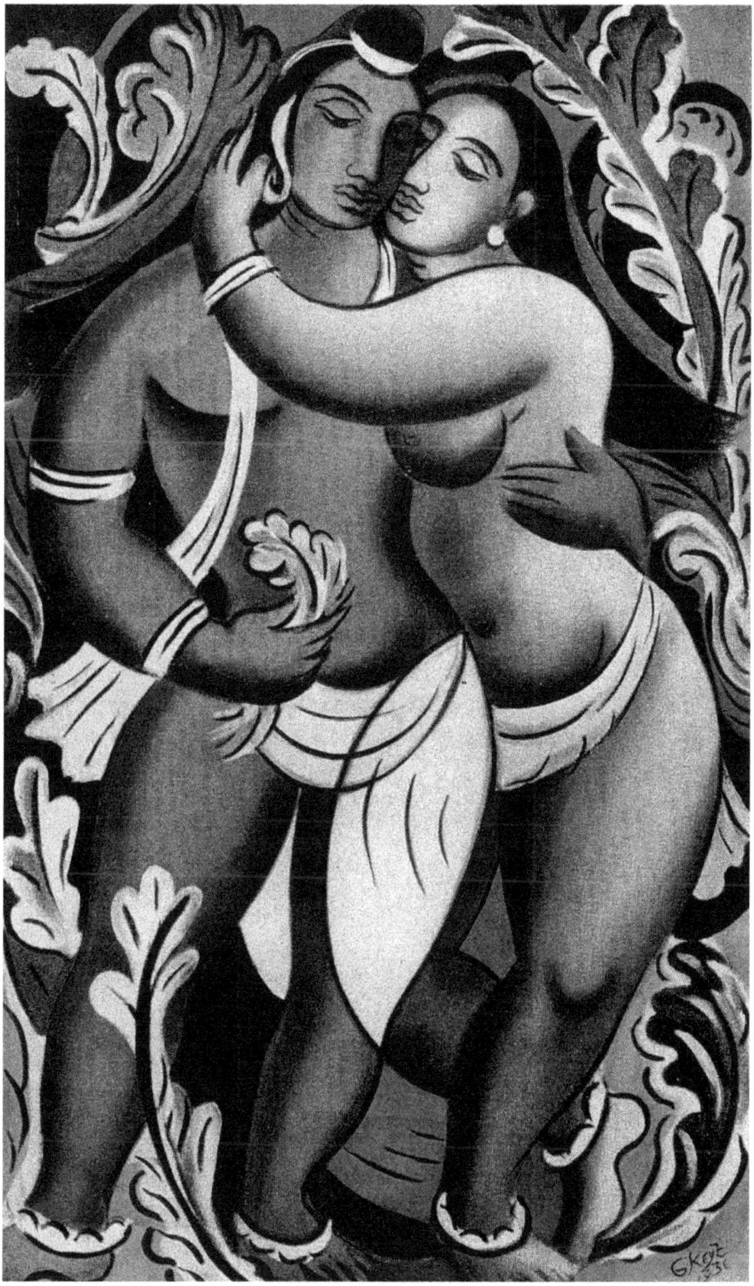

Plate III Sringara Rasa. Oil on canvas, 1936. 60.96 × 99.06 cm

Courtesy: Martin Russell Archives.

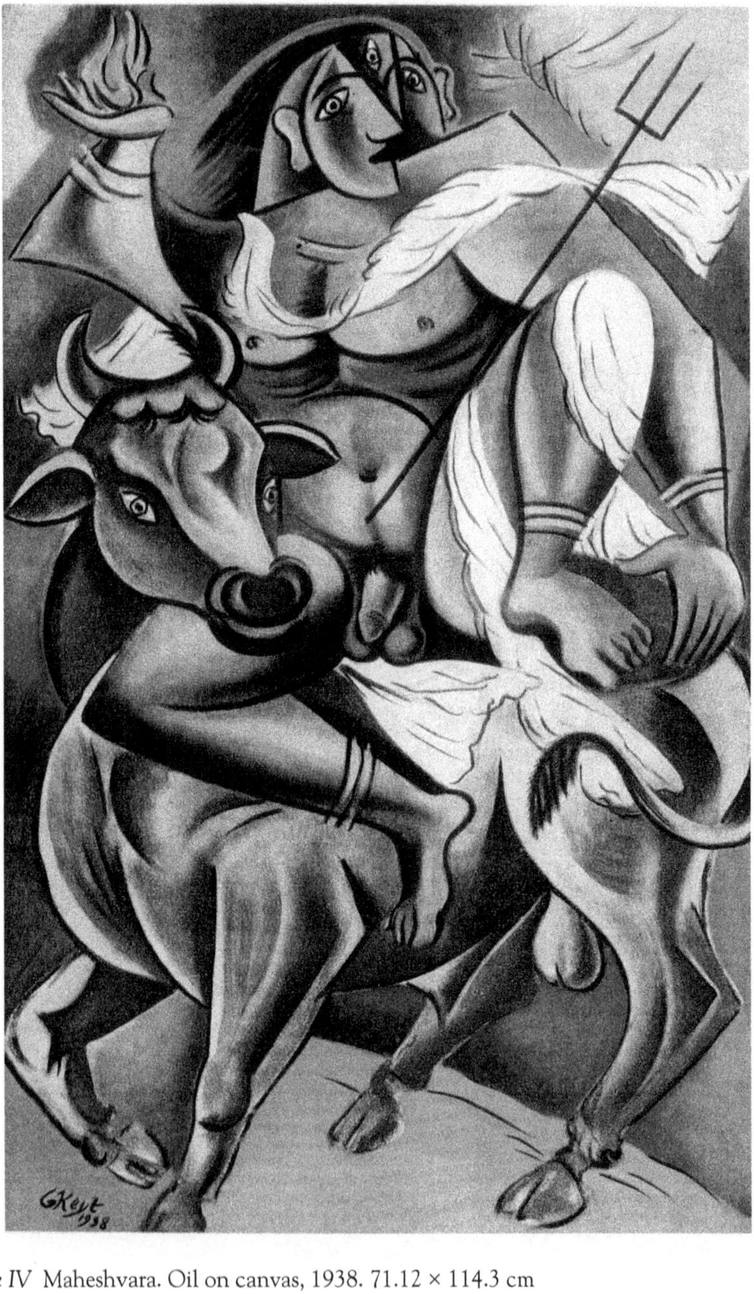

Plate IV Maheshvara. Oil on canvas, 1938. 71.12 × 114.3 cm

Courtesy: Martin Russell Archives.

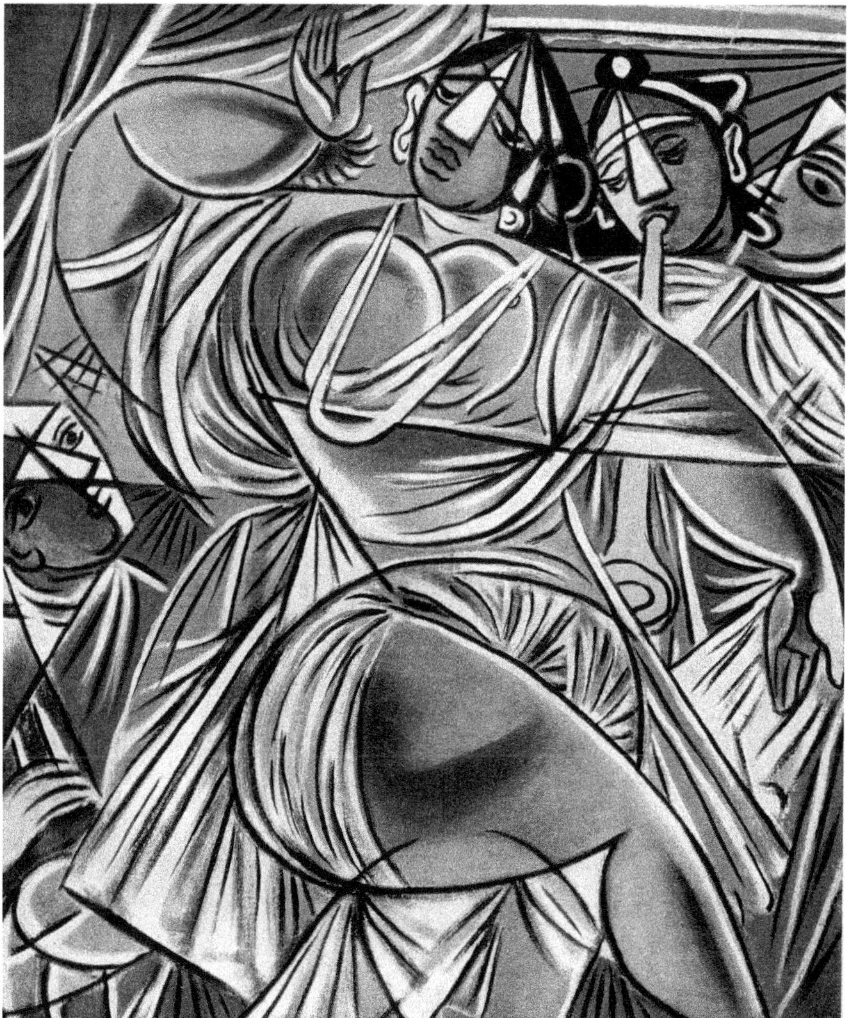

Plate V Jalaja. Oil on canvas, 1938. 63.5 × 76.2 cm

Courtesy: Martin Russell Archives.

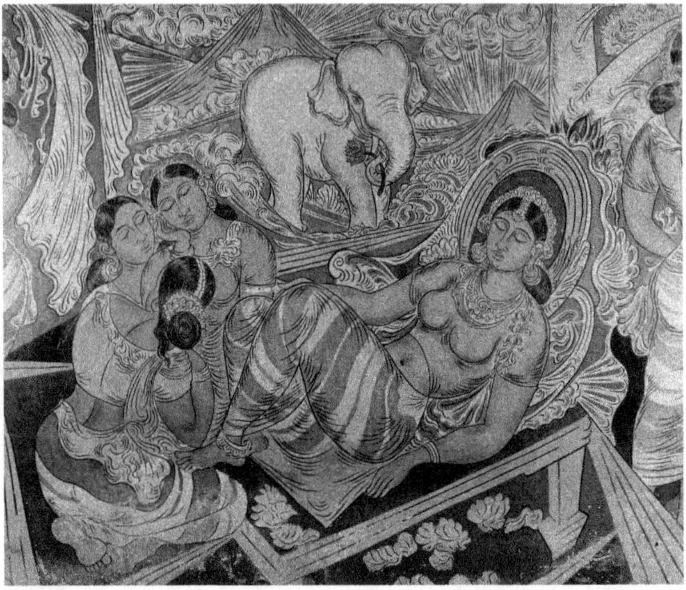

Plate VIa Mahamaya's Dream. Mural from Gotami Vihara, 1940

Courtesy: Martin Russell Archives.

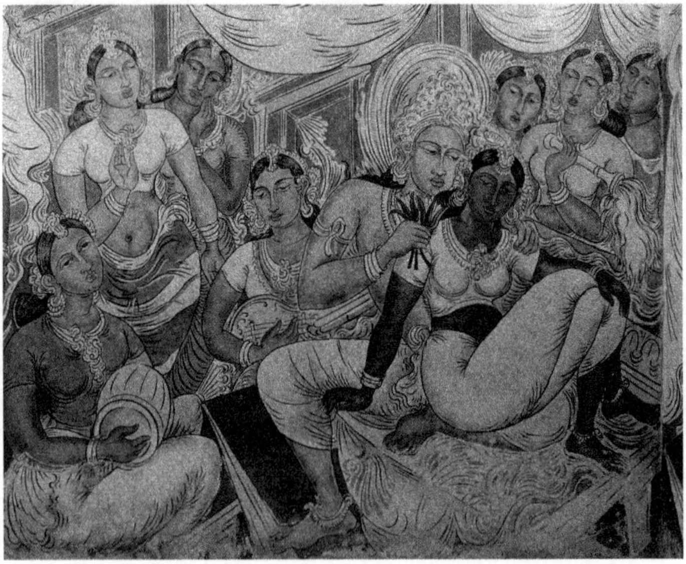

Plate VIb At the Palace with Yashodhara. Mural from Gotami Vihara, 1940

Courtesy: Martin Russell Archives.

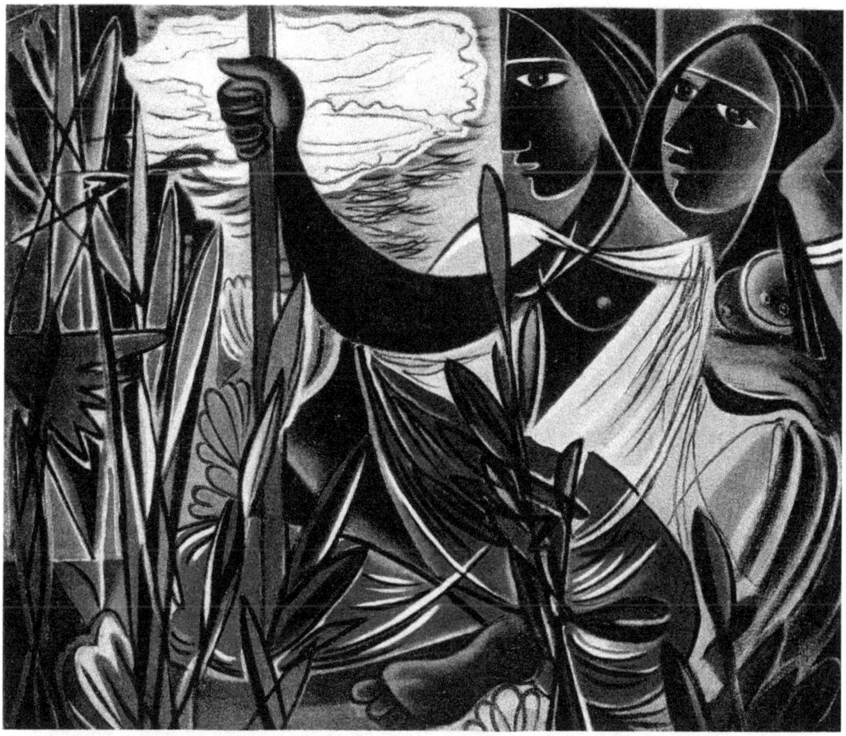

Plate VII The Journey. Oil on canvas, 1943. 91.44 × 76.2 cm

Courtesy: Martin Russell Archives.

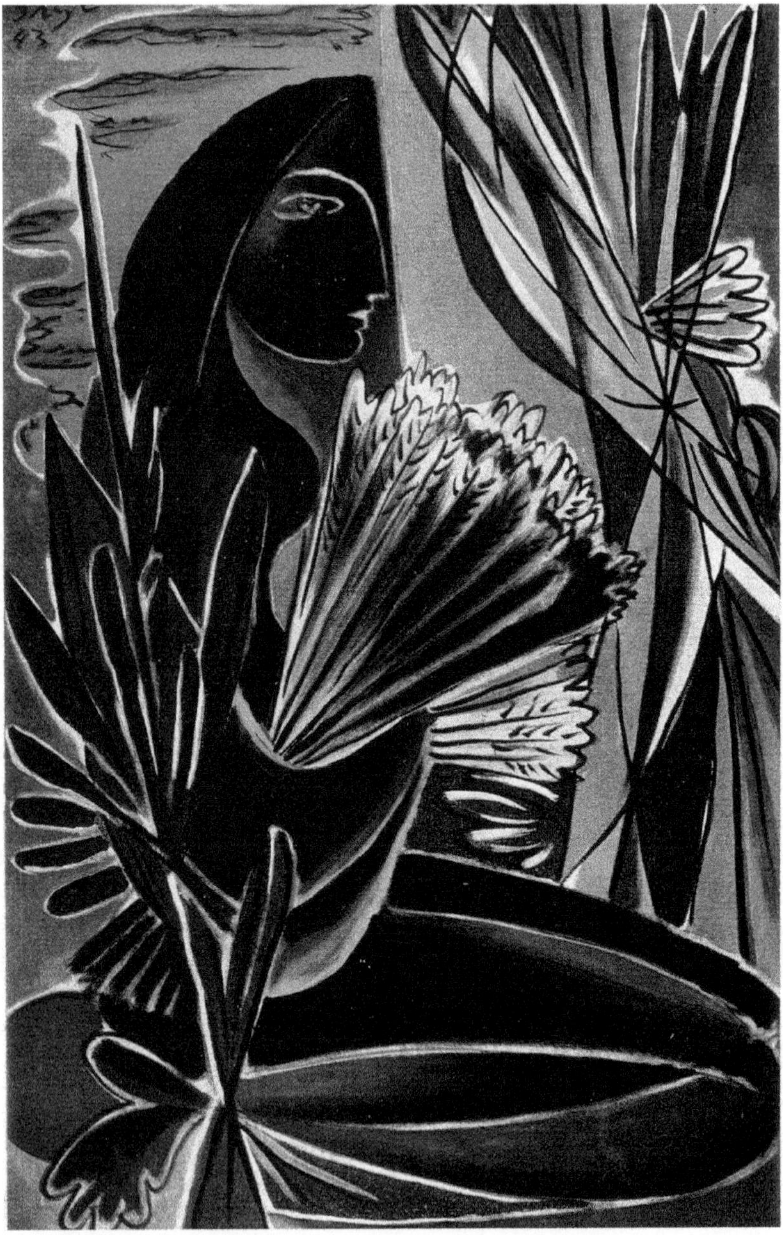

Plate VIII Woman with Sheaf. Oil on canvas, 1943. 48.26 × 76.2 cm

Courtesy: Martin Russell Archives.

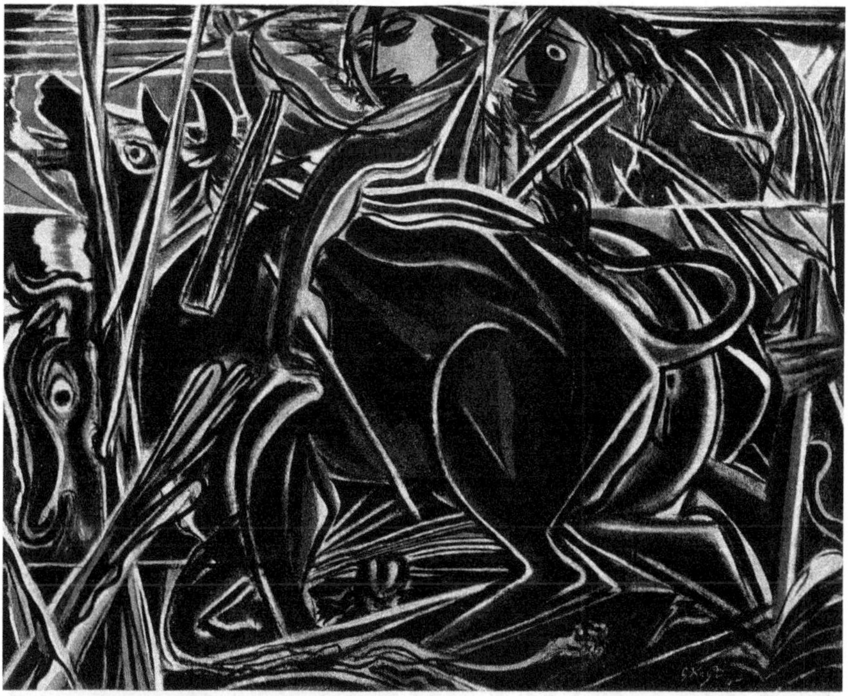

Plate IX Ploughing. Oil on canvas, 1944. 76.2 × 60.96 cm

Courtesy: Martin Russell Archives.

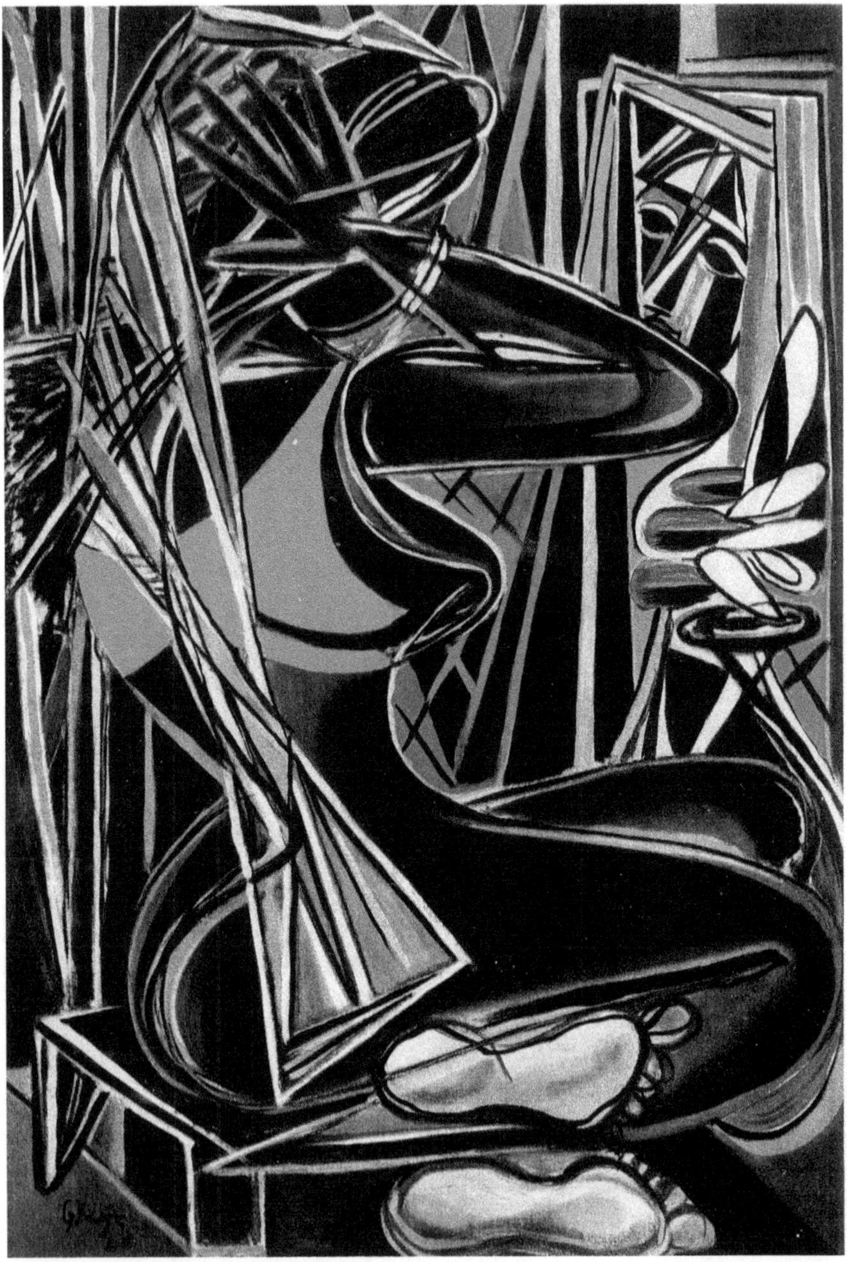

Plate X Sringar. Oil on canvas, 1944. 55.88 × 81.28 cm

Courtesy: Martin Russell Archives.

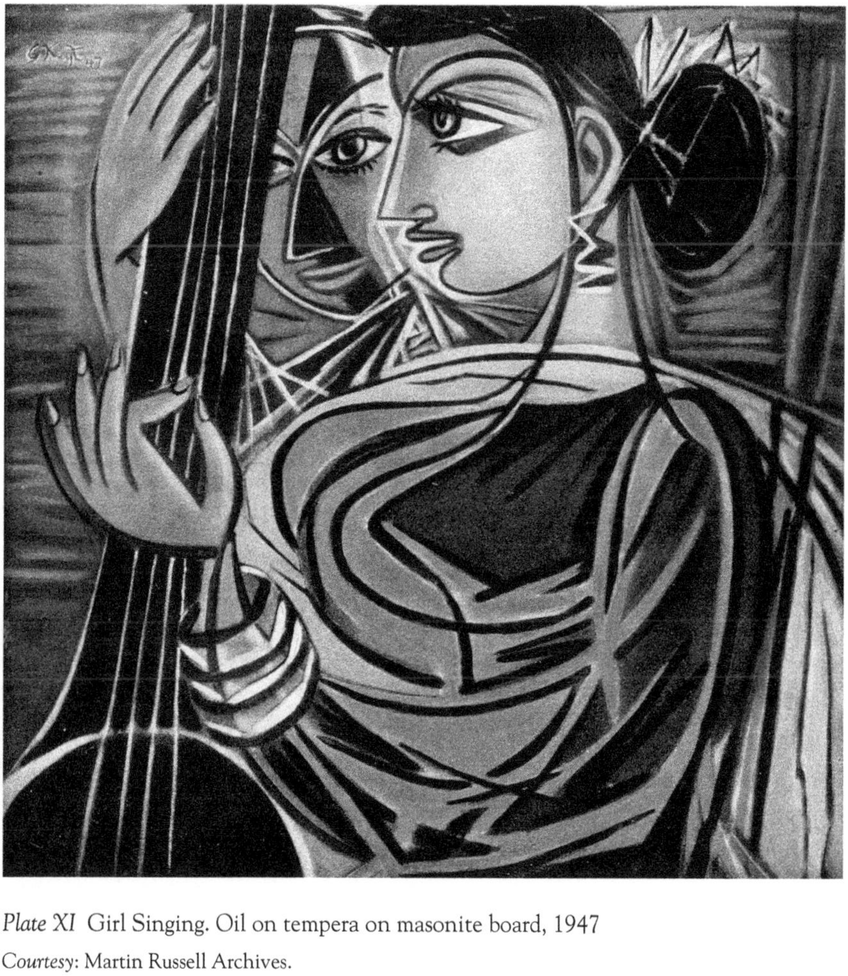

Plate XI Girl Singing. Oil on tempera on masonite board, 1947

Courtesy: Martin Russell Archives.

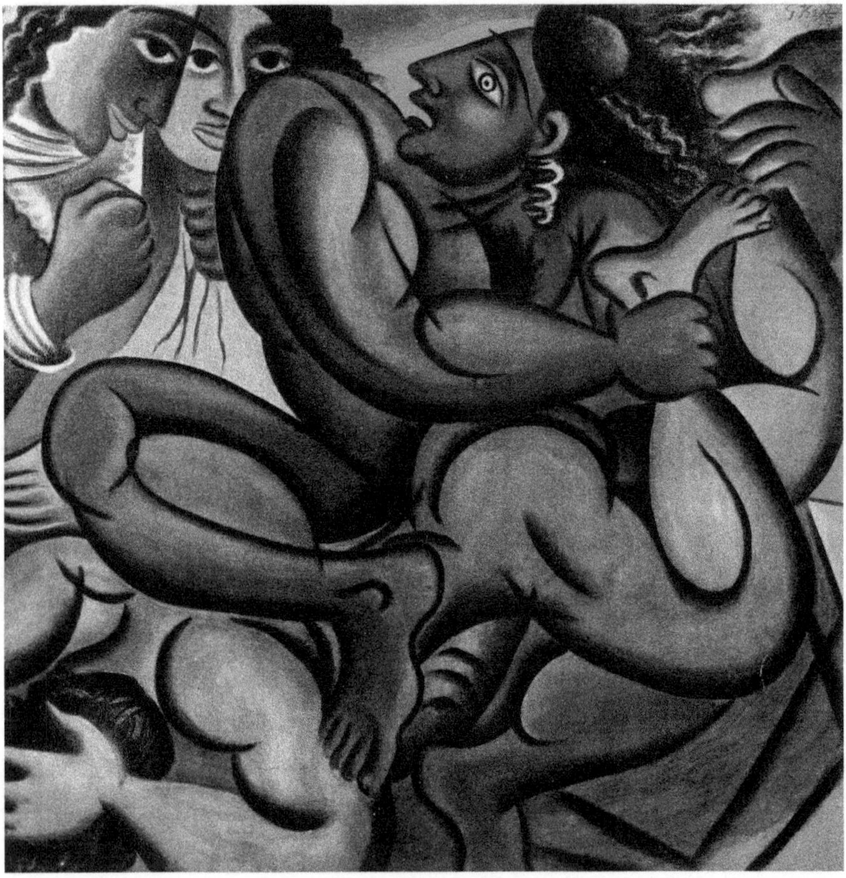

Plate XII Bhima and Jarasandha. Oil on canvas, 1943. 78.74 × 78.74 cm

Courtesy: Martin Russell Archives.

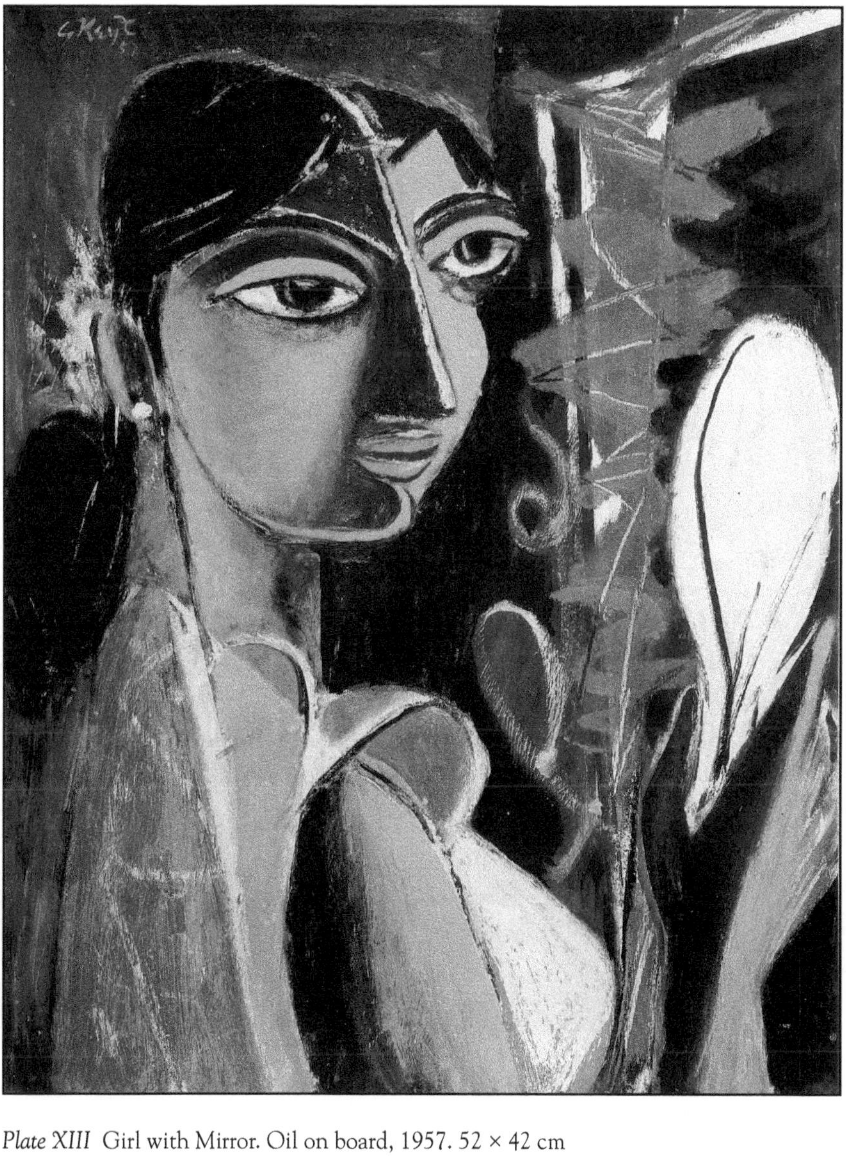

Plate XIII Girl with Mirror. Oil on board, 1957. 52 × 42 cm

Courtesy: Martin Russell Archives.

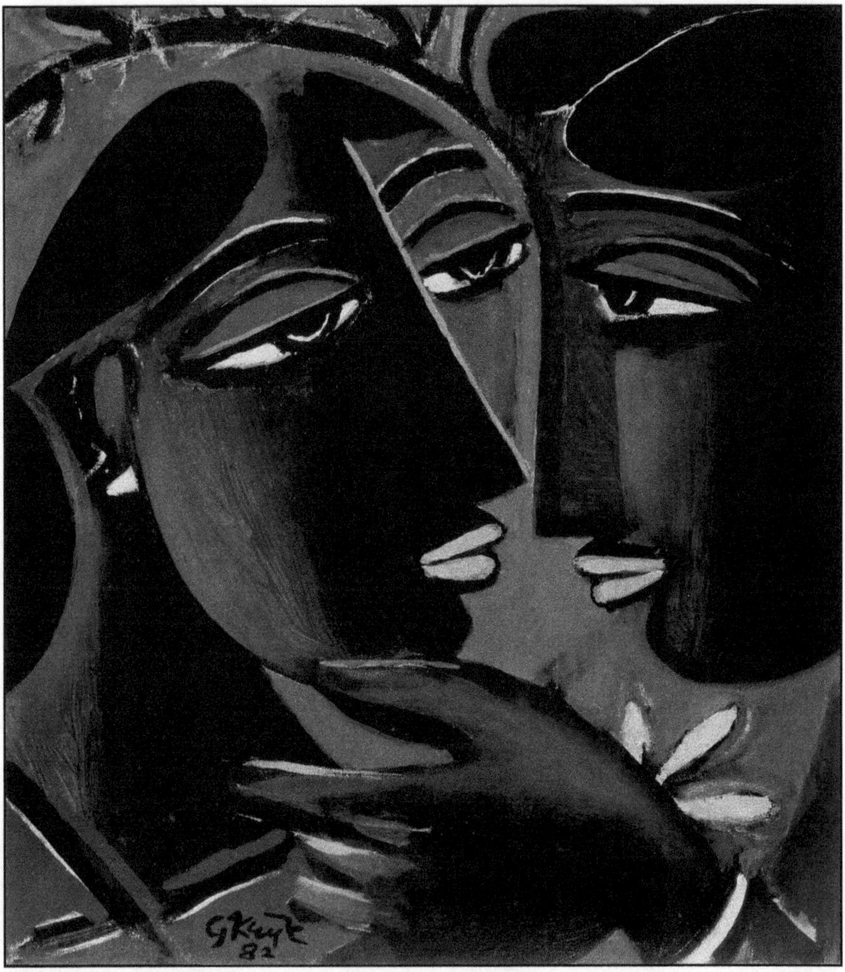

Plate XIV Friends. Acrylic on board, 1982. 39 × 39.5 cm

Courtesy: Martin Russell Archives.

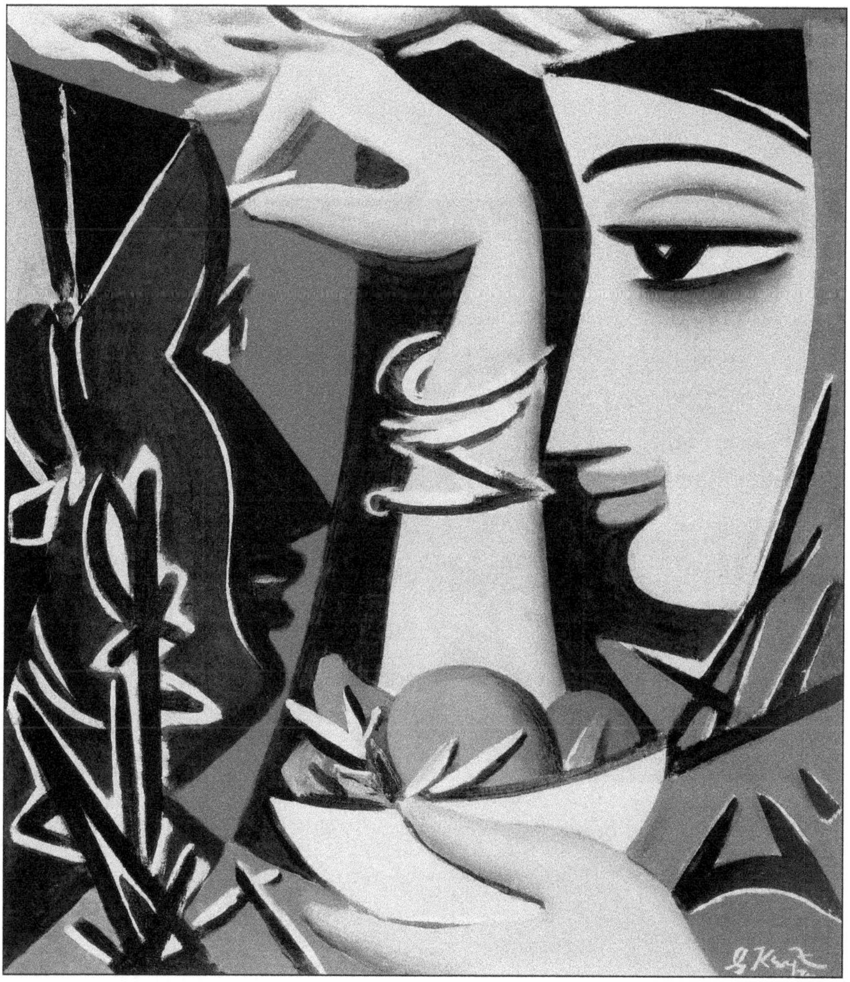

Plate XV Tilak. Acrylic on canvas, 1974. 45 × 41 cm

Courtesy: Martin Russell Archives.

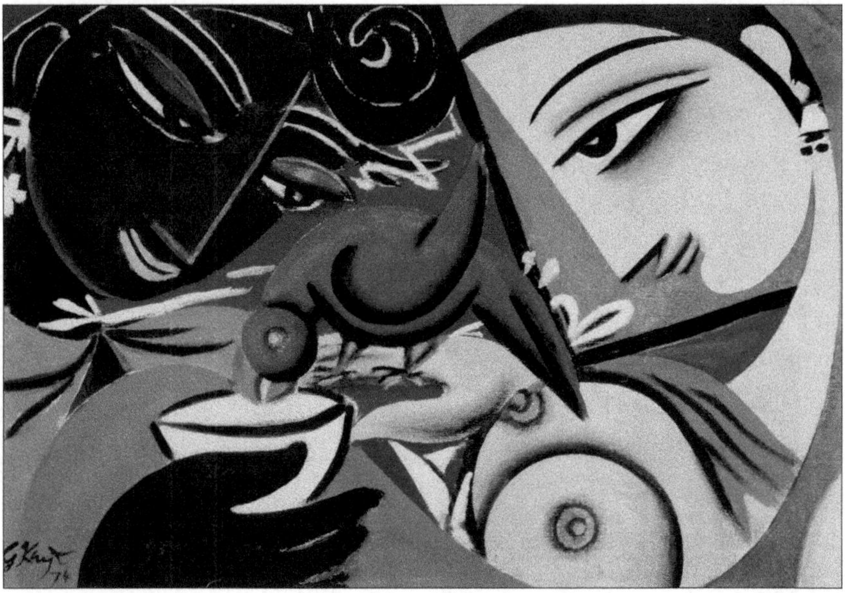

Plate XVI Radha and Krishna. Acrylic on canvas, 1974. 45 × 65.4 cm

Courtesy: Martin Russell Archives.

8

MARTIN'S JOURNEY

Many years later when the course of his life would change considerably George was to look upon Martin (1918–2004) as his closest and best friend. He had met him when he was 42 years old and had turned into a fully fledged painter and a domesticated man living an isolated life in a village near Kandy.

The closeness he felt for Martin can be gauged from the fact that he wrote to him continuously from Sri Lanka when he left the country, addressing him often as *namaste mere purane mitra* (greetings my old friend). Indeed he turned to him when in dire trouble particularly in his later years when life became unbearably difficult. How had this come about? They had grown up in completely different circumstances. Martin was a chess master and an Etonian who also happened to be the nephew of the great philosopher Bertrand Russell. He came from a wealthy upper class business family, where his father was a partner in Cull and Co. bankers to Chester Beatty and Henri Dreyfus. His father Gilbert Russell, a merchant banker, was the son of Lord Arthur Russell, brother of Hastings, 9th Duke of Bedford. Martin's mother, Maud, was painted by Sir William Nicholson, Orpen and McEvoy, and in 1937 had sat for a portrait by Matisse which hangs at the Southampton Gallery. She had contributed for the floor mosaics at the National Gallery made by the artist Boris Anrep and the two were said to have had an affair. He had also created her mosaic portrait playfully titled *Folly* at the Gallery alongside portraits of Bertrand Russell, T.S. Eliot, Greta Garbo and others.

Julian Russell, Martin's son, felt it was a common thing in that period,

> My father had been brought up in the English liberal arts tradition – dinner parties, affairs, my mother (Martin's wife) had gay friends at time when it was forbidden. One part of the family was

> upper class English, the army. The other was into liberal arts. Our house was covered with paintings. He had been brought up with his mother buying art. My grandmother was buying Picassos and she said, 'What is Martin doing buying unknown Asian art.'[1]

At the age of 17 Martin was taken to the great post-impressionist exhibition at Petit Palais by his mother (Maud Russell) and according to his account, 'She asked the girl selling the catalogues a question. She said "I'll ring up Vollard" who said – in translation – "ask the lady to come and see me". Vollard introduced her to Matisse who made a charcoal drawing of her.'

Voyage to Singapore

To revert to Martin, he joined the British Army in 1939 but was released the following year as he had asthma and became a temporary civil servant at the Ministry of Information. It was at this time that Duff Cooper became Minister of Information and Martin as his private secretary went with him to Singapore in 1941. At this time Cooper had been appointed Chancellor of the Duchy of Lancaster and was sent by Churchill to Singapore to report on the coordination of the numerous British government departments active in the Far East. Cooper was accompanied by his wife, Lady Diana, and by Russell as his private secretary.

According to Martin's obituary,

> On the way to Singapore, bad weather forced their ship into Lisbon, where they stayed at the British Embassy. One evening, having dined out, Russell asked a taxi driver to take him back to the embassy. He was deposited at a building that was in darkness; he walked through the door and found himself standing in front of an enormous portrait of Hitler. It was the driver's idea of a joke.[2]

Cooper was to leave in haste as the Japanese were about to capture the island and it is here that things began to change for Martin. He rejoined the army there in January 1942 to work in the cipher office. In his own words,

> By great good fortune, a few days before the island was captured by the Japanese army, I met Admiral Spooner in the street. He said, 'You shouldn't be here at all', and made arrangements for me

> to be evacuated. I was moved by the Army and Navy via Sumatra and Java to Ceylon. I disembarked from a river steamer in Colombo on 10th May 1942.[3]

According to Julian, 'Martin went on a river steamer from Singapore to Sri Lanka. They had to burn the wood to get it across. He was in intelligence so he had to send some fake messages. All quite boring for him.'[4]

He checked himself in at the Galle Face Hotel, Colombo, which was largely empty and reported the next day to Ceylon Army Command Headquarters, which had taken over the Museum. Since Martin's parents had visited Ceylon in 1939 and knew people there he was introduced to the upper crust without much effort. He met Jerry and Hilda Naidoo where the former was a proctor and the latter a pianist and possessed two grand pianos! Through them he was to meet Lionel Wendt who sought legal advice from Jerry and also taught music to Hilda.

> Hilda and Jerry took me to see Lionel Wendt at 18 Guildford Crescent, opposite the Museum, where the army employed me as cipher officer. . . . I was not entirely ignorant of modern art. My father's family, the Russells, had made collection of paintings for centuries, but regarded modern art as incomprehensible or absurd. My mother was half Jewish and half German, and she began to appreciate modern art quite late about 1935, and took me to see a most important exhibition in Paris, at the Petit Palais. Henri Matisse made two drawings of her, so when in Lionel Wendt's glorious sitting room I saw two magnificent oil paintings, *Nara Narayana* by George Keyt, and *Homage to El Greco* by Ivan Peries, I was smitten. I was a hardworking army officer in a strange country, threatened by invasion from a cruel and almost barbarous enemy, and I was sometimes living in private houses, sometimes in hotels and sometimes in army huts, but I brought some pictures by Ivan Peries, although I had nowhere to hang them.[5]

Meeting Lionel

Lionel Wendt befriended Martin because he

> perceived I was a sensitive soul, and he invited me to come to his house one morning to see his collection of pictures. The

> Wadsworth was amongst them, also *Nara Narayana* by Keyt, and *Homage to El Greco* by Ivan Peries. I liked them very much. When I arrived to see them, I entered through an open French window, to find him playing the piano in a most authoritative manner, such as I had never heard in an English house, even from my brother, who later reached high standards. I did not interrupt him, but remained standing until he had finished the piece.[6]

Subsequently he was to meet George Keyt at the opening of the inaugural exhibition of the '43 Group in November 1943.

> At that time I did not quite understand Keyt's work, because it was so non-European, but another member of the '43 Group, George Claessen, now living in London, pointed out to me that Keyt's work had a 'poetic' quality. The word 'poetic' used by Claessen has been embedded in my memory ever since. I bought all the Keyts in the show, except one, *The Journey*, which I was told Lionel Wendt himself wanted to buy.[7]

In the meantime a neighbour of his mothers' in Hampshire, Lord Louis Mountbatten, was appointed Supreme Allied Commander, South East Asia, in 1943, and established his headquarters at Peredeniya. As a result Martin was moved from Colombo to the Allied Land Forces Headquarters at Kondesalle which was only an hour's walk from Amunugama where Keyt was living with Manike. Martin began walking there in the evenings once or twice a week for a meal, and began buying his latest works which he hung in the officer's mess.

Those were heady days for George and Manike. They would have Martin and other friends over for company in the evenings and talk late into the night. 'George Keyt was a mentor of my fathers. He was very well educated and quite clever. That was the primary relationship.'[8]

Later Martin would buy a small house near their place which he called *Srinivasa*. This house would be retained by him even after he left Ceylon and went back to England. 'He was quite adventurous and lived in a village. A village girl would bring water from the river.'[9] Perhaps Martin would have liked to stay here forever and tried hard to convince his mother that it was a whole different way of perceiving things which she had to understand. Among the few British officers posted in the subcontinent during colonial times who saw things differently, he would surely be the most comprehending. In a letter to his mother he complains of her patronizing attitude towards India:

> I have found it very difficult to write to you from India because of your unsympathetic attitude to Indian things. It seemed hardly worth writing when I knew you would not believe what I said or agree with my opinions. My last letter was an attempt to overcome these difficulties . . . I do not think I caused so much trouble as Raymond [his brother who went to live in Malta and died there], but I would like to remind you that this was due to my management of severe neurotic afflictions silently, without giving way to public manifestations, and to ask you for more understanding . . . First, you devote a page to 'that India those English civil servants seemed to run quite well' That exasperates me. Of course they run it quite well! . . . Most Indians of intelligence not only admit this, they [welcome] it! What is the good of your writing this to me? I know what the civil servants did well, I know what they did badly or left undone . . . I have met two civil servants on intimate terms since I came here. One was Shiveshwarkar, the Administrator of Junagadh whom I stayed with for three weeks . . . He is a Maharashtrian Brahmin who joined the civil service after winning high mathematical honours at Cambridge. Integrity and impartiality could go no further . . . He gave Muslims perfect security, and protected them against communal animosities. The other civil servant I met was W.G. Archer. He is a fine type of Englishman, sympathetic to Indians, an authority on aboriginal folk poetry, and [is an immense] enthusiast for Indian painting and [in particular] for the miniatures. He has of course a big knowledge of Indian [affairs] in some fields – administration, political, legal etc. But I could not compare him favourably with Shiveshwarkar as an administrator . . . Archer is conscious of his ignorance but I believe this is exceptional. It is typical of British attitude to [deplore] that Archer should be an authority in the aboriginals – the least interesting aspect of Indian life. We have always shirked Hinduism. Now that India is again independent we cannot shirk it in any longer, particularly as India will possibly remain within the Commonwealth.[10]

Martin made another strong complaint to his mother,

> Now I want to answer a remark in your letter that irritated me beyond measure when I read it. 'Folk songs, popular poetry, tales

> of [heroic] exploits till exist in a number of countries. You needn't go further than Yugoslavia and Bulgaria. . . .' I think it is fantastic to compare Yugoslavia and Bulgaria with India. In any case Y and B have nothing to do with me. . . . I am living in the land of the Buddha whose importance is not less than that of Christ or Socrates. All civilizations East of India is based on India or influenced by India . . . It is however a pleasure to find a culture of high intellectual value co-existing with a folk art which is derived from it. It gives a [certain] grace to life which is lacking in many countries.[11]

In an interesting comparison between an English and a Ceylonese village Martin writes,

> In England the village atmosphere is utterly different from the village atmosphere of Ceylon. In the England the villages are associated with cricket, beer and the maypole tree, also with soup and rent. In Ceylon the most conspicuous thing about the villager is his beautiful command of Sinhalese. Knox, the first or one of the first Englishmen to go to Kandy, in the 17th century, remarked that every man of the Hamuduruwa caste, though he worked in the field, was fit to be a king . . . Another thing about the Sinhalese villager is the superiority of his women, beautiful creatures, shy, intelligent, just as Keyt has evoked them. Marriage is a civil affair. It has no religious significance in Buddhism. The girls are not expected to be virgins – what a horrid thought. Nor are they expected to be promiscuous (unlike Archer's idiotic aboriginals). Any relationship with a Kandyan girl must be based on politeness, shyness, intimacy. . . . That is why Keyt's *Nayika* paintings are felt to be almost sacred. So don't scoff I beg but admire the consummate technique which unites Indian art with modern art, and folk art with Art. Keyt's work is uneven – but so is the work of all artists (excepting Braque and Rouault who maintain their own special levels quite consistently).[12]

Martin's involvement with the arts in India and Ceylon in a way was intuitive and perceptive at a time when it was unheard of to think of anything beyond Euro-American art.

He attempted to explain this to his mother, equally well grounded in Western art, who found it difficult to understand it or why Martin wasn't

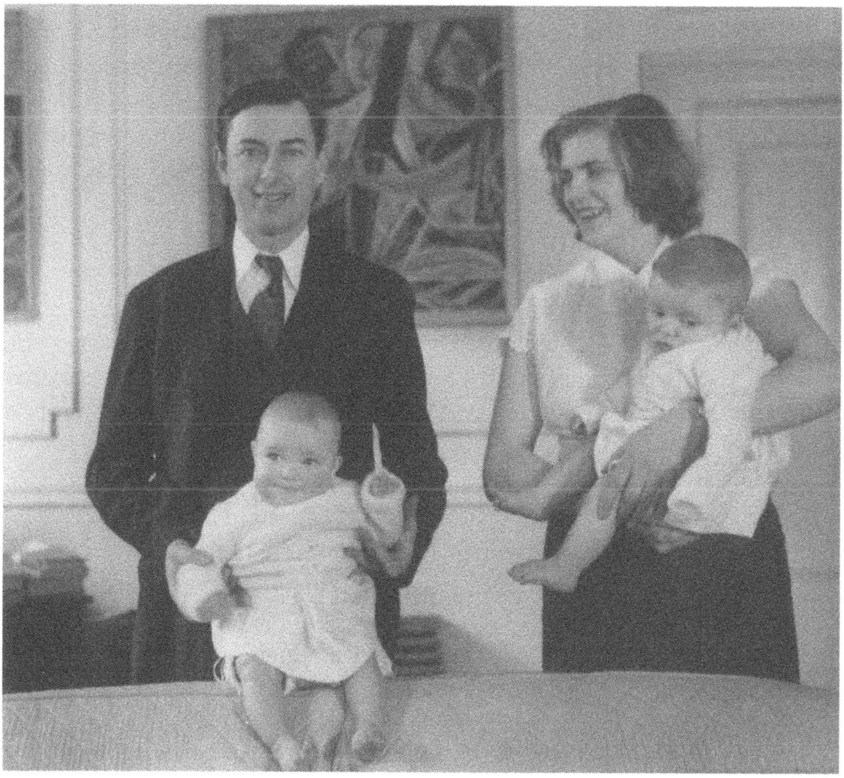

Figure 8.1 Martin, Anne, Julian and Stephen.
Courtesy: Martin Russell Archive.

returning. When in August 1945 the atom bombs were dropped on Japan, he was to return to London on Christmas Eve in 1946. In an interesting interlude, on his way back he visited Thailand where a Siamese lady sculpted his head in clay and had it cast in bronze. In the meantime he found a valuable head of Buddha lying in the fields and sent it back to England labelled 'Head of Martin Russell'. The head by his sculptor was sent back labelled 'Head of Buddha'.[13]

The book on George

During his stay in London, the Bombay art magazine *Marg* managed by Mulk Raj Anand and Anil de Silva asked him to write a book on Keyt. Martin wrote part of it at his favourite place, the Mottisfont Abbey at

Hampshire. It became essential for him to return to India to enable him to complete the book and he moved to Bombay where George and Manike were staying. The book came out in 1950 but he continued to stay in India until the end of 1952 after which he returned to his house *Srinivasa* in Sirimalwatte. He went back to England in March 1953 but for the rest of his life retained a long and intimate association with George mainly through correspondence.

Martin's account of what met his eyes in India when he was living there is a record of a period when society and culture retained a pristine link with each other and their rootedness in an ancient tradition. At the same time, there was an enviable exchange with international developments which was later to be more restricted. What is more, the people were optimistically intent on a change in their society. In his account of Karachi Martin writes,

> The customs authorities charming and efficient. The streets clean (Hindu sweepers still at work). The dogs well fed and cheerful. The sacred cows still amble on the pavement. The hotel is crowded with English businessmen so that I have to share a room and a table. There is one most excellent smart restaurant with a dance floor. Excellent food. High prices. Chianti is the cheapest wine at twenty-five shillings a bottle. The bookshops appallingly bad – the standard is sub-edgarwallabe. Books on India are almost unheard of, but tomorrow I go by train to Lahore where the bookshops are better.

From Karachi Martin travels to Lahore, Rawalpindi and then Murree. About the latter he wrote, 'Marvellous wild country – the people sturdy but living an incredibly primitive life and yet active and humorous.'[14]

> Also I went to Taxila where I found a most excellent small museum and was most carefully shown every object by the Indian in charge – a refugee from East Punjab . . . The art of Taxila includes the extreme Eastward finds of work in the Gandharva style and some pre-Gandhara sculpture, very good and very interesting. Also much Gupta work from nearby Buddhist monasteries of which I visited two, with excellent specimens. The old town of Taxila is about as big as Cavendish Square – or perhaps twice as big! . . . It had a main street about as big as the drive at Mottisfont with smaller side streets at right angles. It was in perfect condition – a great credit to the Archaeological Survey of

> India – with all renovations carefully marked and dated. When I say 'perfect condition' I mean that although only the bottoms of the walls remain – a few feet only in the case of the top city – they had sown grass and drained the ground and prevent any new deteriorations.[15]

When he reached Lahore by train the following day we get a totally different account,

> On the following day I returned by train to Lahore. Many Pathans carrying rife and ammunitions over on the train, having no doubt come down from Peshawar. One complete coach was reserved for 'Azad Kashmir' (Free Kashmir). From this and other things I hear it is absurd to pretend Pakistan is not helping the tribesmen . . . There were a few Hindus in Lahore but it will be a long time before a Sikh can show his face.[16]

Travels in the country

By December 1948, Martin is in Delhi where:

> I am sorry to say appalled by vulgar ostentation and incomprehensible mistakes of styles in the British-built city – Lutyens I'm afraid. Hindu, Buddhist, Islamic, Greek, Christian motives mixes in hideous confusion: we were all the more sensitive to these outrages through having seen so much fine architecture in the previous fortnight – Sanchi, the forts at Gwalior and Agra, Akbar's palace at Fatehpur Sikri, the temples at Brindaban, the gems at Mathura, the streets of Jaipur – that it is astounding suddenly to be confronted by the bad taste of our own age.[17]

By 24 December 1948 George, Manike and Martin set off in his American Ford, with the three sitting in front and mountains of luggage at the back, on a tour of India. They would load and unload every day, leaving by 10 or 11 in the morning and arriving by dusk. Their first stop was Nasik and then Dhulia and at this juncture Martin exclaimed,

> How enormous India is! What lovely country, what fine people, so distinguished compared to the rest of drab humanity. The Mahrattas appeal to me most – upright active men and women: Poona

> is their traditional capital but they populate Bombay and stretch as far as Indore and further. . . . The Dak Bungalow where we stay are maintained by the Government for travelers, not unlike the Ceylon Rest Houses, but usually simpler. The Keyts can manage Hindi so have few linguistic difficulties. Rice, mutton, dhall, and wheat pancakes accompanied with chapattis are our staples, cooked in village style and delicious. You should see how I thrive! Rice suits me marvelously as a diet. My asthma has disappeared completely.[18]

They stayed everywhere in Dak Bungalows where they got simple but delicious village food. These were the days of petrol rationing and they ran out of 'coupons' for it. They had been assured of getting it in Mhow but found instead a large fleet of stranded vehicles! 'Some attribute this to the overissue of coupons . . . some to the condition of the railways and to the recent Bombay dock strike.'[19] At the Dak Bungalow near Indore the

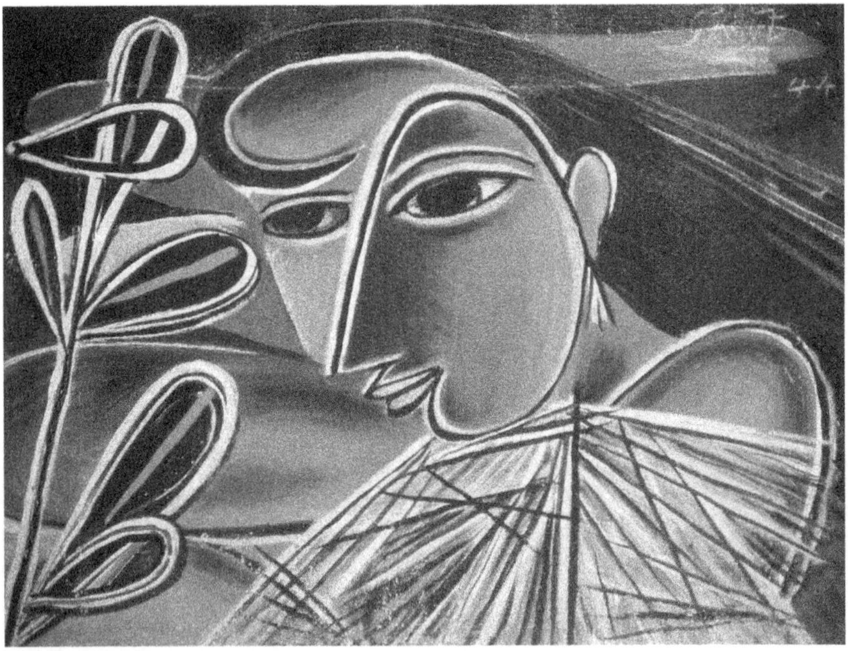

Figure 8.2 Portrait of Russell's soul in the guise of a Kandyan peasant.

George Keyt.
Oil on canvas, 1944.
Courtesy: Martin Russell Archive.

Police authorized the issue of petrol to take on to Bhopal where they got the required amount as there was no shortage here as Bhopal was on the main line from Bombay.

They stayed in the guest house in the grounds of the Nawab's palace and were very comfortable. Martin writes,

> Pandit Malaviya is a good friend and I think the best man in Bhopal . . . I did not care for the Muslims . . . hangers-on of the Court, except for two – Dr. Tamuri, the archaeologist, who is a distinguished man, and Sir Om Narain Vissariya, the Prime Minister – the name is Hindu but who appears to be Mohammedan.[20]

At Sanchi, they didn't visit the stupas but went instead to a nearby town called Bhilsa.

> Here the great Gupta Emperor, Chandra Gupta 2 paid a visit in 401 AD . . . His Minister of War had a cave cared in the rock to commemorate the visit . . . there is a huge carving of *Varaha*, the boar incarnation of *Visnu*. These strange incarnations, so repugnant to European taste were not represented in Hindu sculpture until the Gupta age . . . There is at Bhilsa a pillared by one Heliodorus, a Greek Ambassador . . . who lived at Taxila and worshipped Vishnu.[21]

The threesome continued to Saugar and thence to Chhatarpur. Martin writes,

> 'The old Maharajah is dead; his state is now merged with Vindhya Pradesh; and the young Maharajah lives in retirement in Khajuraho on an income of 15,000 pounds a year tax free. Khajuraho is the furtherest object of our tour, famous for its temples of the 10th and 11th centuries, for the carvings that adorn them. In the abundance of carving they remind one of Gothic but the abundance is much greater – perhaps 800 on one temple – and the temples too is comparatively small – much smaller than Romsey Abbey. They present difficulties and aesthetic problems . . . The quality of the sculpture is sometimes only of ordinary good craftsman's labour and sometimes very fine. There is a tremendous richness and vitality, joy beyond and joy in life, scenes from mythology being freely interspersed with exquisite erotic sculptures. Men

> and women are freely shown enjoying intercourse in all sorts of positions; often the man carries the girl, sometimes she bends and he possesses her from behind, sometimes a complicated position is shown including a man and three girls, sometimes it is only a tender caress or a kiss. It is noteworthy there is no representation of our perversions. Perversions were evidently thought obscure, indeed absolutely contrary to Hindu thought. We spent the nights in a small Dak Bungalow. It was without furniture and we all noticed how much more comfortable this is! – at least in a small house. I slept outside on the verandah, at the back was a small courtyard in which we washed in privacy: plenty of water is always made ready in India for washing, so we remain spruce and shaved under all conditions. We left Khajuraho very early one morning and motored the whole way to Sanchi in a day, about 200 miles. In Saugar we had lunch and applied to the Magistrate for petrol.[22]

Emergence of thought

The years Martin spent in India proved to be fruitful not only for George but for the cultural life of a newly Independent country. Perhaps one of the first intellectual magazine which was begun in the country was *Thought* and Martin became its main initiator and founder. The magazine was the brainchild of both Martin and an Indian publisher from Bombay, Narayan. Perhaps Martin met him through Mulk who was a mutual friend. At any rate the two struck up a friendship and hatched a plan to bring out a weekly paper devoted to reflective pieces on politics, literature and the arts along the lines of the much respected *New Statesman*. It was in 1949 that Martin first mentions it to his mother,

> I have taken a 36 % share in the weekly paper of the *New Statesman* kind to be brought out in Delhi. The other proprietors are Indians, the chief being a friend by name Narayan. We have obtained a brilliant editor called Arthur Moore. He is really the senior journalist in India being formally the editor of *The Statesman*, the most important Indian daily paper, which is published simultaneously from Delhi and Calcutta. He quarreled with the European Association [of Journalists] during the war and had to resign (as he was a friend of Gandhi's he did not approve of the

> repression [against Indians]. A tall and distinguished man not dissimilar to Mr. Branson, our paper is to be called *Thought* . . . Although himself an Indian, Narayan prefers to have an English editor . . .[23]

A few months later the first issue was out and Martin wrote,

> *Thought* has come out amidst insuperable difficulties. The press we established ourselves was owned by a Muslim who was being cheated by his Hindu business manager – not of course cheated because he was a Muslim, but because Hindu happened to be a scoundrel. We made representations to the Government, but fruitlessly, for they instructed the Custodian of Evacuee Property to seize the press. The effect of this and the subsequent litigation – on the following day the Delhi Magistrate ordered the Government to release the press – was to prevent publishing there. We moved at short notice to a tiny press in the bazaar and have produced several issues on time! The Police Commissioner then agreed to help by unsealing another press which had been suppressed by the Government for printing Hindu Mahasabha literature – the propaganda of Hindu nationalism. We shall start printing there immediately.[24]

But paramount among the difficulties faced by the paper was the lack of finance because of the mismanagement of the business side. Martin decided to resolve the situation by going to Delhi.[25]

This visit proved fruitful and the paper began to improve but

> the literary section is very inferior. Most Indian literature is in the vernacular – in the Indian languages – certainly the best is, and it is virtually unknown in English. It will take time to ferret it out and get it translated and written about. Some of the films are good but here the prevalence of European standards of criticism make it difficult to get good reviewing. The proper person to review an Indian film would be Shakespeare or a Marlowe – but such people in India don't know English and can't write for Thought. Moreover previously nothing has been written about India – with few exceptions – except in disparagement. Very few people – non-Indians – have come here to appreciate the food, clothes, women, films, music, eroticism, painting, sculpture etc. without

> ulterior motive. Most either become devotees of Indian religion or adopt a generally supercilious attitude – or even become downright critical. This is the result of Europe's unhappy contact with India – that of conquest – with all the debasement of disparagement implied. The marvelous luxury and beauty of Hindu civilization in its prime is virtually unknown. . . . Even today the music of India is (to my mind) unsurpassable though of course entirely different from ours. I'm afraid I shall be here most of this year – it can't be helped![26]

While being beset by financial difficulties the paper also had a paucity of good writers in those early years of cultural life. Yet it managed to retain an independent stance and also critique the government as well as the establishment. The bigger problem was to get the right editor for the paper!

> What is more disagreeable is that we have had a severe quarrel with our former editor Arthur Moore. A quarrel with a man of 70, active, obstinate and not strictly honest is no joke. The amount included are small, say only 2000 pounds at the most, but our Company cannot afford such a loss, besides which we are not willing to be cheated. We are prepared to bring him into the Courts but as he has great reputation, was our own editor, broadcasts often, was editor of *The Statesman* and was for years ahead of the European Group in the Assembly, it is a grave step to have to take . . . I have got Sir Maurice Gwyer, the Vice Chancellor of Delhi University and former Chief Justice of India to act as conciliator or 'honest broker'. He is not very active at the moment as he has developed laryngitis and cannot speak![27]

Following this Ram Singh was appointed editor of the paper and Martin hoped that it would now be on even keel for:

> He is an exceptionally honest intelligent hardworking man, by origin a Jat from the United Provinces . . . During the war he was anti-Fascist and supported the British war effort, unlike the Congress. He is therefore not popular, but I have a high regard for him. Unfortunately his Hindi is better than his English, and in the long run it will be necessary to give him a sub-editor who knows English really well to revise his writing. This may be a matter of some delicacy.[28]

Martin went on to appoint the literary editor who was none other than the famed Hindi poet and writer S.H. Vatsyayan and went on to explain his appointment to his mother.

> The great point about him is that he was sent to prison for trying to blow up Lord Halifax's train. Although the attempt was unhappily a fiasco – a hole was blown through the floor of one compartment without a derailment – he doubtless did his best. Subsequently he seems to have made his peace with the British authorities and became Captain Vatsyayana during the war. He is the most silent man I've ever met and seems to be a person of profound convictions – apart from his conviction for conspiracy. However, what his convictions are I have not yet discovered, but I hope to learn them through the columns of my paper.[29]

Travails of a publisher

By May 1950, Martin was still struggling to keep the paper going. He could not return to England as planned because,

> My main preoccupation is *Thought*. This though mostly ill written, shows continued signs of improvement and may become in the end the best political and literary weekly in India. I have had a difficult time with it. [At first] it was under Arthur Moore, and though I was a minority shareholder I gradually had to accept the main responsibility for it. This was by no means agreeable, as I did not agree with the politics in very important respects especially when he advocated Pakistan's rights . . . and the management and financial administration was disastrous and even dishonest. Then came Diwan Chaman Lall, India's newly assigned Ambassador to Turkey. Chaman Lall rapidly changed the paper completely and did not carry on with his share of his agreement with the group which owns *Thought*. I wrested *Thought* out of Chaman Lall's hands and as it showed signs of life decided to keep it going myself and restore it . . . under Indian editorship.
>
> Unfortunately just before I did this our best journalist and writer resigned from the staff, and although the paper is better it still limps badly. The present [writer] is a man I respect but when his leading article is entitled 'Reshuffle an Eyewash' I feel despondent![30]

The circulation remained stagnant and the paper was losing 5,000 pounds a year though Martin felt this was not excessive. He continued to be optimistic,

> Fortunately the outlook is not wholly discouraging. First . . . Minoo Masani, who was a member of the Viceroy's Council at one time and is a forthright and intelligent person, has offered to join . . . *Thought*. Secondly, I have appointed [someone] to improve the English and I have hopes that our literary editor, S. H. Vatsyayan, who is a poet and short story writer in Hindi will make the literary column good. Thirdly, a really nice man has offered to join the paper for a month or so as Manager, which would make a world of difference. I think it will therefore be best if I keep *Thought* going for another 12 months, since if in that time it becomes self-supporting it will, as an influential paper, be an asset worth owning . . .

Martin had many visions about it,

> I am registering and new Company and I hope to call it *Srinivasa Limited*, which will be my own company with my own picked directors and will take over *Thought* from my present associates whose dishonesty I would not mind if they were reasonably competent. . . . *Srinivasa* (the new Company) should be working by the end of June.[31]

The matter of his staff for the paper remained problematic until the end. Many years later in the late 1970s he was still justifying the appointment of S. H. Vatsyayan for his paper. He wrote to Martin Gilbert in Oxford from his residence at Dungrove Farmhouse, Dorset, on 25 March 1978,

> I think that Lord Irwin's letter dated 26th December 1929 to Churchill, in answer to Churchill's telegram of congratulations, may require historical qualifications. Between 1948 and 1952 I was the effective proprietor of a small Indian weekly newspaper in Delhi. The editor was Ram Singh, now dead, on whose advice I appointed a Hindi writer called Vatsyayan to be literary editor. (The name Vatsyayan is the same as that attributed to the author of *Kama Sutra.*)
>
> Ram Singh told me that Vatsyayan had been one of the conspirators to kill Irwin. Vatsyayan told me that he had been the scientific adviser to the conspirators. I cannot be exact about what

he told me, but I believe he chose the amount of the explosive, the writing, the switch, the electrical batteries required to effect the detonation, etc.

The conspirators wished to kill as little life as possible, so they decided to detonate the explosive under the Viceroy's carriage only, rather than derail the whole train. Therefore Vatsyayan placed only a small amount of explosive on the line and set up two poles (like telegraph poles, but no doubt smaller) in line with the explosive and placed himself with his batteries and his switch at a safe distance from the most distant pole from the railway line.

So soon as what he thought was the Viceroy's carriage came in line with the two poles, he detonated the explosive. According to Vatsyayan, the reason the explosion occurred under a carriage not occupied by the Viceroy was that the conspirators had received inaccurate information from a previous station (I recall Vatsyayan said it was Allahabad) about the make-up of the train.

Vatsyayan told me that he and other conspirators were arrested, but that the Indian C.I.D. concocted so much unreliable evidence that what is now, in America, called plea-bargaining occurred . . . Plea-bargaining was unacceptable to British justice, so all the conspirators were acquitted.

This footnote to history has very likely been written elsewhere but the reason Vatsyayan gave me for not blowing up the whole train is of moral integrity, the reverse of what Irwin supposed immediately after the event. Vatsyayan may be alive and active, but I broke off relations with him for reasons which I shall not mention.[32]

Stay at Maiden's Hotel

By September 1950, Martin had housed himself at Maiden's Hotel in Old Delhi and was very comfortable there.

Maiden's is an exceptionally pleasant hotel without having any outstanding merit. This part of Old Delhi is about 6 miles from New Delhi and lies outside Old Delhiwallas. It is country like – trees, even undeveloped stretches of jungle, with peacocks, jackals etc. There is one large paneled dining room with numberless small tables which rather inhibit conversation, but it is air-conditioned and has a comfortable bar with upholstered wall

> benches. [I avoid the gin and whiskey which tends to be diluted.] In any case: I regard the whiskey habit as a bad one in the tropics. It provides the simplest road to chronic drunkenness! And it ruins the appetite. My system is to rely on sherry, chianti and brandy. The wines are less poisonous, if poisonous at all! . . . And there is good Dutch beer. In the evening there is a grill room open with a band and dancing from 9.30 till 1 p.m. or later. I don't dance, but one can entertain there. The champagne is an amenity. Isn't it fortunate that champagne travels so well? It seems to be just as delicious here as in Paris. (Heidsieck are great exporters to the East.) Sometimes I go down and have an omelette about midnight. I have a room with writing room and bathroom on the first floor. It was very hot here, but is now becoming very pleasant with wind, rain and white clouds.[33]

The *Thought* office was close by to the hotel.

> I sit on a small verandah and perform the functions of a managing director . . . Our circulation and revenue are improving. I daresay *Thought* may become permanent. Curiously enough there is little opposition to the idea of an Englishman owning an Indian paper, except from Communists, Trotskyists etc. Although I never intended it to so, *Thought* has become the most violently anti Communist paper in India! We are virtually the only pro-American paper. I freely attack Nehru who strikes me as likely to become Asia's Maserzk.[34]

But by November Martin's enthusiasm was deflated,

> *Thought* is better, but shocking things still happen. Did you see the cover of our Diwali issue? It was done in my absence. The thing I like in *Thought* are the political notes in the first five pages, the short story when written by a Hindu and the Bombay art critic. But I still doubt if it will survive.[35]

The paper was running increasingly into financial insolvency and Martin himself required funds which he requested his mother to send.

> Of course I shall now have to change my life; no more of luxury, no more of generous donations, no more of picture- buying, and

> no more of *Thought* [always written in caps]. The latter is not yet closed, or sold, but I am hoping for the latter. It is difficult to close it, because it has achieved its object to a considerable extent, and is justly beginning to show signs of recognition. Three important advertisements now support it, Tatas, Shell, and Associated Cements and I am sure others will follow. If I sell *Thought*, it will fetch about 2000 pounds, or I may be able to find another backer. In any case I don't regret that part of my expenditure, though I cannot continue it beyond the month. Politically *Thought* is valuable for India. It has also been a strange adventure for me.[36]

His mother obliges by crediting his account with the required money and Martin responds gratefully, 'Thank you so much for acting so promptly. It should have been a great load off my mind but curiously enough I felt instead the sudden weight of responsibility of having so much money again.'[37] He continues about the paper, 'I have had another discussion with influential friends about *Thought*. They want it to be kept going because it represents the only intelligent, respectable trend of thinking in India against capitulation to Communism.'[38] He continues,

> Do you know it still costs 500 pounds a month? We considered various measures to reduce the loss to 300 pounds and to find another backer who won't wreck the policy or debase the standards. I also want someone to take the political responsibility off my shoulder. In an election year, my position is . . . invidious. Fortunately the Indians have no [policy] against the British – rather the contrary in fact.[39]

In the dips and highs that signified the paper in these years, the month of July 1951 was again one of brightness. The financial position had improved with an advertising contract from Caltex, one of the two big American oil distributors in India at the time. Some of the British firms in Bombay and Calcutta had also made enquiries about their circulation and area of distribution. Martin felt more was to follow particularly from an Indian business house which remained unnamed. The paper itself was drawing attention from important quarters.

> The Indian Embassy in Washington have issued one [of] our leading articles on the Kashmir situation to the Press there. I met Sheikh Abdullah not long ago. Your description of him once as

> an 'Indian puppet' is wide off the mark. He is a fool on some matters but he is an upright honest man and without question the natural leader of the Kashmiris. He has much autonomy in Kashmir. So I am happy the Government here should like our article. Our circulation took a bound in June, probably as a result of our article on June 1st called 'Mr. Sivaraman's Suppressed Despatch'. Nehru replied at length in Parliament to our accusations.[40]

By early 1953 Martin had left for England but the paper struggled along with Indian owners. For its times it was probably the most influential thinking publication which critiqued the government and its policies and aroused 'thought'. As it gave way by the mid-1960s to other important weeklies and quarterlies, like *Seminar* and *Encounter*, in many ways it had paved the way for thoughtful and responsible journalism.

Resettling in England

Indeed at this juncture if anything was a thorn it was just that his mother's attitude towards him had become cool and unsympathetic.

> I don't know what you mean, saying that India has been disastrous for me 'mentally and materially'. Materially to some extent; but why do you say morally? My impression is the opposite: that my moral character has benefitted despite all the discomforts and difficulties . . . I have had here.[41]

Martin returned to England in 1953 having left behind a trail for not only art but reflective thinking. His own situation on returning, however, became unstable since his financial capacities began to be tested. He worked in the investment department of the British South Africa Co. for a while but then in the early 1960s decided to set up his own firm. The beginnings were somewhat comical with Martin's own lack of experience creating many *faux pas*. Indeed when he asked the Bank of England how he might start his own bank he was told, 'It's quite straightforward. You go to De La Rue, ask them to print some cheques for you, and then you persuade someone to clear them.' Martin Russell soon became the founder and chairman of M B P Russell, an investment bank in London which managed investment accounts, mainly for private individuals.

After a few years when the bank took on a new assistant while all the partners were out at lunch, the assistant entered into a series of transactions on the options market without covering them; and, by the time the partners returned, half the working capital of the bank had wound up! Russell and his partners managed to raise capital from another source, but lost control of the bank and it went into voluntary liquidation in the mid-1970s.

Martin was left with little means for his inherited wealth too had narrowed considerably. In fact his mother felt he had wasted his time in India and had not made, understandably enough, a financial success of *Thought*, and she did not feel it was justified that he get much of her money. On his return he found that she had given money to various relatives but left him with little to buy a house.

> I should be surprised that you should buy houses in London for Raymond, Alexie and Mary but not for me? If you will think about me, I believe you will recognize that I have never asked for anything for myself. If however you had bought me a house I should of course have lived in and should undoubtedly be living there now. The impression you gave me was that you did not much want me to live here . . . You simply said that you were not buying a house for me because I had not (you thought) decided whether to live in England or not. As my absence abroad was the result of military service this was an odd way of putting it. At the end of 1947, when I was about to return to India, I actually asked you to get me a house in London, and you rebuffed me.[42]

What is more, despite his dissuasions, the Mottisfont Abbey which was a picturesque family retreat had been given over to the National Trust and became a heritage site which could be visited. It was clear that Martin was not trusted enough by his mother to make a success of financial affairs in the manner of his father, a banker. His dream in 1947 which he wrote about to his mother could be prescient:

> In my dream Mr. Marx came to see me about my investments, but when I looked in my dressing case for the lists he wanted to see I was quite unaccountably unable to find them. I apologized, but he seemed strangely unperturbed. When I had made a further search, I went to look for him, he had disappeared. When I have an unusual dream I always attempt, usually quite successfully, to find a rough Freudian analysis. On this occasion I was quite unable to do so. Now, however, I feel I can read the parable, and

I cannot help believing that the dream took place at the same time as his death.[43]

Martin was left to devote himself to what he was best at – the evolution of art in South Asia and in particular that of George Keyt. He spent most of his time dealing with galleries and museums trying to interest them in a different vision of art. It is to his credit that not only did he succeed in drawing attention to Keyt's works but also to the art of the subcontinent and created notions of other forms of modernism which had emerged in Asia.

Bliss of matrimony

Martin had married in 1954, Anne Swinton Lee, a woman who was known to have driven a jeep into France during the war. Anne Swinton Lee was the daughter of Brigadier Stanlake Swinton Lee. She had fought in the Second World War between 1944 and 1946, in the French Army. She was twice decorated with the award of *Croix de Guerre*. Anne was in many ways a person who took a great deal of risks. 'She was part of the decoding machine apparatus during the war. Then she became an ambulance driver and drove into Paris two days after D'day.'[44] In London they were quite the modern couple: 'She was part of the modern feminist period. My parents were quite liberal, bohemian couple – the 50's bohemia' added Julian.[45] For the family Asia and Asian art was nothing foreign, 'We grew up with educated Asian people. I was lucky. These were intellectual people.'[46] Soon after the couple had twins Julian Hugh and Stephen Raymond and some years later a daughter Laura Diana followed by Emily Esther. It was a humming household though tragically, Stephen passed away when in his forties.

When the family became insolvent, they shifted to Dungrove house in the countryside at Dorset. A picturesque cottage which was done up elegantly by Anne, it had many paintings primarily by Keyt on its walls. 'Every corner of the house was covered with these wonderful paintings by George Keyt of beautiful, naked women.'[47] The outhouse became a comfortable work hub for him from where he would sit with his secretary and dictate many letters. For Martin being in Dungrove farmhouse, life as compared with London slowed down considerably. As he wrote,

> My severe difficulties date from 1982, when I learnt that my Father's wishes as expressed in his will had been set aside by my

> mother. She should have given me advance notice, particularly as my Father had appointed me to be a Trustee of his Will.
>
> I have now struggled on for over five years, and I find things intolerable. I am forced to live in a house I don't like, over a hundred miles from London where all my interests lie.[48]

'He started rich and became poor. That's his life story. He should have been an academic. His father was a banker.'[49]

Despite his misgivings however, he remained active with the promotion of Keyt's works until the end. When Martin passed away in 2004, he had the satisfaction of having achieved what he set out to do which was to have put Keyt on the international art map. Till the end his achievement lay in establishing an alternative, rich and ever-expanding vision of Asian art.

Notes

1 Conversation with Julian Russell, London, August 2012.
2 Obit, *The Telegraph*, March 9, 2004.
3 Account by Martin Russell for a catalogue of an exhibition of Sri Lankan paintings, April 30, 1998.
4 Conversation with Julian Russell, London, August 2012.
5 Account by Martin Russell for a catalogue of an exhibition of Sri Lankan paintings, Colombo, April 30, 1998.
6 Martin Russell, Notes for Manel Fonseka about Lionel Wendt, April 27, 1995.
7 Ibid.
8 Conversation with Julian Russell, London, August 2012.
9 Ibid.
10 Letter to his mother from Taj Mahal Hotel, Bombay, August 29, 1948.
11 Ibid.
12 Letter to mother from Taj Mahal Hotel, Bombay, August 29, 1948.
13 Notes by Martin Russell titled, Martin Russell, Curriculum Vitae.
14 Letter to mother from Palace Hotel, Karachi, January 28, 1948.
15 Ibid.
16 Ibid.
17 Letter to mother from Dak Bungalow, Vindyapradesh, December 31, 1948.
18 Ibid.
19 Ibid.
20 Ibid.
21 Ibid.
22 Ibid.
23 Letter to mother, January 30, 1949.
24 Letter to mother from Poona, April 8, 1949.
25 Ibid.
26 Letter to mother, Taj Mahal Hotel, Bombay, January 7, 1950.
27 Letter to mother from Maiden's Hotel, Delhi, February 10, 1950.

28 Letter to mother from Taj Mahal Hotel, March 25, 1950.
29 Letter to mother, Bombay, March 25, 1950.
30 Letter to mother Taj Mahal Hotel, May 17, 1950.
31 Letter to mother, Bombay, Ibid.
32 Letter to Martin Gilbert Esq., Merton College, Oxford from Martin Russell, March 25, 1978.
33 Letter to mother, Maiden's Hotel, Delhi, September 18, 1950.
34 Ibid.
35 Letter to mother from Gunnepana, near Kandy, Ceylon.
36 Letter to mother from Airline Hotel, Churchgate Reclamation, Bombay, June 10, 1951.
37 Letter to mother from Bombay, June 14, 1951.
38 Letter to mother, June 14, 1951.
39 Ibid.
40 Letter to mother, Maiden's Hotel, Delhi, July 26, 1951.
41 Letter to mother from Maiden's Hotel, Delhi, July 1, 1951.
42 Letter to mother, 22A Ebury Street, London S.W.1, December 12, 1953.
43 Letter to mother, on the train, Geneva-Paris, August 26, 1947.
44 Conversation with Julian Russell, op. cit.
45 Ibid.
46 Ibid.
47 Conversation with Julian Russell, op. cit.
48 Letter written from Dorset, January 13, 1988.
49 Conversation with Julian Russell, op. cit.

9

INTERNATIONALISM AND FAME

The 1950s was a period of euphoric heights and stultifying depths for George. On the one hand he was more rooted than ever to the land and became a cultivator as well as a landowner. On the other hand George began to make a dent in the international world which elevated him to another sphere of experience. Surely the maddening intensity of these days would be unmatched!

On their return from Bombay, George and Manike went back to their simple home at Sirimalwatta. He also contemplated buying some fields at a place called Abana. His letter to Martin had a different tone altogether, 'I'm just back from a tiring but very pleasant journey to a place called Abana' he wrote on 11 August 1953.

> into which I was hustled by Jayana to see the wonderful fields he's been so excited about – certainly very beautiful country and quite out of the usual towns and villages, with a great river feeding the fields. I was desperate enough, seeing the failure of my field here, to draw on the little money I have in the bank and invest in a field there, as I was assured by the headman that side and also the cultivator and his son, known to Jayana, that I wouldn't stand to lose as those fields simply don't depend on the rain at all. Of course it will mean that from about April or May next year I shall continue to get some paddy, which will be of great help. Also I am being hustled into investing in a bit of land about 9 miles from here where some very good and reliable people will cultivate it – vegetables etc. and give me half the produce and also try to sell the surplus crop and share the profits with me . . . So that if all this works I shall be relieved of the anxiety lying so heavily on my heart at present, in regard to Manike and the children especially.[1]

Home and hearth

George was now a father for Manike had borne him two sons, Prem and Sachin, and although he loved them dearly his anxieties about providing for them had increased. The letters of this period bring up his isolation and his troubled state incessantly. The fact that Prem didn't keep well was cause for worry, 'have been very anxious and busy over poor Prem who still continues ill – so scraggy through starvation you can't recognize him . . . I feel he is taking a turn for the better – only vomited twice today. Fever very low'.[2] He also delighted in his children,

> Prem is now 5 years, and can read words of 2 syllables in Sinhalese (he knows no English whatever) and counts upto 80 and do small additions and subtractions in sums, all of which is a great achievement considering my case at that age! Sachin is 2½ years and is very talkative and looks like a Sikh child with his long hair . . .[3]

Meanwhile Harold and Peggy, who were foster parents to George's earlier children from Ruth, Diana and Flavia, were having their own difficulties. Harold in a letter to Martin,

> I thought Flavia might be ready to try for admission to the Conservatoire next year when the academic year begins in Paris. She was sixteen this year in October. I am beginning to have doubts, however, whether it would not be wiser for her to try for admission in 1956. She is still very immature and lacks a sense of responsibility. She is definitely gifted and artistic, but fails to achieve what she is capable of owing to lack of concentration. . . . What I have said about Flavia applies to Diana, who is much more lethargic. She gave up her plan of studying medicine and has been working, on and off, under Bertie Weerawardene at Turret Studio. Weerawardene got his experience under Lionel Wendt at Chitrafoto. Turret Studio is rather cramped and Diana finds it impossible to get experience in dark room work during the usual hours.[4]

Harold recounts an interesting encounter which Diana had,

> A young man, who quite by accident saw her at Bombay en route to Colombo by air, fell in love with her at first sight. He followed her here and was so importunate that Diana accepted him but, as

far as Peggy and I can judge, she is more flattered by his ardour than really in love with him. He wants her to marry him soon and live with him in one flat with his parents, married brother and a sister. This has made us realize what a world of difference there must be, in environment and outlook, between a Gujerati household and ours. I have manage to enlist Roshan's help and her advice is to send Diana abroad for a year . . .[5]

Martin was vehement in his reply,

Of course Gujerati households differ a great deal according to the Gujerati involved. Most Gujeratis spend very little money, and almost all are vegetarians, though one would occasionally meet a Gujerati who was a meat-eater and who maintained a large and comfortable household. I think it is very unlikely indeed that Diana would be happy in an average Gujerati household unless she was prepared to a adopt a completely Hindu outlook. The Gujerati attach a lot of importance to caste, not necessarily in any religious or superstitious sense, but as a practical method of regulating social customs. The caste system might not suit Diana at all, and if she goes to India to marry a Gujerati she should recognize that she will encounter a way of life utterly different from anything she has previously experienced . . . My first twelve months in India were really very unhappy as the result of the difficulty I had in adapting myself, and some foreigners never do find sufficient compensation in Hinduism for the strangeness to them of the Hindu outlook. I think that one should go to India more to experience an extraordinarily romantic atmosphere than to make one's home there permanently.[6]

When it is decided that Diana study in Cambridge George writes to Barbara disapprovingly,

They [Harold and Peggy] are going away again to Europe for 6 months as my elder daughter wants to be in Cambridge university – medical tripos – and my second daughter wants to study music in Paris; and my sister and brother-in law have to make the arrangements, though why it should take 6 months I can't understand . . . The earlier the better I expect as Flavia is only 13 and Diana 16. How much better to have gone to Lucknow to

> study music – 'oriental' I mean. But that was sneered at. Anyway there is time for it, and I expect a good knowledge of European music will be helpful in so many ways especially in order to refute it in the end.[7]

As it turned out Flavia did not, much to her dissatisfaction to this day, study in Paris but in Munich.

> A friend of Harold Peiris, who had been at Oxford and spoke in Sanskrit told him 'Don't send her to France where the men are not wealthy. Send her to Germany and they were worse. I was admitted to the Detmold music school and most of the students there were 10 to 15 years older than me. Harold was always keeping in contact. There was a casanova who was always following girls and a girl called Elly and me in particular. All of a sudden I was sent off to Munich and I had to again go through an entrance exam and I got in with shivering fingers. It was worse than Detmold . . . I wanted to go to England or to Paris.'[8]

Boat of despair

George wrote despondently to Martin,

> Let's break the boat [of despair] and be blissful in a harmony among ourselves on the broad sea independent of being compelled to be so like people in primitive communism seen even here even now in certain village are. Not that we are like that, really; but what I mean is that we should break the despair by lessoning so much of the uncertainty which causes it, when we can lessen the uncertainty. Despair is so terrible a bourgeois quality, where one must sit around moping or indulge in defeatist humour and, of course, drink like hell the while and smoke and smoke innumerable cigarettes![9]

To add to his despair was the fact that Barbara decided to leave for London for good. He writes,

> I'm terribly cast down for my sake, to hear you will be taking a job in London. I only hope you'll be able to help us some time, to cause us to be all together again. But I doubt it. Do you think

> Martin will come again? He says he will come and keep Srinivasa going.[10]

He refutes the suggestion to go back to his old life,

> I cannot do what is still demanded of me – throw up Manike and all this life and return to where I'm supposed 'to belong' and so reinstate myself in security, 'social' and otherwise and be in a position etc etc – so that I depend very much on you and on Martin – not that any change for the better can make the slightest difference where our love is concerned! Only that my present condition is such, as if ill, that I am in greater need . . .[11]

He implores her again but knows it's of no use,

> I feel so sick to think of you not succeeding in getting a job here. But then you want to be where Martin is – and had you a job here I expect you would have chucked it to go over the seven seas and all that . . .[12]

He discusses her job situation,

> So now it's come to the stage where you're having it out with Hawkins. Your job in Bombay, I expect, is more or less finished. Is it so, my dear? I wouldn't advise you to give it up if it means you have to be forever in England as a result. But you know best. All I know is that I want you here – and you must come before you do anything else – and that I have a feeling that Martin does mean what he says, keeping Srinivasa for his return . . .[13]

Barbara finally left for good for London in October 1953 six months after Martin.

By early 1954 George was to repeat more often his own loneliness, lack of financial resources and particularly his worry about Manike and the children. He writes,

> Simply hadn't the heart to write confronted as I am, more and more, by such a void as (as I like to console myself in feeling) such inevitable and undeserved extinction not only where my work is concerned but my spirit too. Simply nowhere to turn and even 'rich men and princes' and great geniuses must have somewhere and

someone to turn to for help from time to time! And there has been the recent discouragement and the frustration of my very necessary visit to Europe, so necessary as a break away too for my health's sake (after everything had been planned and even arranged) merely due to my not being able to raise a paltry 6 or 7 thousand rupees.[14]

He felt isolated and persecuted.

The malice towards me, so harmful to poor Manike too, is growing and darkening my surroundings with the vegha of innumerable columns of smoke. If I die tomorrow Manike and the children will be in a position worse than abandoned. Her own people are a subhuman crowd of outmoded vultures. Her sister has turned against her and the children, Ukku Mainka, Koin Mainka and Tenneknoon, were all put up against her, because we just couldn't continue giving money and provisions at the rate we were doing.[15]

George's worry about Manike and his new family becomes increasingly intense. When he recovers some money from the sale of his Abana fields which had been at a loss but still bought in some income,

this will be some added provision for Manike and the children until Prem and Sachin can grow up and improve things materially – they haven't a soul in the wide world, beyond myself, to see to their future now that you have cut yourself off more or less. As you know Peggy and Harold decided not to have anything to do with Manike since Prem was born. Manike's own people are pure beasts and are only out for what they can get and are always involved in wicked litigation. There's a limit to my helping even Manike's sister and so they keep away anyway, they still live in the 16th century in the worst sense! Please always keep in touch with Manike and me as your relationship with us surpasses every others', however loyal and sincere, being *sampurna* as only Lionel's was.[16]

Isolation of Manike

To Barbara he wrote more fully about his sister's attitude to Manike,

I have always taken her about with me, but have only done it less after Prem came to us because of the inconvenience to

> her – though more now as Prem is bigger. I only avoid taking Manike to my sister's place – although we used to go together when we first returned from Bombay – because of the sudden change of heart there over Prem's birth . . . If I take up the sort of stand you very rightly desire it will mean a breach and Manike will suffer as she will feel responsible for it, and I certainly don't want a repetition of the nightmare which occurred in Bombay.[17]

Indeed in one letter to Barbara he writes about the soirees at Peggy's place where attempts were made to introduce him to other eligible women. On one such occasion,

> I was glad to be there because in the sort of 'salon' that ensured they made a special feature of bringing Sita Jayawardana and me together. She's a nice girl although she dances bogus Katak and every other kind of dance besides and writes up a society column in the 'Times' and does radio singing (bogus Sinhalese folk songs being a society girl in Colombo) and painting on a 'prolific' scale – exhibiting too – and wears special cholis to 'team' with her specially designed hand bag (herself the designer) and deep saris an almost authentic veni and such a provocative bindi on her neat brow, a bindi resembling her own vulva, vertical and the correct crimson when ready to receive. She recognizes me as the greatest painter and a true genius, and so isn't she a nice girl?[18]

Clearly nothing came of this but a few laughs!

George was preoccupied with his hearth and home. While Prem was a musician Sachin was also talented. George who loved children would spend a great deal of time with them. Prem however became a cause for worry when he grew up as he drank too much and later died to George's immense grief. He was however also very fond of Sachin and in some way the children were a consolation against the isolation felt.

> In any case you can do what think fit regarding the property or estate when I die; but one thing is essential, that you and Anne take Manike and the children away from here. A great child-expert of a doctor who came to see me the other day, and to whom I confided my fears about Prem (his being born so soon after Manike's convalescence) looked very grave and told me that Prem must be very carefully brought up, excessive kindness, as he noted

> too the completely unbalanced way in which Prem behaves when a little excited, either anger or pleasure or wanting something; though the younger child appears to be quite normal and quiet, though awfully obstinate when made angry . . .[19]

The nitty-gritty of living in the village was beginning to get him down.

> My hands have been full, as the saying is, for the last 6 or 7 months with every conceivable sort of bother but the right kind, that is my own work. Simply no way of doing my painting as, apart from my bad health and my worries, I've not been given the chance of concentration and even worse, a retreat from my constant isolation – a protracted retreat to enable me to assemble myself and move among incentives to work.[20]

By mid-1955 he wrote to Martin who had had twins, Julian Hugh Russell and Stephen Russell,

> I'm happy and relieved to know that you will have a parampara – yes, after September – and long after we are in some other plane of existence in Samsara, ourselves no more in this life, your twins . . . such a happy thought. But alas for me and the possibility of my parampara – the girls on the one hand now turned against me and my world, and poor Prem and Sachin, on the other with ghastly uncertainty before them, unrecognized by my people, avoided, ignored and doomed to my kind of extinction, depending entirely on Manike and me! Anyway I've left what little remains or will remain of my atma-projection in the way of pictures to you if that will help Prem and Sachin – and please assure me that if M and I die too soon you will like a true Buddhist take Prem and Sachin . . .[21]

He turned to Barbara for discussion and solace. She was way out of the conundrum he had gotten into. While his love for Manike remained unchanged he felt an almost paternalistic concern for her and her state after he had passed away. Gone were the days of ecstatic union and a spell-binding encounter with the 'other'. Instead his affection turned towards her welfare and the two sons they had given birth to. On the other hand the life in the village was one of continual problems and he found that he was no field cultivator nor could he deal with the large extended family which came along with Manike.

Despite his isolation and worry, however, George continued to paint incessantly.

> Naturally, all my continual bother has slowed down and even halted my work very much, although, visitors coming here are always surprised to see 'a continual stream of creative work' or as Jayant said 'an inexhaustible stream' but then they always tend to see my work retrospectively and somehow there is work up to date linking up my efforts since 1927 or so. But I assure you my dear Martin, that had I been less subjected to stupid and wicked persecution and segregation physical as well as psychical – and you don't know my real life – the *ananda* quality of *rasa*-happiness, the sole source of all art in me, would have expressed itself much more and three worlds would have been flooded in just the same way that the Hindu *rasa* flooded India and overflowed into all the rest of Asia.[22]

International exposure

Yet the international exposure to George's work couldn't have been better. He exhibited along with the rest of the '43 Group at the Imperial Institute in South Kensington in November 1952. He however complained to Martin that none of his important works had been shown. Perhaps this was set off by the remarks of the well-known art critic John Berger. Had they been shown in Britain, George would, 'surely be recognised as an artist of important genius'. His words however were of poor consolation for he also felt that George produced arrangements. 'He gathers together elements from Picasso, the Indian cave paintings at Ajanta and the Sinhalese at Sigiriya. . . . He lacks the fire to fuse the elements together because his mood is too nostalgic and his observation too schematic.'[23] George bitterly observed to Martin,

> He's no good really [Ranjit Fernando] and John Coorey told Harold he's got that Berger chap in his pocket. The funny article appeared in Sunday Times – the sort of thing an upper farmboy would be ashamed of. I'm telling you the truth. And Berger was there called a famous 'English art critic' . . . He has done poor old Justin a disservice.[24]

Then elsewhere,

> I've been very unhappy over the way the *Times* here has pounced on Berger's exaltation of Justin at the expense of my art. Had I been financially secure and able to move out of my segregation here, meeting whom I wish, hitting up against right incentives to give my now cramped art new life, etc., I wouldn't have cared a damn – but its months and months since I'm now badly stuck.[25]

Keyt's solo show which was held simultaneously at the Institute of Contemporary Art in London, then an important hub for cutting-edge art, had received a warm response. William Archer, Curator of the India section at the Victoria and Albert Museum who had introduced and written the text of the catalogue, mentioned 'a fervid appreciation of physical form, a passionate exploration of poetic romance and a certain close connection between his idioms and those of traditional Indian art'.[26] And a rave review written by William Graham appeared in *The Studio*, 1954.

> The genius of George Keyt lies in the wholly original manner in which he finds inspiration in ancient Eastern art. In Sinhalese and Indian mythology he has found themes capable of expressing a modern philosophy of life through his own emotional and poetic imagery. His work has a sensuous poetry, with frequent allusions to the ancient forms of song and dance, conveyed with a characteristically Oriental calligraphy.[27]

John Russell made a sumptuous summing up in the *Sunday Times*:

> The Grand Tour still passes through Italy: but for the novelty which delighted the picture-financiers of the 18th century we must now look further afield. Perhaps Ceylon is the place? Painters abound there: and at the moment three galleries (the I.C.A., the A.I.A., and the Beaux Arts) have laid open their walls to the work of Ceylonese artists. The most expert of these painters is undoubtedly George Keyt, whose pictures now fill the I.C.A. Gallery. His scenes from folklore and mythology are minutely prepared, brushed with commanding confidence, and suffused with a dark and quasi- ironical vitality which has won the heart of at least one young English collector. They are not drawing room

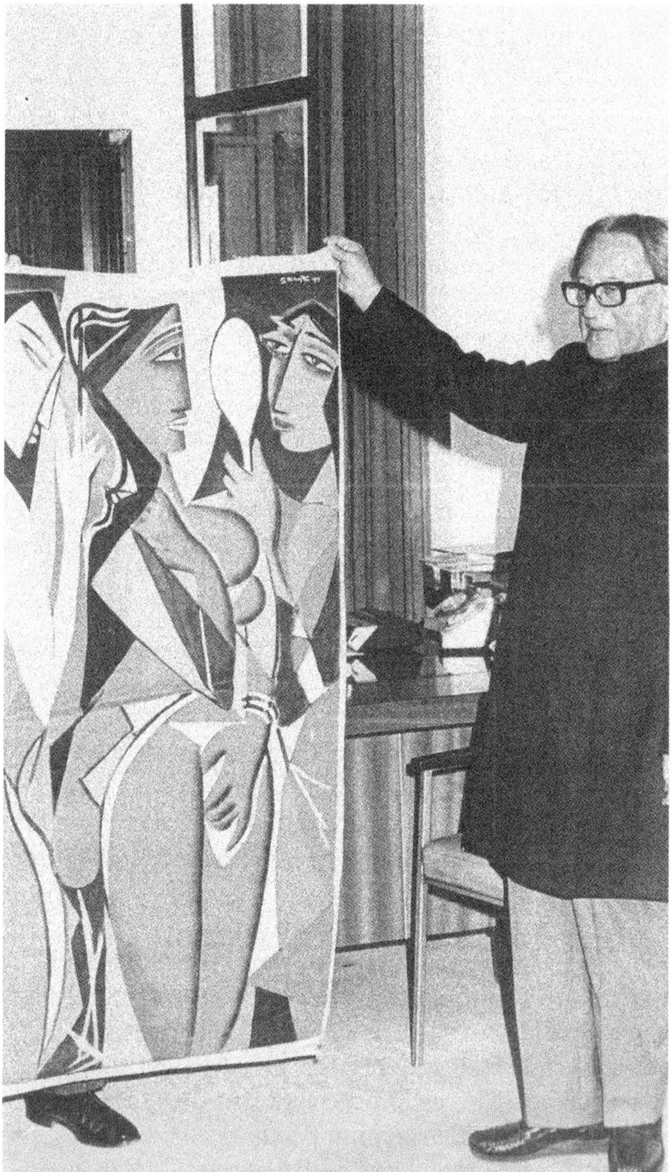

Figure 9.1 George holding his painting at the National Gallery of Modern Art, New Delhi, 1975.

Courtesy: Martin Russell Archive.

> pictures, but instruments of wonder, in which there lurks, nonetheless, a disquieting humour.[28]

Paris show

The group show went on to Petit Palais in Paris and largely through the efforts of Ranjit Fernando was received well. One of Gabriel's paintings was bought by the museum as well as that of Ivan Peiris. George however was not impressed,

> What you say about the 43Group is quite right – I shall remain a member, out of loyalty to the dead and some of the living such as Harry P, but refuse to show abroad with them. I feel more proud to be represented in the Indian section of the V. and A and be aware of the warm *bhakti* of people like Archer and Penrose and your true and consistent devotion and friendship than be bought for ghastly places like the Tate and that Petit Palais nonsense in Paris.[29]

It could well have been that George, never overly generous about his fellow artists, wrote this out of rile because his work was not bought by the Museum! He was however intent on having a solo show in Paris. And he urged Martin to enlist the help of Cartier Bresson and his Javanese wife Ratna in Paris. On this count he urged Martin, 'I love Henri and Ratna and they're always inviting me there and sending their undying love and all that, but always some damned inconsequential thing turns up to deflate my bank balance.'[30] For George,

> She is the *Shakti* [Ratna], in some ways, and is certainly loved, honoured and submitted to by her lord who is the gentlest and sweetest of all the truly talented and industrious bipeds in the three worlds and they are certainly true friends of Manike's and mine so that you can rely on them. When they heard that Monroe Wheeler (of the Museum of Modern Art, NY) was coming here, they sent an 'embrace' and their love, so that although I didn't care for Monroe Wheeler and preferred Evelyn Waugh who accompanied him to see me, I was nice to the polite snob.[31]

Henri and Ratna were at that time one of the most popular couples in Parisian social circles and were inseparable though they were to divorce in 1967 and Henri was to marry the thirty years younger Martine Franck in 1970. Known for his photography of the decisive moment, Henri's work in India was well known. He had met S. H. Raza in Srinagar and the exchange they had had influenced the young artist struggling to find expression. Yet the intimacy he shared with George was probably greater and went beyond the communication over ideas. In the frequent exchange of letters between Martin and Bresson, the exhibition seemed as if it might well take place. But despite their warm invitation to George to have a show in Paris, Henri and Ratna turned to Martin to get a sponsor and eluding official ones Martin knew few galleries in Paris. Martin felt that it shouldn't be official,

> I am certainly in favour of trying to arrange an exhibition of George Keyt's work in Paris . . . But I am reluctant to try to arrange and exhibition on official lines as I feel it is usually a mistake to associate an artist with any official organization. What we really wish to do is to interest an art dealer or the owner of a gallery somewhere in Paris to the extent that he will agree to hold an exhibition for us on mutually acceptable terms.[32]

Keyt also suggested that his old friend Anil de Silva be contacted in Paris.

> I agree about Anil, though I assure you, as she is a real *bhakta*, that she can be of great help – only see that nothing in the way of pictures or money falls into her hands. She has a lot of influential friends etc and her active *rasa* coupled with her love for me will result in something I'm sure. She sent me a most fervent and loving letter. With all her drawbacks she is one of the few people who really care for and whose company I enjoy.[33]

He wrote again about Anil, 'I noted with (modest) pleasure the picture on the wall behind you which poor dear Anil used to gaze at with tearful eyes at 25 Cuffe Parade in Bombay and which dear Rathin Mitra used to study so much to no purpose. . .'[34] He went on to emphasize:

> I think all my things should be shown. You don't find outside influences in Picasso's work causing the rejection of such work from exhibitions? My work, whatever the influences, are my own work – and if some pictures seem to show a Western influence

(which in any case must be investigated well, as in a sense there is universality too in good art) that is no reason why they should be kept out as in the I.C.A. show . . . My work is never, like Justin's 'ecole de Paris' (or better, echo de Paris) even if on that account it isn't so readily accepted and acclaimed by the Maurice Collises and Bergens and what not in Europe (England to be precise).[35]

Neither Paris nor Rome could host the show so keenly sought by Keyt. Nor did George despite his fervent desire get to visit Paris, still the Mecca for the art world, for lack of resources. A reasonably successful show of his works, however, was held at the Rotterdam Kunstkring. Martin inaugurated the show of more than 50 pictures and he seemed to have made an impression. George did complain to Martin about the lack of publicity and he admitted to it,

It is quite true as Harold says, that the show in Rotterdam was not sufficiently publicized. This in a way was my fault but I was desperately busy at that time. I hope things will be better in future now that I have settled down and shall have more leisure. I understand that your wonderful *Abhisarika* was sold in Rotterdam for 45 pounds, i.e., approximately 650 rupees less commission.[36]

Yet George wanted Archer to have the work which hadn't been possible,

I'm sorry Archer couldn't buy the *Abhisarika*; I like that one too – where is it now? I cannot yet decide about being out there with you, but there are chances – I'm having a little place built out in the garden for me to work – it is now absolutely impossible to work here . . .[37]

Village life

Good innings internationally alternated with extreme isolation and frustration in his life in the village. He wrote,

I wish you would write to me more often. You cannot imagine how much I miss you, Manike too, doomed as we collectively now are to such separateness and isolation among the people of this land we find it so difficult to like anymore, even though the land of our birth. My illness reached its climax a few weeks ago, what

> with a bad throat, some infection, and following the crushing of that, at Marawila – a sudden fever and a feeling of death which within a day quite crippled me so that I couldn't even stand![38]

George was ambitious but in the real sense he felt his work was good and should make a mark internationally. Yet he would never compromise and wanted it to be on his own terms. He also wanted his own people to see the work and gain from it. His interests in national identity and homogeneity would after all be the most effective in his own home. In this context it pleased him immensely when in late 1954 a large exhibition was held in his country at the University of Ceylon, Peradeniya. He wrote,

> I don't know whether you had news of the exhibition going on at the University, but in case you haven't allow me, my dear Sir, to tell you lovingly that it has been 'an unqualified success' as Mr. S de Soysa said, and that over a thousand three hundred people have already turned up to see it – including not only some of the futile elite and others but undergrads both male and female and students and teachers from schools and colleges around including, I'm thankful to say, a number of 'vernacular' teachers male and female; and as people are still flocking to it – and this is in spite of the gate money to be paid for entrance – and the show has been extended another three days. So it has been a triumph both ways, that is to say financially too . . . There are 67 pictures on view in the Senate Hall – madly hung though painstakingly by Mr. Peiris and Mr. Goonatilaka and some other enthusiasts. As people are still flocking to see the show – and today is the last day of the ten days – an extension of another three days has been affected, Jennings entirely agreeing.[39]

In mid-1955 he was still exalting about the show to Martin,

> I want you to meet a friend of mine at present in London, called Mr. Ralph Peiris, of the University here. It was he, together with Mr. Goonatileke, who got up that superb exhibition of my work, at the University in October and which was such a success, about three thousand people visiting it in only 10 days!. . . Please show him my paintings which are with you and my things at the V and A etc, and enlighten him generally and enlarge his life and cultural experience in London.[40]

Despite his isolation he had a stream of visitors,

> At the moment I'm quite static; but I hope to be dynamic again, and so resume the *shabta* and *kriya* which I abandoned 8 or 9 months ago, and paint again too – the nuisance is that I'm so seldom happy now – among my recent visitors were the Prince Ludwig of Hesae and the Rhine and his wife, and Benjamin Britten and Pears the singer – I got up dancing for them – they were very nice and all that, but I somehow didn't find them so welcome – may be my fault. Dear Bill Archer wants a copy of a *Nayika*, the one with the red background reproduced in the book; however, I cannot do it . . .[41]

He was quoted by Jose' Ortega de Gasset in his brilliant book on modern art *The Dehumanization of Art and Other Essays* which had caused quite a stir.

> And I must incidentally mention here that I was surprised to see that some of the things I've said about contemporary art were in Jose Ortega de Gasset's excellent and courageous and brilliant book on modern art called the dehumanization of art. I wrote my aphorisms towards the end of 1946, whereas de Gasset's book (the translation) appeared in 1948 and I only saw it the other day when it was brought to me . . .[42]

The feverish intensity and burgeoning ideas of this period for George were at a heightened pitch. His own developing thoughts on modernity were reflected in his art,

> Yes, I expect it's alright for the pictures for the Venice Biennale, though I can't help feeling that my stuff will look quite out of place among, not only the other '43 Group stuff, but also (and more) among the European work which must be so 'modern', not having been done as counterpart objects of magic ceremonies and so forth thousands of years ago by Maya and other semi-civilized and barbarous and aboriginal races during the 'childhood of the world' but on the contrary as 'art' and quite empty of the spiritual

intestines of the old stuff the outsides which so intrigue the modern artists and ethnologists and researchers and historians and so forth (though I allow the ethnologists and research scholars etc. try very hard to reassemble the invisible intestines). 'Psychology' is the last resort where the moderns are concerned.[43]

Notes

1 Letter to Martin, Gunnepana, Sirimalwatta, August 11, 1953.
2 Letter to Martin, Gunnepana, April 11, 1954.
3 Letter to Martin, Sirimalwatta, September 19, 1955.
4 Letter from Harold Peiris to Martin from Siriyakanda, Boralesgamuwa, November 19, 1954.
5 Ibid.
6 Letter to Harold Peiris from Martin, 2 Montpelier Walk, London S.W.7, November 26, 1954.
7 Letter to Barbara from Gunnepana, July 5, 1952.
8 Conversation with Flavia Keyt, London, April 2013.
9 Letter to Martin from Gunnepana, September 26, 1953.
10 Letter to Barbara, October 15, 1953.
11 Ibid.
12 Ibid.
13 Ibid.
14 Letter to Martin, probably early 1954.
15 Ibid.
16 Letter to Martin, December 26, 1954.
17 Letter to Barabara, July 11, 1952.
18 Letter to Barbara, Gunnepana, December 23, 1951.
19 Letter to Martin, August 27, 1956.
20 Letter to Martin, undated, probably 1954.
21 Letter to Martin, July 13, 1955.
22 Letter to Martin, December 26, 1954.
23 Quoted in Neville Weereratne, *43 Group: A Chronicle of Fifty Years in the Art of Sri Lanka*, Lantana, Melbourne, 1993, p. 111.
24 Letter to Martin, undated, probably early 1954.
25 Letter to Martin, February 2, 1954.
26 Mentioned in Weereratne, op. cit., p. 111.
27 Weereratne, p. 111.
28 John Russell, 'Peregrinations,' *Sunday Times*, January 17, 1954.
29 Letter to Martin, September 14, 1954.
30 Letter to Martin, September 22, 1954.
31 Letter to Martin, October 11, 1954.
32 Letter to Cartier Bresson, London, April 28, 1954.
33 Letter to Martin, February 2, 1954.
34 Letter to Martin, probably sometime in 1955.
35 Ibid.
36 Letter to George from London, June 3, 1954.
37 Letter to Martin, September 14, 1954.

38 Letter to Martin, May 8 1955.
39 Letter to Martin, October 22 1954.
40 Letter to Martin, May 8, 1955.
41 Letter to Martin, probably 1955.
42 Letter to Martin, September 22, 1954.
43 Letter to Martin, undated probably in 1955.

10

NEW PASTURES, FECUND FIELDS

He was in his late sixties and she was much younger. When they met they didn't realize that a storm would break over their heads and last for the rest of their lives. And break it did! No one quite knows how they met, but they had many friends in common. Martin Russell mentions in a letter that he had first introduced them,

> One of the daughters, Mrs. Diana Beirne-Keyt, who is married to a New York stockbroker, tells me she thinks he left his estate to an Indian woman friend, Kusum, at one time married to an Indian called Narayan. I had introduced Kusum to both Narayan and Keyt in Bombay.[1]

When George met Kusum Narayan in Bombay she was married to a well-off businessman Narayan who was different in that he was also interested in literature and the arts. Books lined his home, he listened to music and he had been the chief financier of the quarterly *Thought* which was an important stimulant for its time. Narayan had met Kusum and fallen in love with her, according to a mutual friend, Asha Seth, at her mother Stayawati's place, who was a freedom fighter.[2] Petite, bright and involved with the arts Kusum was to bring a different glaze to his house. They had a son, Deep, together and to all events led a pleasant sociable life enjoying the pleasures of living in a social whirl in Bombay. Yet, it seems Kusum felt frustrated as she was ambitious and liked the good life and found that both were lacking with Narayan and that his fortunes were volatile and unpredictable.[3] According to one account Narayan was a self-made man from Kerala. He was not educated but was interested in politics and knew politicians. He felt inclined towards the humanities and possibly married Kusum who had winning ways because she was Satyawati's daughter.

Narayan himself had Bombay's intellectual bohemia congregate at his place. People like JP Narayan, Rudolf von Leyden, A.S. Raman, the art writer, and Martin Russell would be present at Narayan's home. Indeed his walls had paintings by artists like S.B. Palsikar and Shiavax Chavada. According to Asha's daughter, the well-known photographer Ketaki Seth, 'He was very unlike a businessman. His flat was lined with books and music.'[4] When Kusum left the household it created a devastating impact even on Ketaki who was a child. 'I remember it made an impact. Everyone in the house was affected. Uncle Narayan moved out of Darshan apartments and shifted to the Yatch Club. He spent the rest of his life there. All the soirees stopped.'[5] Subsequently it seems he shifted to Pune with his son and passed away sometime in the late 1970s.

When the couple met George he could possibly have been with Martin who was the co-owner of *Thought*, or with Mulk who was a close friend and admirer of George. It was little known to both of them that this would lead to such earth-shaking changes. In a letter to Barbara, George recounts his meeting Kusum,

> I came back [from India] on account of Manike's illness; but went again several times alone in the fifties; and in 1960 stayed for nearly a year, when Kusum fell in love with me and played hell over Asha Malaviya [Asha Seth] and Leela and the rest; and again in 68 and the seventies, with Kusum, doing so much . . .[6]

Despite their age difference and the fact that they lived in different countries and were married, Kusum fell deliriously in love with George. She found his work original and distinctive and his overwhelming persona overtook anything or anyone she had known in her life. The attraction was mutual, for her petite and lissome figure, appreciative and intelligent audience attracted George too. In the painting *Kusum Reading* (1968), we have a fair, petite and attractive young woman bending over the book *Gita Govinda* and overlooking her a man, bewildered, anxious and devoted. The Cubist dissection of space above, which reveal the man's demeanour in shifting panels is also the stamp of the artist's modernist preoccupations.

For many this was the best work that came out of George's relationship with Kusum,

> The best thing that came out that period was a portrait he did of her . . . she is seated on a couch with her feet up . . . it is a straightforward, clean, beautifully compressed . . . in his recognizable style

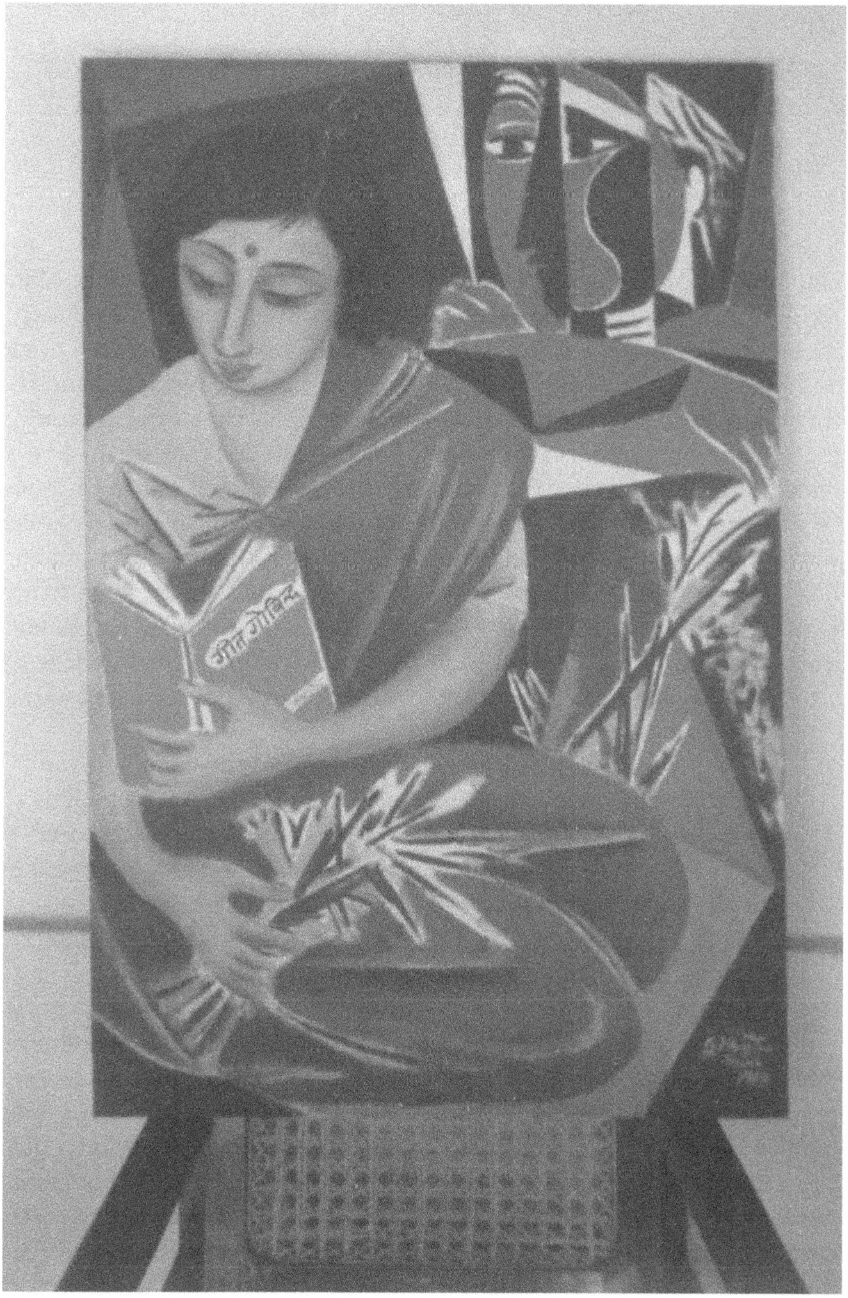

Figure 10.1 Kusum Reading.

George Keyt.
Oil on canvas, 1968.
Courtesy: Martin Russell Archive.

> but there is an elegance and ease with which he has approached the subject which must mean a little bit more than a mechanical approach.[7]

The India show

George left for Sri Lanka, however, for there was concern about Manike and the extended family and the demands of his land. What is more, though he could work as well in Bombay, Sri Lanka was where his home and friends were present. Kusum, obsessed by him, followed him and the three co-habited for a while at Sirimalwatte. Manike always accepting, took this in a matter of fact manner. But many found that she had been relegated to looking after the house and the needs of George and Kusum, 'When we went to meet them, she was a domestic in his house. Kusum was in front of the house and she was at the back.'[8] This arrangement, however, soon proved impractical and George and Kusum migrated to Colombo where the two were to marry according to accounts by Islamic rites, following which they lived in Colombo and Galle for the next six years. George described their place in Colombo in a state of happiness,

> This is a very nice place we live in – sort of semi-rural and yet with everything necessary available all round – the best Colombo suburb I think. The flat we have is large with lots of wall space for pictures and three bedroom and big bath etc and nice kitchen. The old home we left was nice but too much of interruption all the time – people dropping in without notice even though there was a telephone not being sure whether or not we are in![9]

This led to urbanity, sophistication and a level of communication he had not had with his earlier partners. It also led to a high point in George's professional life. Kusum wrote to Martin, 'George has just finished a big mural (7'×18') for People's Bank. It is very beautiful. We are intending to go to Anuradhpura on the 20th of this month till the 25th. I am looking forward to this holiday as I have never visited the ancient city.'[10] He exhibited at the Commonwealth exhibition at Kensington in 1974 where there were two sections of one-man shows – that of Keyt and the other artist who also had a solo was M.F. Husain. The show was held from 26 February to 24 March 1974 and Keyt had displayed 30 paintings and drawings. After 1954 this was the second major exhibition of his works. The following year a large show took place at the National Gallery of Modern Art (NGMA) in New Delhi in 1975. Of the 61 exhibits, most were done between 1971 and 1975 and the bulk of it came from the artist's collection and from Kusum. It drew an appreciative response from audiences in India. The catalogue text was written by the director, Dr L.N. Sihare. It was during the exhibition that he met the famed poet Keki N. Daruwalla who came to see his show and invited him and Kusum home for dinner. If the poet in him was aroused by the encounter it also led Keki to compose a moving poem on him:

> The eye of the blue Gopal keeps track of me
> as if mounted on a swivel- gun.
> I walk six paces to the left
> six paces to the right
> and the eye of the indigo cherub follows me.
> The eyeball is just a black, inverted cone
> Yet it stalks me like a taut bow.
> Have I walked into a haunted cave?
> Wrong, it is I who am the haunted ghost,
> a spectral wisp in the house of the living[11]

The verses which evoke the sensual Krishna and Radha paintings of Keyt end with the evocative lines:

> There is a lilt in the line that comes
> from the wellsprings of joy.
> No room for dark angels here,
> nor horizons pocked with tragic omens.
> All pain is swallowed
> in the delicious pulp of the gourded body.
> Shiva and Shakti
> Purusha and Prakriti wander
> through the unchartered south seas of the soul
> where the black sails of the night
> shall never be hoisted[12]

Thereafter the show travelled to Bombay and Madras while George was still in India. He returned to Sri Lanka on 20 January 1976. Later some of these works were acquired by the NGMA though not without a tussle for

Kusum both initiated the process and later acted as an obstacle. In a letter to Barbara some years later Martin writes in more detail,

> I do apologise and feel sorry for having used the expression 'absolute rubbish'. My difficulty is that George and Kusum have given contradictory instructions, and put me on notice that they do not know what they are doing. Kusum was mentally upset when she was in London, and I have been told by George that she has had lithium treatment. She 'bequeathed' certain pictures to the Museum of Modern Art in Delhi, and I received instructions from George to send them there, and peremptory demands from Museum and the Indian High Commission in London. Subsequently George told me that such a transfer could not be legally effected without a deed sworn before a notary, and that he was leaving the pictures to me in his will. When he was in London he and Kusum 'donated' pictures to the Commonwealth Institute at a ceremony to which I was not invited or even told about. Later George asked you to retrieve the pictures for him. Now he says in an informal letter he has once again 'donated' or 'bequeathed' pictures to the George Keyt Foundation. I cannot act on such inconsistent and erratic behaviour. For all I know George's three wives may all have a claim on them. Meanwhile I have been paying for the transport and storage of pictures since 1954, also for repairs and restoration. I need a formal legal instruction from whoever may claim ownership, and sworn evidence of ownership . . .[13]

George's associates and friends claim that Kusum did keep a tight hold on his painterly activities,

> We went to meet George and she was very particular that wherever we went she was behind us. We said we wanted to see the studio so she came but she said, 'Don't touch anything'. So we didn't touch a piece of paper or drawing. Because if we went George would give us a sketch or something but no way would you get anything with her. And the last time we met her in the hospital with him in Colombo. He was dying then and we took a book to sign. He looked okay, mentally he was okay. . . . she was a difficult person to come to know . . . even when we went to the hospital she was sitting there in the chair day and night in the

> hospital. And when we wanted him to sign she said, 'No, don't tire him too much'.[14]

That at one level Kusum was a hard-headed businesswoman who looked after her interests will not come as a surprise. As Martin wrote to Flavia, 'George, in a letter to me, has revoked his gift of certain important pictures to Kusum, because he says that the gift was obtained from him under duress. Please keep this matter confidential.'[15]

George writes in an exasperated tone two years later,

> regarding those paintings and drawings which are entirely in your custody and do not belong to Kusum even though in order to humour her, since she wasn't quite normal after her recurrent attacks of psychosis and I was on tenterhooks all the time in London must I have to assure you again that there must be attestation by a notary to make those lists valid legally and that they cannot be contacted in a court of law, and that it was in full knowledge of this fact that I agreed to and signed the lists just in order to be left in peace by a half insane person who now does not even remember the incident in your house and hasn't even mentioned or alluded to the fact, now that she is mostly sane and only has a slight and temporary – few hours – set back once in three or four weeks? For God's sake don't upset things for me by writing to Kusum because it will precipitate the ghastly nightmare I went through again and again and am only now somewhat free.[16]

London travel

Between June and 3 July 1977 he participated in the Commonwealth exhibition titled *Commonwealth Artists of Fame* to celebrate 25 years of the reign of Queen Elizabeth. George was the only artist represented from Sri Lanka and was invited to send five paintings. Another major show took place at the Patrick Seale gallery between 14 September and 5 October 1982. Sponsored by Martin Russell, there were 43 works on display, of which most were made in his peak period between 1926 and 1953 with only three from the 1970s. As Martin pointed out in the catalogue,

> He contradicts Kipling's assertion that East and West cannot meet. From the West he has borrowed idioms which unlocked for him the traditions of his own culture. His vision of humanity's

> place in the world and in eternity is totally of the East. The West has shown him a short-cut to the ancient springs.[17]

He was to point out an important difference between Picasso and George,

> Keyt was born only twenty years later than Picasso, so that they were artistically contemporaries. There are qualities in common – long life, prolific invention, a love of expressive distortion. But whereas the art of Picasso is systematically destructive of Western civilization, Keyt's affirms and extols a vast and ancient but, at the same time, a current way of life.

George was delighted to hear that his paintings had been cleaned and restored before being exhibited. Martin recounted an amusing incident,

> The results of the cleaning are delightful. All manner of colouring and poetical effect has reappeared. . . . The restorer charges 8 pounds an hour, and *Jalaja* took 7 hours, so the expense is not great compared to the value of the pictures. The other day when she was sitting here discussing these matters she suddenly let out the most bloodcurdling scream I have ever heard . . . The cause of this was that a fly had alighted on one of the pictures.[18]

George also showed continuously in Sri Lanka during this period for it brought him great pleasure to show in his home country. George had been commissioned in 1984 to make two large paintings for President J.R. Jayawardane, which were set up in the Presidents' House in Colombo. His felicitation volume with his personal autograph came out in 1977. The same year the Indian Prime Minister Indira Gandhi came to Ceylon for the non-aligned summit conference and visited him. She had earlier spent nearly an hour at his exhibition in Delhi.[19]

And yet there was trouble brewing in his marriage in a manner which would be irreversible and set his world upside down. The first signs of it appeared when he visited London for the first time along with Kusum in the last three months of 1978. Kusum had a massive breakdown here and its onset henceforth would come unaccountably for the rest of their lives together. As he wrote to Martin and Anne,

> You couldn't have been more disappointed than I was not to have been able to be with you at your cottage. I was *so* looking forward

> to it. But surely you were told why I couldn't come? . . . Anyway, I'll tell you again and in confidence. K's mental illness, which was pretty bad, was fairly recent. Worse, Martin, than Manike's, as it took the form of violence too, and a rushing out etc. At times she becomes abnormal. As I said, the dregs of the psychotic condition appear to be still there, and a stirring occurs at times, and all comes up to the surface. Now you understand, dear Anne, why she declined the invitation, and the way she went on. She wasn't alright at the time. And she cannot be left alone at any time – not since her illness. At the moment certainly not – and I don't know for how long. The doctor said I should be *very* careful as a setback cannot be ruled out. Anyway, she appears right most of the time. But something happened that night at the dinner. She mustn't know I told you. Martin, you have been my oldest and best friend and nothing on earth can ever estrange us. But for the time being I am in a dreadful predicament and you and Anne must please understand. . . . I cannot go about to meet people . . . I get so easily tired now for one thing; and I can't leave K alone. I have to be careful. I never expected things would take turn out like this and so looked forward to meeting you.

As a postscript, 'When normal it is unimaginable that K can be anything else and it is so pleasant. She's been alright now for some time. But her jealousy over me surpasses even Leela's [Shirveshwarkar] – in those days in Bombay you remember Leela?'[20]

Conundrums and dead-ends

A mutual friend wrote to Martin later,

> After he returned from England last year [in 1978] from his short visit to you, George came into a lot of trouble. He was as you know staying with Kusum here in Galle, in a house he had taken on rent, a short distance from my home; and I used to see him often as in the old days. Then Kusum fell ill, and had a kind of nervous breakdown. George decided to wind up and retire to his village retreat in Sirimalwatte, which rather left Kusum high and dry, and I was very sorry for her. Of course Kusum was to stay at Sirimalwatte with George, but this never was a happy solution; and after a few days Kusum was obliged to return to India to

> her people, for a spell, where she is at present. I have heard from George she has had a breakdown there.[21]

Indeed George had written about it himself to Martin,

> Kusum is away at the moment in Bombay, from where she will go on to Delhi to settle some of her affairs – such as some ancestral land and Insurance etc and will return, I think, in about 1 ½ months at least. I shall then go back with her to Delhi and explore the possibilities of settling there – my true home; so that I can go to the Lotus feet of Lord Hari.[22]

But they were not to settle in Delhi. As he wrote to Martin,

> Since I returned, and this in strict confidence, Kusum was ill twice. Once after we returned from London, and again after that, after she returned from Delhi (where she went alone to look into some possibility of business there and disposal of land etc. all of which was a flop except her looking into and coming to a settlement over her insurance which has 'matured'.) She is alright now, and very normal, more than she was in London, as I have set about administering the necessary drugs *secretly* through the agency of a trustworthy servant – she would not hear of taking any treatment after the disaster of the Dunedan's Nursing Home where in March 78 she was forcibly put – just had to be forcibly put by my sister – where no real proper treatment was given but only sedations all the time by an old humbug of a doctor – it's a private nursing home for the fashionable. But now a real up-to-date psychiatrist – an old admirer of mine – has observed and diagnosed her treatment as nothing serious, not schizophrenia – serious and incurable – but only recurrent mania and preventable by necessary drugs containing chemicals which combat the chemical distortion in the patient causing the mental derangement. In 3 or 4 months I'm going back to Sirimalwatte. Kusum is being given a fashionable 'boutique' in a 5 star hotel in Madras by her very rich cousin, big businessman; and with great difficulty I got out of going with her; but promised to follow since she cannot live without me. But let me tell you in confidence, I may not follow.[23]

In a despairing tone he wrote to Martin later,

> Kusum had quarrelled badly with her only relatives in Delhi and Bombay when she went back from here, intending to stay there. She made such hell for her brother and his wife and children, over a land dispute etc. and before that, in Bombay over some insurance money, with Narayan; that her people completely broke with her – this just before a terrible attack of insanity in Delhi. They put her into a nursing home, paying the huge bill and when not yet hundred per cent normal, paid the package and sent her back here. They wrote after that telling her they did not wish to have her or have any dealings with her ever again. So that, though she holds Indian citizenship, she cannot go back and stay there as he has no place to go to – Narayan having divorced her . . . Before all this, of course, when I first married her, it was all so different. Her people welcomed me with such warmth . . . and disparaged Narayan like hell. But now it is all different. She cannot go back. I have no foothold there economically. If she does go back, it may be after my death.[24]

George tended to worry about Kusum and her condition and with reason. Anticipating Martin's visit to Sri Lanka he wrote,

> With Kusum here – and she's not quite well and I don't know when she will go, as she says she has to go in the end – I am very uncertain about myself – that is to say my movements; because she has become quite helpless and static, quite helpless; and there isn't anybody else to look after her – no one here, and incapable of communication as she is ignorant of Sinhala; and no one to give me a helping hand and see to her if I move out; because my sister and the rest are dead against her. All this in confidence please.[25]

A long letter from George to Martin written on 14 September 1980 from Sirimalwatte speaks of his considerable distress,

> And I was in a terrible mess owing to the upheaval of the time, Kusum's malady, and my having to run out of Colombo and go to Galle, and the disastrous consequences when my work was

concerned, and my diminishing economy and my then being in London and my happiness there too being clouded by K's behaviour – her hypermaniac state following on her last attack as depressive manic psychosis, which you and poor Anne had a taste of . . . I had to leave Galle where I was beginning again to work in earnest and did a mural etc. K again having an attack and in the meanwhile antagonising people as usual and after K returned from Delhi and I came here (after 7 years, to find mutation and fragmentation of house and property). K went again to Bombay and Delhi, quite well, and even met Indira Gandhi who inquired after me, and tried to do some useful work; got ill there again, after 6 months there, and has now come back in a queer condition; and myself trying to send her back to her people. But all this, dear Martin, in absolute confidence. I have hardly anything with me here; and people came and bought the paintings I did here when K was away, and also the few paintings I had with me, though the money coming in had most of it to be spent on recovering the land and paying for the house here which was mortgaged; though the bungalow on the hillock of this land and the houses along the street and the cottage in the land and the lovely and salubrious farm in Wawrina, so valuable now, could not be returned; and the paddy fields too. All the damage was done by Prem in my absence, abusing his power of attorney. I'm getting back some paintings of mine from the Kalagane's gallery of the Alliance Francais in Colombo and also from Harry Peiris, to have with me; as I intend working again although my spacious and dear studio is not yet available, Prem having leased it in my absence, and a year more less to run out before I recover it. I am compelled to work, somehow, in a little cabin sort of room (outhouse in the land which I restored at a cost of Rs. 2000). So when you come I can give you the 10 books and see what can be done about the show you are trying to get up. Of course it can be a small show. . . . Shall see to in the meanwhile the problem of Kusum – though don't refer to this – what can be done; because I certainly very much wish to be in London again, dear Martin, and make up not only for my own debits there, If I may so put it, but for dear Anne's disappointment too . . . I have to remind you about Dr. Sihare's proposal regarding the exhibition at the National Gallery of Modern Art in Delhi in the new section called the Gallery of Asian Art where he wants to give me prominence. When you come can you have a look at it and Dr. Sihare

> in Delhi, I wonder, on your way here? You are coming with Anne? You'll be, I'm afraid, unpleasantly surprised to see in the present condition here. Just like my poems in *Image of Absence* – I shall return to a place grass unjabiri – sort of prophetic like many other things in *Image in Absence*! Something will have to be done since I don't yet feel like going to *Vaikuntha Svarga* to be at the feet of Lord Hari. But I do feel at times like going at once.[26]

They would now sleep in separate rooms,

> Kusum and I have one portion – the large studio where I sleep; and attached room with bathroom; Kusum sleeps the attached one. There are 3 other rooms, a large kitchen, a veranda, and a sort of living room. There's an outhouse here where I work.[27]

George was never to return to London or to Europe again. As the critic and friend H.A.I. Goonetileke pointed out, 'For an artist who had so successfully fused the East and West within the confines of his easel, the European interlude was exceptional in its briefness.'[28] Nonetheless he had made several excursions to the National Gallery and was enthralled by the works of the masters. He also did a round of the Tate, the British Museum and the Victoria and Albert Museum. He visited Oxford twice with Martin and Anne and also as a homage to Shakespeare went to Stratford-on-Avon where he saw his favourite play *The Tempest*. He walked and walked in London – to Westminster Abbey and St Pauls 'for inward reasons; and so much more in being entertained by Bill Archer and others; and seeing the ghost of Sherlock Holmes in Baker Street . . .'[29]

Radha and Krishna

George was now the most well-known artist in Ceylon and no visitor would leave without seeing his work. Yet the work itself had changed considerably from the earlier days of inventive modernist forms etched in rhythmic flowing lines to those of vapid figures of Krishna and Radha equally well executed but without the layered overtones and deep sensuousness. From 1973 onwards when George and Kusum shifted to Colombo and Galle, he used acrylic rather than oil paint and made what Martin called 'propaganda on canvas'.[30]

No other modern artist has painted episodes from Lord Krishna's life with such consistency and adroitness as George Keyt had. His peak period in art in fact had been reached with the paintings of Krishna and Radha, the milkmaid and their divine love in the early 1940s. In works like *Krishna Painting Radha* (1948) we have the blue god painting Radha's full breasts in a modern version of the famed Pahari miniatures made by the descendants of Nainsukh. The interplay of eroticism, love, tenderness and fusion of two individuals could not have been more masterful. In his *Gopika Vastra Paharaha* (1952 oil on canvas) we have the bashful milkmaids hiding their nudity and at the same time revelling in it as Krishna watches from above in a glorious celebration of eroticism. Keyt spoke of divine love and merged it with eminently human gestures making it both profane and contemporary. In his visualization of the celebrated 12th-century Sanskrit poem the *Gita Govinda* in the late 1930s, the forms themselves bifurcated and replicated to reveal the sublime fusion of the two lovers in their divine conjunction. Keyt's own explanation of the poem elucidates,

> The physical aspect here is not something distinct from the spiritual, nor is it on that account a parallel in any sense whatever to the sort of love that is sexual in the manner of the 'Ars Amatoria' and other such expressions of 'profane' love in Europe. But on the contrary there is the endowment of the physical side with all the real and enduring qualities of the spiritual . . .[31]

Of course George, aware of the original intent of the *Bhakti* cult which was a reaction to the over-dominance of puritanical Brahminism in the 12th century, ends his notes with 'The personality and symbolism of this much loved deity, and the great Bhakti cult, were in times past among the most powerful and beautiful reactions, on the part of the people of India, to the bloodless abstractions of the Brahmins.'[32] In these proliferating works on Krishna there is a profound undercurrent of a sense of loss, a feeling of an imminent absence which makes the coming together an act of grace. In paintings like *Sri Krishna and the Gopis* (1936) the blue god in his swirling yellow robe twirls around the grieving milkmaids, both joining and separating in the inevitable emotions of joy and pain. The *virahadukha*, or the pain of separation which fascinated him in the *Gita Govinda*, was at the core of his own paintings of Krishna and Radha.

In the paintings of the blue god and his milkmaid that now began to emerge in the 1970s, however, there was an absence of these richly layered epiphanic creations. He still painted flawlessly, the agile draughtsmanship etching out the forms in their swaying rhythmic movements. The lovers were now piquant and pouting and their act of love-making nothing more than sexual revelry. As a critic put it,

> The fluid speed and impatient vitality of his appetite for improvisation have, sometimes, tended to impart to his compositions an air of arid nostalgia or repetitive arrangement. The fusing fire seems to desert him, though the distinct elements of the painting are strictly delineated.[33]

It was as if life had gone out of these works and made them a mere delineation of forms which now began to seem repetitive. Yet his paintings began to fetch high prices and were sought after for their consistent attention to detail and their competent handling of the composition.

These were not good days for George. The turbulence inside matched the chaos outside. He was in the throes of a failed marriage, which could not be severed. His friend Martin in faraway Dorset wrote to him but not very frequently though he was always involved with George's affairs. To add to his distress was the fact that Barbara was not very well. She had emerged in 1980 after thirteen years of silence when there had been no communication with either Martin or George. It seems her husband John Buchanan had died a few years ago and she got in touch with them after that. But now she was ill. He tried to comfort her,

> With great care, dearest girl, there is really nothing to fear. I know of 3 cases – Harold Peiris being one – where life continued normal; but great care was taken. Exercise is good, you know, and a little stimulant in the way of a glass of claret a day.[34]

If there was any woman George remained consistently involved with through the years it was Barbara. At first it could have been an affair of the heart but he was to be genuinely concerned about her welfare as a person in the following years. She was one woman who did not recede to the back of his mind. What is more, he seemed to feel that Barbara after the long years was still involved with Martin. He wrote to her fervently,

> You know how for a person like him he somehow behaved so worthily and even courageously, and I should say even, consistently where his feelings towards you were concerned. I repeat for a weak person like him, for whom you used to feel so sorry when you used to see the way he had to endure things and the reverses

> he used to be put to, but he kept coming to you for relief and in the hope of getting the happiness only your love could give him – well, my dearest Barbara, all I can say is, try once more . . .[35]

Flavia who used to see Barbara frequently in London corroborated that she was in love with Martin,

> When I was a small girl of seven I fell in love with Martin. He was so handsome – he came in his uniform. And he was so shy also. He was with daddy all the time. . . . In London Martin had this exhibition. Anne was there and Martin was very fond of her and they had something going. And I had an English girlfriend with me. And he hadn't asked Barbara to come and she was very sad and upset . . . She looked much younger than she was . . . she had light skin and wore dresses.[36]

Flavia remembered her later years,

> She couldn't walk along all of a sudden. It comes from drinking too much alcohol. I met her last in her apartment. It was a nice place. She used to telephone and say she didn't know what it was but she couldn't walk. She died before Martin. I didn't know she was 80. I thought she was much younger . . . I think she still liked Martin somehow. When Anne was in Dorset he used to meet her here somehow.[37]

On the edge

Apart from a failed marriage there was considerable stress financially. As his sister Peggy wrote to Flavia and with some concern,

> George came here the day before yesterday and stayed to lunch. He brought Sachin his second son, with him. I got a shock to see him. The wild man of Borulla was everywhere – his hair all crumbling and like this (draws a sketch of a man with his hair standing) . . . He was quite wild as a child. What has happened I really don't know. He was dirty and sweaty too. George may dress oddly but he has a refined look. How he spawned these horrors I really don't know.[38]

Peggy wrote in much the same vein again,

> George arrived last morning with Sachin. George was a most unsavoury sight – His dhoti was torn and dirty – his long shirt like dirty soft sujon all crushed and dusty. His waistcoat that was once orange is crowned with dirt and most buttons missing. His scarf that was once black-grey with sweat, dirt and dust. His nails both and fingers and toes like claws. His finger nails were turning up! I got Sachin to pare them short. G objected he said his fingers were like those of the Ajanta frescoes. I took no notice. His toe nails couldn't be cut as they were like hard wood. I helped his son to saw them of when he got home. G's house is crowded with women. Why in God's name can't they see to him. He is now 81 years old and needs some attention. As for Sachin – he was better than last time – his hair had been slightly trimmed and the clothes cleaner. He is eternally chewing beetle – day and night and needs to wash his face.[39]

But four months later Peggy writes on a more optimistic tone,

> George was here yesterday with his son Prem and daughter-in-law. George was looking clean – even the clothes and face clean! He was sleek and well fed!! And would you believe it he actually brought me a few avocado pears as a gift!! First time in his life. He is quite well off and is selling and painting murals for an order somewhere in Bentota. I am sorry to say I think he is a miser – his Jewish blood no doubt. Prem has got fat, he had grown his beard again – looking an oily Pakistani but very polite. His wife Sudharma – a nice pretty woman and such good manners – much too good for him. George seems happy collecting money and in spite of his wife Kusum, who occasionally runs around naked, quite calm – he seems to take it in his stride.[40]

Martin had come to Sri Lanka along with Anne and Emily in 1981 where he seems to have had a good time according to his plan. As he had written to Flavia before the trip,

> Anne, I and Emily are booked to fly to Ceylon on Friday, 6th February, returning to England on 6th March. You will be able to get

> into touch with us either through the Naidoo's or at the Queen's Hotel, Kandy where I propose to stay and write another monograph about your father. Anne and Emily will, I expect, pay a visit to the jungle with Jerry but afterwards I expect they will be based with me in Kandy. . . . I propose that the four of you should kidnap your father and bring him to London without any female companionship, because, as you point out, he can stay with Galina . . . I did kidnap George once before. I simply went to his house in a taxi and suggested that we should go to India. He readily agreed and without doing any packing got into the taxi and off we went.[41]

In many ways George had traded his worry about Manike for Kusum and in fact not bothered too much about Manike after that. Perhaps she had receded to the back of his mind while other more troubled thoughts overtook him. He wrote to Martin about repairing his studio at Sirimalwatte but nothing about Manike, although he was in a way back with her. Yet George wrote to Barbara about her confidentially,

> You were astonished that money was stolen here of all places, now you will get the shock of your life if I tell you that the money – not once but several times, and big sums always in 4 figures, stolen – was taken by no one outside of this place, but by one, and I have proof, by one inside this very house. I could never bring myself to accuse or rather tell the person . . . to put back the money, because not only would I feel just too bad but because there would be indignant denial and what other consequences in the melodramatic vein and complaints all around such as I cannot imagine!. . . . May I mention the name, in absolute secrecy, dear Barbara? Manike! Incredible you think? No. And what for? For reasons connected, I know with her incurable insecurity complex, against the time when I should be lost . . .[42]

Perhaps she realized that she had lost him already and that there would be no recovery.

To be fair to him, though, he continued to feel responsible for Sachin and entreated Barbara to get him a job with the Asian section of BBC in London. He praised him to the skies,

> I can absolutely recommend Sachin that he will be an asset then; and even in time, give public recitals, like Ravi Shankar and

> others in London with a good impresario behind him – and the rest of Europe. And you, my dearest and best, will be the originator of it all.[43]

The fact that he needed the necessary promotion was however only one reason why Sachin found it difficult to get a steady job. The troubled home life and most of all the fact that the children belonged to both worlds and yet to neither may well have contributed. According to George's nephew and solicitor Michael Sproule who now handles his estate, 'Manike's sons were neither here nor there – they could not be considered fully village nor full part of the upper class milieu. He didn't put Sachin in Trinity College in Kandy but elsewhere . . .'[44] After George passed away, Sachin was to write to Martin for help in his straitened circumstances complaining that the monthly allowance his mother was getting was stopped.

> And as I have no job I am in a critical condition. I have no other house for my late brother Prem's children and I want to make a (Samadhi) monument with my father's ashes. And there is Prem's second wife also demanding for a place to stay . . .[45]

Meanwhile Prem, his eldest son, had not behaved too well either. He described to Barbara the manner in which he turned violent,

> Anyway here I am again, after making a resolution to get away for good following an unimaginable climax to so many enactments of a sort of ghastly nightmare created here by Prem at night – rarely interrupted by normal times – he forged my signature on more than one cheque and cashed them . . . I got wind of it, thanks to Sachin's suspicion and went and got blind drunk as never NEVER before, and came back and created an upheaval in the course of which, when checked by Sudharma [his wife], he assaulted her and whipped out a knife and started stabbing her and seriously injuring Manike too; and when eventually put a stop to by my rushing up and striking him in the face to divest him from further stabbing.[46]

His peace of mind disturbed beyond limits, George along with Kusum decides to leave. As he wrote,

> I left with Kusum when he abused in filthy language, fortunately in Sinhala which she can't understand, and going for me too

> before that . . . We only returned the following day from Sangakkarnas', who took us in. Returned on Prem's assurance that never again . . . He and Manike and Sachin came looking for me. Sudharma had a lucky escape. Had the wounds inflicted been a few inches higher, the doctor said, she would have been dead.[47]

Flavia's account

The person who emerges from the shadows and begins connecting to George is Flavia. She seems to visit Sri Lanka every year and meet him and also spend time with him perhaps recovering the lost affection of childhood. It was clear that Kusum was not popular with Flavia.

> My father was very bohemian and was a bit frustrated. He did awful drawings when he was with her. The drawings of women were all pink. He was not so nice when she was with him. She made him work a lot to make money. And then she disappeared when he died.[48]

And when did she meet Kusum?

> We met her when they were living in that house together. Lucia couldn't speak English and she couldn't speak Sinhalese and they had awful fights. And he wanted to make amends with my mother when he was old. So we had arranged for them to meet at a nice house which belonged to a friend, Dr. Kambilratne. My mother came early, she was very excited. And he came late. And she asked him, 'George do I look as I did before?' And he said 'Yes you look the same.' And then they didn't eat both of them. And as they were about to leave he suddenly got an appetite and ate up all the plantains. 'George can I come and leave you back' And Kusum was there and this woman. 'Ruth I don't think this is a good idea. I can't take you up there.' Lucia, Kusum and my mother also going up. And so with a lot of difficulty we managed to keep her in the car and he went alone up. It was so funny. And then it was a very short thing that he got friendly with her and then afterwards he broke off again and didn't have any contact. But he said he must make amends, he must meet my mother.[49]

It was astonishing that she could keep a remarkable distance from her past which must at one point have been difficult. Yet Flavia seemed to view George in a playful humorous vein.

> My father was also very idiotic. My mother was beautiful. She looked like a Madonna. She had brown hair and very white skin. And her sister had blonde hair and she lived in London and she died when she was 94 . . . Kusum was very bad for him. . . . She would get hysterical. Rosweta [Flavia's friend] wanted to meet daddy and we went to the sea beach. 'Why are you girls sitting so long in the sun' he said. And all of a sudden Kusum got into an awful state. Rosweta got so frightened she wanted to go back. And then I saw this woman was no good for daddy. She stuck to him till he died and then she went away . . . I don't know from where she came. But it was his fault also. Why take away the wife of his friend?[50]

In an interview she reminisced about the time when he met her for dinner at the Oberoi Hotel in Colombo where she was staying.

> He came dressed in a yellow and brown waistcoat – all kinds of colours. Everyone was dressed in white – no-one dresses like that. He insisted on meeting the cook. The cook came and stood near the table and wouldn't go. And everything was 'acha, acha'. He said he could speak Urdu but the only thing he knew was 'acha'. I thought he would tell him the food was good in Urdu. The cook kept wanting him to say something because he had made an Indian meal. I had a room upstairs and he wanted to stay there. I said 'no' so he went to Alfred House and stayed with uncle Harold. And the whole night he wouldn't stop speaking his thoughts. Poor Uncle Harold. Aunt Peggy went to another room . . .[51]

Flavia did not stay with Peggy, George's sister, but at the Oberoi in Colombo instead. The reasons for this are mentioned by George to Martin,

> Flavia was very disappointed at your not being able to come while she was here. I was with her in Colombo for 2 days; and she'll be here in Kandy from tomorrow. She's awfully and very justifiably annoyed over Peggy not allowing her to take a beautiful

> *Jalaja* picture of mine from Alfred House, where my pictures – though left even after the indiscriminate sales they made of many of them – look sadly neglected, disgracefully framed, and hung all wrong. In a word out of place completely. Flavia dislikes staying there for very valid reasons, and is in the Oberoi Hotel instead; but goes there. They sold a lot of her pictures too, bequested to her from the Wendt collection . . . The important *Govindamma* painting they sold for a song to one Henry Pieris (no relation of theirs or Harry's) and used to keep it turned to the wall on account of it being a nude! I found Flavia just the same – childlike and all that – and mad about my work and very loving and devoted; and a complete stanger to any sort of decorum. But you know her quite well. She has inherited a little too much of my mothers' nature and behaviour and beauty, especially the unrestrained and unconcealed tendency to laugh at absurd people and absurd things in general – that is, people and thing which are stuffy or on the respectable plane, on their being funny or odd without knowing it.[52]

But the last word on her is from Martin,

> Flavia tells me she is leaving for Ceylon on or about 15th February, which is very convenient, as she is a powerful source of energy and is devoted to you and all the people I know in Ceylon. When I was in Munich she gave a demonstration of Kandyan dancing to me and a friend of hers late one night. She said she had learnt it from Jayana. She had a recording of Kandyan music to accompany her. Her dancing was really exquisite and she looked so happy. I was quite stunned.[53]

Notes

1 Letter by Martin Russell to Paul Walsh, London, June 19, 2000.
2 Conversation with Asha Seth, Mumbai, July 10, 2011.
3 Ibid.
4 Conversation with Ketaki Seth, Mumbai, July 12, 2011.
5 Ibid.
6 Letter to Barbara in London, September 11, 1982.
7 Interview with Neville Weereratne, Melbourne, November 2011.
8 Ibid.
9 Letter to Martin from Colombo, August 12, 1974.
10 Letter to Martin from Colombo by Kusum, November 9, 1976.

11 Keki N. Daruwalla, *The World of George Keyt, George Keyt: A Felicitation Volume*, George Keyt Foundation, Colombo, 1977.
12 Ibid.
13 Martin Russell to Barbara from Dorset, May 31, 1989.
14 Sybil Keyt, artist and wife of Neville Weereratne, Melbourne, November 2011.
15 Martin Russell to Flavia Keyt, November 22, 1979.
16 Letter to Martin, Sirimalwatta, August 26, 1981.
17 Martin Russell in the Patrick Seale catalogue, London, 1982.
18 Martin Russell in letter to George, August 23, 1982.
19 Letter to Martin, June 14, 1976.
20 Letter to Martin and Anne, from 7 Sydney House, London, October 20, 1978.
21 Cyril Abeyawardene to Martin from Galle, May 24, 1980.
22 Letter to Martin from Galle, March 15, 1979.
23 Letter to Martin from Galle, June 28, 1979.
24 Letter to Martin, February 28, 1982.
25 Letter to Martin from Sirimalwatte, August 1, 1980.
26 Letter to Martin from Sirimalwatte, September 14, 1980.
27 Letter to Barbara from Sirimalwatte, July 8, 1982.
28 H.A.I. Goonetileke, *George Keyt, A Life in Art*, The George Keyt Foundation, Colombo, 1989, p. 13.
29 Letter to Barbara, Sirimalwatta, September 11, 1982.
30 Martin Russell in Patrick Seale catalogue, op. cit.
31 George Keyt, Preface to the *Gita Govinda*, published by the George Keyt Foundation, 1996.
32 Ibid.
33 H.A.I. Goonetileke, *George Keyt, A Life in Art*, George Keyt Foundation, Colombo, Sri Lanka, 1989, p. 13.
34 Letter to Barbara from Sirimalwatta, undated.
35 Letter to Barbara, December 13, 1982.
36 Conversation with Flavia, London, April 2013.
37 Ibid.
38 Letter to Flavia from Peggy, December 26, 1981.
39 Peggy to Flavia, Colombo January 10, 1982.
40 Peggy to Flavia, Colombo, May 19, 1982.
41 Martin to Flavia, January 6, 1981.
42 Letter to Barbara, August 25, 1982.
43 Letter to Barbara, September 7, 1982.
44 Interview with Michael Sproule, Colombo, February 2011.
45 Sachin Dutt Keyt to Martin, Sirimalwatte, Kandy, undated.
46 Letter to Barbara, Sirimalwatta, November 27, 1982.
47 Ibid.
48 Conversation with Flavia Keyt, London, April 2013.
49 Ibid.
50 Ibid.
51 Ibid.
52 Letter to Martin from Sirimalwatte, February 16, 1981.
53 Martin Russell to George, January 5, 1981.

11

THE FINAL YEARS

Nothing could be more poignant than the last decade of Keyt's life. He yearned incessantly to be with Martin but neither his finances nor his personal life allowed it. His uneasy companionship with Kusum continued and he was unable to deal with either her dominant personality or her fits of manic conditions. By 1988 the couple had moved in with George's second son Sachin and his wife Vasanti because living in Amunugama had become very isolating for them. Staying in Piliyandala, about ten miles from Colombo, seemed like a good compromise and bought them into contact with an urban milieu. But this was to last only for five years after which they returned to the Kandyan village on 23 January 1992.

George's depression made him want to see Martin or Barbara and neither was available. As he wrote,

> It is such a long long time that I hear from you and it relieves me to think that you are still there even though I have not seen you for so many years – my oldest friend, associated with me in so many wonderful things in my this last of my many lives.[1]

His personal life had reached the lowest depth as Kusum continued to hamper his progress in various ways which only Martin was aware of. Yet he painted incessantly and his work continued to be brought attracting a great deal of interest. Perhaps the best definition of these troubled years could be that of continuing to survive.

George's forays into the Western world would also define the making of modernism in South Asia. In Zurich to find a gallery for Keyt, Martin's encounters were in many ways path defining. According to him,

> The two galleries I went to see were in the charge of most capable women. The pictures they were exhibiting were lousy, but it was

> obvious that they were only pandering to contemporary debased trends, against their more educated feelings. The first woman I saw was the owner of the Gimpel and Hanover Gallery, the Pope or *Doyenne* of art gallery dealers in Zurich. She *was* very percipient. She carefully looked at all the picture in my book about Keyt and commented that in the twenties he had been painting in the style of the twenties, in the thirties in that of the thirties, and so on for some sixty years. She said it would injure the artist to put on a small show because the work would be written off as imitation of styles in Europe. She recommended a major retrospective exhibition to enable the public to see the whole evolution. She particularly wanted it to be seen in relation to the Ceylon background, the very roots. This gave me the idea that in such a show I should exhibit not only Keyt's own miniatures which had such an influence on him; also reproductions of the Ceylon frescos and some specimens of the textiles and village paintings. This has never been done before, although all the ideas are in my book. The lady was a dry old Swiss who said the pictures would not find a market in German Switzerland as the older generation who had the money had had no Eastern or Colonial experiences.[2]

In a letter to George he described the path which took him to these two galleries,

> In Zurich I called on Dr. Wille of Sotheby's, who proved a tower of strength and a dynamo of energy. He immediately called in his assistant, a young man called Ralph J. Dosch, a Swiss German, who looked at the illustrations in my book and expressed the view that the modern work was too much like that of Picasso to have a market in Switzerland, where, he said a collector would not like to have a picture on his walls that looked like a Picasso but was not one. Dr. Wille was not convinced by this line of argument, and took the book and catalogue home to show his wife, who is a painter. He came to the Hotel at 8.15 the following morning to have a cup of coffee and return the book. He said his wife agreed with his assistant, but he himself was still not in agreement, so he introduced me to the proprietors of two galleries, Frau Rotzler of the Gimpel and Hanover Galerie and Frau Pon of the Galerie Nicoline Pon. . . . The main picture in her private sanctum had some chicken's feathers adhering to it, in fact sticking out of it.

> It was a calculated insult to the kingdom of birds, but may have been intended as an insult to humanity as a whole. But the lady was most intelligent and perceptive. She went through the book with care . . . In the meanwhile, on a Saturday morning, Dr. Wille had made an appointment for me in Basel, which is an hour from here by train. From the station in Basel I took a tram, and arrived at a very splendid gallery called the Fine Art Gallery, owned by a young Swiss French called Daniel Blaise Thorens. He had a much better show on his walls, examine the two book and the picture with care and appreciation and said he saw no difficulty about the resemblance to Picasso and other artists. In fact, he produced a catalogue of the paintings of a French artist called Samartino whose works showed a strong resemblance to Picasso's without, as he said, having anything to do with Picasso. I suggested to Monsieur Thorens that if he had a show of your works in his gallery we should also include some bronzes, miniatures and textiles to show the influences or remind people of the influences which were local and not European. He said he was coming to London in the next month or two and would like to see the collection . . . I hope to see another Zurich gallery tomorrow – the Mexican Art Gallery, so called. It was recommended by Dr. Wille because it already has a clientele accustomed to non-European art. I shall write to you separately about that and any other thoughts and suggestions.[3]

In a separate letter to George,

> The real name of the Mexican art gallery is the Galerie Valentin, but Frau Valentin died some time ago, and it is now run by a woman friend of hers who spent fifteen years in Mexico, Hanni Grogli. She uses the second floor of an old house in a beautiful part of the City on a small hill. She was a charming woman, and very appreciative of your work. At one moment I thought she was going to say it was influenced by Mexico! She did get as far as saying that *Sajiya Tala*, was reminiscent of Mexican painting. She showed me some Mexican paintings and none of it was in the least like *Sajiya Tala*! She said she could not give a show for you because her clients were not accustomed to your style of work – she clearly meant the Hindu and Kama aspects. However, she asked me to invite her when you did exhibit, and gave me the name of a man, Herr Barr or Baer, at the Museum Rietberg here

> which has a permanent exhibition of non-European art, mainly Chinese, Indian and African, so I shall go there tomorrow, partly to see the collection and partly because they are bound to the names of the local connoisseurs. The current show in Hanni Groeli's gallery consists solely of paintings of cats, all very fluffy and whiskery. There were a number of live cats in the gallery, one of which, a ginger, was a Mexican cat, believed to be the only Mexican cat to have lived in Zurich for fifteen years . . .[4]

Martin also visited Museum Reitberg whose well known Indologist director Eberhard Fischer was away at that moment. He was however fascinated by the Museum,

> I must tell you what the Museum is like. It is in Villa Wesendonck, where Wagner often stayed, and for long periods, and composed much music. Although in Zurich, it stands in a large park, and is now a municipal museum, with a small but magnificent collection. I wish Sri Lanka had anything as good. I went through all the rooms. The main exhibit are from Bharat, and wonderful they are, and beautifully displayed . . . The Chinese and Japanese collections also contain some good pieces and it was interesting to see them in galleries adjacent to the Indian as showing the influence India had. . . . I told Brigit Bernegger the object of my mission . . . she volunteered the suggestion that the Museum might lend sculptures and miniatures to an exhibition of yours, which proves she appreciated the wonder and importance of your work, but she said of course the decision to lend would have to be taken by Dr. Eberhard Fischer.[5]

The concluding note of the letter, however, would be taken up by George later. Martin wrote,

> A thing I have not mentioned in these letters is the prevalence of artistic chauvinism. This was first mentioned to me by one of the people I saw here previously – I cannot remember who. I referred to this when talking to Brigit Bernegger, who said it was nowhere worse than in Switzerland! How funny. There used to be no artistic chauvinism in England, although we were quite proud of our writers. It was quite a joke that only foreigners could compose music or sing or paint or dance, and I believe the great Russian

> dancer Markova was in fact a Miss Marks from the East End of London, who had been ordered to change her name by Diaghileff. At the opening of your last show in London Flavia when asked by Patrick Seale what your principal language was, replied 'Yiddish'. Lionel [Wendt] was far-sighted when he left so many of his pictures to her – the quizzical sense of fun is a feature in common.[6]

The Picasso debate

As Martin had pointed out to a business acquaintance earlier,

> Salesmanship requires a particular kind of persuasiveness, and this has to be supported by arguments thought out in advance. For example, some potential purchasers might think that they would be buying a second generation Picasso. One can point out in reply that none of the Keyts actually resembles any Picasso, and no Picasso resembles any of the Keyts. One can also say that the existence of important contemporaries makes the artistic work more interesting and valuable, not less so.[7]

Even a Paris gallery when approached said that it would not be able to host a show of George Keyt,

> unfortunately I can not think of any gallery in Paris who would now be interested to exhibit Keyt's work, particularly as galleries are reluctant to take on additional artists whose careers span (roughly speaking) the mid-twentieth century, unless those artists got very well dug in at a much earlier point of their career. I feel that this would be especially so in the case of an artist whose work has so much in common with that of Picasso, even if deeper study revealed that resemblance as merely superficial. Picasso of course dominated the plastic arts in France for half a century or more and showing Keyt might be seen as over exposure of a well known style . . .[8]

Ironically, the keynote of international modernism was that it was not pivotal and created pluralization and hybridization in each country where it was located. Hence the giant of modernism, Picasso, had a radiating influence all over the world where the resemblance to his style only served to create more styles. Yet Euro-Americanization did not recognize autonomous, self-directed Modernism which could reinvent itself in each country where it was located. George had no patience with this argument,

> How silly about Picasso and my work being like his! Have they ever seen the Kalighat pictures – traditional – of Bengal, or the Hindu sculpture, especially of the South, or the Basohli and other fine miniature works – good God they would have said Picasso! And Picasso of what period in all his confusing periods? They are all so used to seeing and hearing about Picasso to its darkness they

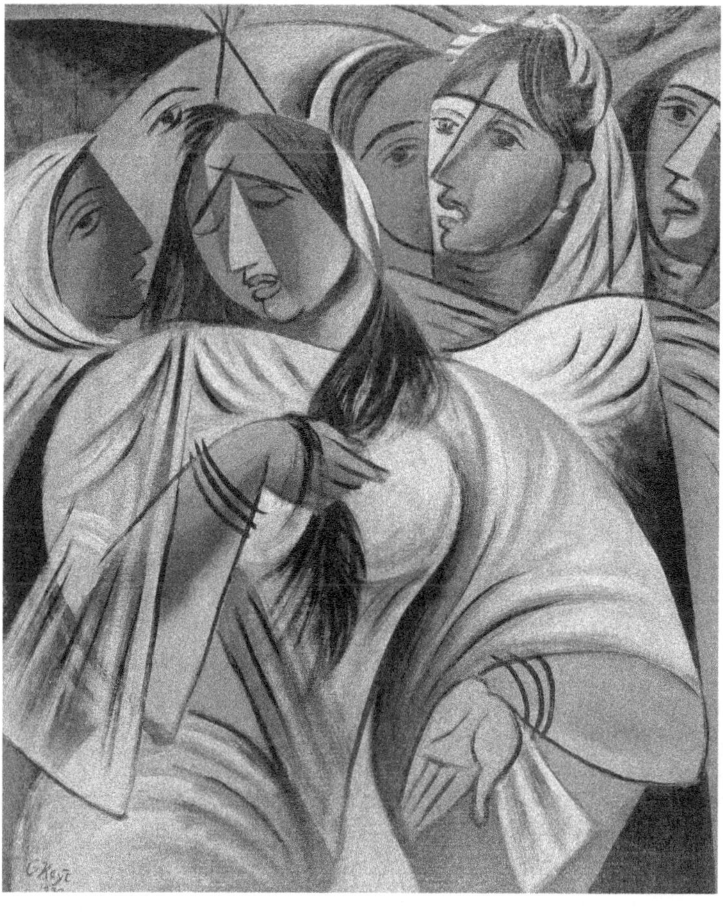

Figure 11.1 Draupadi.

George Keyt.
Oil on canvas, 1938.
Courtesy: Martin Russell Archive.

> are in which all other art is concerned ancient and modern, that anything not academic in the European sight is Picasso! Whereas Rembrandt, Tagore's work too influenced me – especially the juxtaposition of negative lines etc . . .[9]

The Swiss show never did get held but Renee Margies, the Swiss collector and a friend of George, acquired the large painting *Gopika Vastraharana*. George covered his disappointment with a layer of transcendence,

> I don't suppose anything will ever materialize where the Zurich exhibition is concerned. But I am now prepared to accept the Void which existence is in the end, and submit to a condition I always wanted *nishbriya* – beyond all activities. It is true that I paint as usual and have produced quite a lot of work and countless drawings too; it is true that people come as usual to visit me even though I am now finally settled here in a little home (upstairs) which cost me a lot to help to rebuild; but I have often to put on the mask of affability, aware of the fact that it is all in the end the mask of personality; and *nishbriya* is always waiting for me. And I still continue to live![10]

In another touching letter he writes about his depression,

> I haven't been working much in the last two months and am subject to fits of depression because it now seems that all I have done has been to no purpose in the end and I am not among those I wish to be and I see no way of being among them. Most of all, so strange, I yearn for the past, in the thirties, and my family then and my friends.[11]

New terrains

At the same time his fame was spreading. Indeed Flavia wrote in an excited frenzy to Martin and Anne from Munich about seeing George in a film on German television.

> I had an extremely eerie experience – Dear Daddy appeared on TV in an interesting and 'Dusflugrichen' film on a well-known Brazilian author George Armando a friend of Pablo Nerudas! At 11 pm – Fate? – I put on my TV set on Sunday night – A chap

living in Badria – (horrid place). He related about his travels. Suddenly an interesting photo appeared about his sojourn in Ceylon and lo and behold – an elephant and a photograph of Dear Dads' with Neruda and Armando – How eerie and around the 1960s!![12]

By the late 1980s at Martin's initiative and along with a young man from Sri Lanka, Nathan Sivasambu, the *'43 Group Colombo London* had got formed. Nathan had also organized the *Ceylon Bloomsbury Group* in 1981. He had come to England from Ceylon in 1958 to study at UCL and on the recommendation of his tutor, Professor A.J. Ayer, had done his doctoral thesis on the Analytical School of Logic and Methodology. Nathan had also studied the writer Leonard Woolf who had spent seven years in the Colonial Civil Service of Ceylon and wrote widely on the subject. On 24 May 2011, to mark the centennial of Woolf's departure from Colombo, he had organized a seminar on Woolf. A central theme was Leonard Woolf's extraordinary capacity to understand the mind of the poor jungle villager.

The *'43 Group Colombo London* was formed in May 1987 largely initiated by Martin and supported by Nathan, but news of it had travelled much before that and Keyt was intrigued,

> I saw in the papers on Sunday that the '43 Group had its 'first exhibition in London, in the Purcell Room of the Royal Festival Hall' Please tell me all about it. My name was at the head of the list of painters. I only hope it won't create a wrong impression that it is my first show in London![13]

The Group aimed at having the exhibition in the Lyre Room, below the Festival Hall and opposite the Hayward Gallery in two years' time, in 1987. But George was not too happy about a group show.

> Regarding the exhibition which you wrote about, of course it is a very good idea; but you know Martin, I was never in favour of my work being shown in a group exhibition. My work has about it a peculiar character and very unlike other art and you and Lionel Wendt were among the very few – and perhaps Justin [Daraniyagala] – who could alone really see and appreciate and understand it. Also my dear Martin the political aspect has never appealed to me. If I loved India, as I do, and England, it

> was solely from the spiritual and cultural aspect – the aesthetic side. In politics I see no rhythm as expressive of the Divine. . . . Even Mahatma Gandhi failed to instill morality into politics. See the way India is behaving over the ethnic trouble and warfare now in Lanka![14]

Martin tried to appease him,

> I agree with Lionel that your work is different from that of any one else, but this makes it stand out in a mixed show. You will remember that at the first show in 1943 I bought some paintings by you – very important ones, and very beautiful – but none by anyone else.[15]

Its first event, the '43 *Group Colombo London*, was held in June 1987 where in association with the *Ceylon Bloomsbury Group* an exhibition of the '43 Group was held in June 1987 in the Lyre Room, Royal Festival Hall, South Bank, London.

Open all days and held over a period of ten days, the exhibition drew an audience of 34,000 as recorded by the Planning Department of the Royal Festival Hall.

In Tavistock Square Gardens, a tree was planted on 16 December 2004 to commemorate the centenary of Leonard Woolf's arrival in Colombo. It is dedicated to him and those who created and were part of the Modern Cultural Period and the Classical Period from 1905 to 1967.

According to Nathan,

> This period opened in 1905 with Ananda Coomaraswamy's *The Open Letter to the Kandyan Chiefs* which enjoined the Chiefs when restoring the frescoes, paintings, drawings in the Buddhist temples, viharas, monasteries to restore them as they were without adding new colours and introducing perspective – which was being done. It came to an end with the last exhibition of the '43 Group in 1967.

The Martin Russell Commemoration took place on 19 June 2008 in Russell Square Gardens, Bloomsbury. The tree was planted by Tissa Ranasinghe, Honorary Fellow, Royal College of Art, London. The seminar which followed was held at the Institute of Commonwealth Studies, Russell Square. Chaired by Nathan Sivasambu tributes were paid by Shamil Wanigaratne, and Neville Weereratne who sent his written words from

Melbourne, Australia. A copy of the draft monograph on Martin Russell by the '43 *Group Colombo London* was presented to Martin Russell's wife, Anne Russell, by Esmeralda Claessen on behalf of the '43 *Group Colombo London*. Earlier a seminar on George Claessen had been held in November 2000 to mark his 90th year at the School of Oriental and African Studies. The Sri Lanka High Commissioner, S.K. Wickremasinghe (son of the famed novelist Martin Wickremasinghe), agreed to call on George Claessen at his home to convey his felicitation but unfortunately George Claessen passed away six days before he reached 90. The energetic Siva to this day organizes many events both around the *Ceylon Bloomsbury Group* and the '43 *Group Colombo London* and bemoans the fact that the multiculturalism that he knew and which brought about the '43 Group and other like-minded cultural organizations in Ceylon has been lost forever.

In Colombo another path-breaking organization had been set up – the *George Keyt Foundation* established in June 1988 by Cedric and Sita de Silva with the aim of promoting art and had among other things published his poetry, drawings and other writings. Apart from bringing out many publications on George Keyt, the Foundation has bought out a major centennial anthology on his life and works in 2001.

Its ongoing work includes the *Kala Pola*, or street art, which takes place every year and introduces young and contemporary artists of Sri Lanka often neglected by the galleries. Initially, Keyt himself was cynical and not convinced about the benefits that Street Art would bring to Sri Lanka. However, when he was driven around the first *Kala Pola* in 1993, he was thrilled and happily exclaimed to Cedric and Sita, 'Oh! I should have known . . . how much benefits a *Kala Pola* could bring to artists.' The John Keells Group which supports this also has provided the space in the foyer of its buildings for showcasing all the Keyt paintings owned by the Foundation. To this day, however, no permanent museum has been set up for these masterly works belonging to Keyt's best phase and generously maintained and then sent by Martin Russell, owing to lack of funds. Their languishing in somewhat lackadaisical fashion in the entrance rooms of the John Keells offices presents a treat and yet a sorry spectacle for art lovers.

George had requested Martin to send all the paintings he had left with him to the Foundation and he had sent them all, barring the ones which were part of his own collection. He wrote,

> As I had donated my pictures to the Foundation since they are making a gallery and you have with you some of the best of my work and since I now have no pictures in what was my own

> collection, and since very few people will be willing to donate from their collection; I naturally want you to send to Cedric de Silva . . . the pictures of mine with you.[16]

The positive result of this is that many of his good works are in Sri Lanka itself and a source of study and inspiration to scholars and the public. The negative aspect, however, is that they are not housed in a proper museum and do not get the required care and attention they deserve.

George had already donated four acrylics of 1975, 1976 and 1977 to the Commonwealth Institute in London at a ceremony to which to his annoyance Martin was not invited. With many lengthy negotiations, however, the then Secretary of State, Lord Carrington, satisfied that there had been a genuine misapprehension that the Institute had a permanent exhibition, signed a document releasing three (*Bhikshatana*, *Parvati Learning to Dance*, *Damayanti* and *Hansa*), 'The Institute has one picture hanging in its board room or luncheon room with the joke title *The Three Graces* but there is a Devanagri title on the stretcher which I cannot read.'[17] George's sister Peggy had presented *Sringara Rasa* to the Victoria and Albert Museum which was loaned for the Patrick Seale exhibition.[18] Thus the Victoria and Albert had the above painting, *Krishna Radha* as well as a couple of line drawings.[19] George had also designed a magnificent stained glass wall as the centrepiece of the Expo 67 Sri Lanka Pavilion in Montreal. It still remains in storage at the Montreal Public Library, since Sri Lanka could not afford to ship it back home. A memento to his brilliance, it has not been seen by most people![20] Seven works were donated to the National Gallery of Modern Art in New Delhi (*Dasya Dance*, *Megha Raga*, *A God and a Woman*, *Woman with Mirror*, *Mother and Child*, *Sri Sanghabodhi Gives Away His Head*, *Lamentations over Sri Sanghabodhi*). In a confidential letter to Martin he wrote,

> I am happy for the reason that this was the *only* thing Kusum was concerned about, and all will be solved if this is done. The pictures in the list, which I enclose, are not so important either. But they are good; and I shall be happy to be represented in the NGMA in Delhi.[21]

Dr. Sihare was the director then and he planned to house them in a new wing in The Asia Gallery. This Gallery did not come about but the Keyt paintings are occasionally displayed in the main galleries of the NGMA. In retrospect this was a good thing as Keyt was to earn fame and recognition in India as well. Yet it was with some contentious issues with Kusum that this had come about. The least of them was the fact that though she had donated them they were not owned by her in the first place!

> But Kusum will be very happy, because I plainly told her and convinced her that the list which was signed had no legal value whatever and that it was done in order to humour her at a time when she was by no means quite normal and was still in a large measure in a hypermanic condition – which you too were able to see in London and that it was by no means my desire to sign away the pictures, since I had given her from time to time twenty most excellent paintings as gifts and which are now stored in Galle and in her will bequeathed to the Indian Gallery.[22]

He continued,

> Regarding the paintings and drawings, Kusum quite saw the point and agreed with me when I said that she was now normal I could tell her what the positions was when the list was signed, and that I wanted to pictures to be with you, and that there was no legal basis at all over the list being signed, which I further confirmed through my lawyer. So I destroyed the list. All this with her concurrence. But she liked and wanted the picture in the list enclosed to be given to Dr. Sihare.[23]

Eventually, Martin was to send the pictures over to the NGMA where they are housed. The whereabouts of the remaining twenty are not known but it is likely that they were sold by Kusum after George's death to enable her to settle down in India.

An iconic artist

The rather florid works which were now emerging in his later years did not however deter from George becoming an iconic artist in Sri Lanka. On his 86th birthday there was a tremendous celebration which tired him out. He wrote,

> I have just emerged safe and sound from the birthday celebrations – 16th to 19th. On the 16th evening a meeting and reception at Grants in connection with the Felicitation volume, where the manager of the great People's Bank wanted personally to hand

> me a cheque. There was a birthday cake too with refreshments and drinks. Then on the 17th morning a special interview for T.V. followed with a breakfast special and birthday cake! A T.V. on Gotami murals and me on 16th night and a T.V. documentary on me on 17th afternoon; T.V. interview on 19th night. Of course there was the banquet at the best hotel in Colombo (Ramada) on the 17th night ending up with still another birthday cake and special music![24]

An exhibition of Keyt's other paintings (the erotic ones as well) was held at the Lionel Wendt Gallery in Colombo, with support from the John Keells Group, celebrating Keyt's 90th birthday. The Exhibition was inaugurated by the then president of Sri Lanka, Ranasinghe Premadasa.

The strange division that existed between his work and his life however became even wider. His personal life remained in turmoil and chaos while he became singularly famous as Sri Lanka's master painter. Additionally the 1980s is a period of ill health and worry and anxiety about himself and his family. As he wrote to Martin,

> I am so sorry I couldn't reply to your letter earlier – as you know I was very ill and had as Dr. Katugaha said, 'a narrow shave', having been unconscious for over 12 hours, the result of a 'spasm' in the brain which blocked an important blood vessel causing a complete cessation of the circulation throughout the whole body. I got over it but was not allowed to do a thing. I had been in the nursing home, taken there in an unconscious state . . . Am still under heavy doses of drugs – about seven in all; and am still expected not to travel etc. After this, and also before this, I was subjected to great stress here in this place – large sums of money stolen, defrauded to the extent of cheques being forged and even pictures stolen – all by Prem, who in addition used to create hell here in his ghastly, drunken fits . . .[25]

Then again to Martin,

> I haven't been working much for the last two months and am subject to fits of depression because it now seems that all I have done has been to no purpose in the end and I am not among those I wish to be. I see no way of being among them. Most of all, so strange, I yearn for the past, in the thirties, and my family then and my friends![26]

He desperately missed his studio,

> I am afraid I was very glum when I last wrote to you. The fact is I was in a rotten mood, and with nowhere to turn to in order to remedy it. I was missing my previous studios, both in Sirimalwatta and Colombo, and also Galle, which were very roomy, quite spacious, and containing all the wherewithal around me – I forgot to mention the special studio, outdoor, I made at Sirimalwatta. My present studio is so cramped, at least for me, and lacking the furniture etc. so necessary. Most people think it large enough and very nice. But I don't. Also I feel so cut away, and without transport as Prem made it impossible for me to keep my car. People come of course, and many young people, mostly foreigners, to see me, and who respond. But that's not enough . . . J.R. Jayawardene wants 2 big panels for Presidents' Home in Colombo and I'm wondering how to set about it in my present state.[27]

End of days

Two years later George is not well at all,

> It is days and weeks since I have done anything at all. Just absolutely nothing. And I haven't been well – such strange ailments quite incapacitating me. Even now I am not quite well though tests were right. Such a feeling of my head not belonging to and at times so bad that I have to stand still or sit down![28]

Even his birthday being mentioned in *The Times* does not elate him,

> Regarding the birthday in the Times, I can scarcely feel elated being put among such bedfellows . . . I'm in most desperate need for money at the moment. A deal of publicity has recently appeared about me in the press, but hardly anything has fallen into my coffers. I've got a National Honour too![29]

Almost all his letters end with a desperate wish to see Martin, 'I haven't heard from you for a very long time. I'm very unsettled and depressed and plagued and pestered by the folks at Sirimalwatta – Prem etc.'[30] A deep blow for him was the death of his sister Peggy in 1987. Harold, her husband, had died in 1981 and had been a considerable loss for her as she was very dependent on him. Peggy had loved and supported George through the years with all his upheavals, and he visited her frequently and turned towards her in need. Martin exhorted him to exhibit his portrait of her in the exhibition in London that year. The events were closing around George in a manner which he could not have perceived.

By mid-1993 he was abysmally ill,

> George has been at the Joseph Fraser Memorial Hospital . . . since the 2nd of January 1993. He has to have Kidney Dialysis which takes 4 hours each time – twice a week – he can skip a day occasionally . . . Sri Lanka's former President J.R. Jayawardene opened his 92nd Birthday Exhibition. George left hospital for a few hours to be present to accept the accolades and Sri Lanka's gratitude for his undiminished contribution. George retains an amazing memory and still paints – he has done one each on his two visits from hospital of six days each to the Kandyan village – Pilawela which is his present abode.[31]

Perhaps it shouldn't have come as a surprise when news of George's death reached Martin in 1993. He was 92 and had been ailing for some time. Yet his emphatic presence, vivid, alive, complaining, frustrated made it seem as if he would live for perpetuity and now he was no longer there! The architect and author Minnette de Silva wrote to her sister Anil de Silva vividly describing the last days.

> George Keyt died at the nursing home in Colombo . . . I broke down when the coffin was removed and did not go to the cremation . . . I hate these 'gas chambers' cremations . . . poor Manike was desolated . . . all so complicated with the different families, grand children from different wives and all . . . and Kusum being considered the official wife . . . Manike not mentioned . . . until some of us pushed her forward and had her introduced etc. I am so glad I had been seeing him in hospital . . . he was thrilled with your book and I so regret not having a copy for him to read . . . he knew it all of course . . . He spoke very affectionately of you the last time I saw him . . . remembering the old days . . . he had this incredible memory even for details. . .[32]

Minnette wrote of the last days,

> He had a wonderful death in that he had been painting, on a visit to Kandy in between his dialysis treatment, until the day before

> when he was rushed down to Colombo because he was feeling bad and died two days later on the 31st [July 1993] . . . Another chapter is over. We shall all miss his exhilarating talk. One of the few left who had participated in nearly all my life. We are all feeling very sad.[33]

George lay in state at the National Art Gallery in Colombo for two days and was then cremated. Ruth, Manike and Kusum along with all the children and grandchildren were all present for the occasion. The funeral services were conducted according to Buddhist rites, the Hindu *gatas* and a requiem mass at the church of St. Michael and All Angels for George had observed all three religions and perhaps all at once!

Miles away at his farmhouse in Dorset Martin Russell could feel the impact of the loss and readily agreed to write the obituary for the *Independent* on 13 August 1993 and *The Times* London on 23 August. In the *Independent* he mentions the quintessential Keyt,

> Keyt said to me once that he had to admit, with regret, that his work was 'controversial'. He knew that it would not receive universal acceptance immediately. But although he was influenced by changes of fashion, he never sought popularity. If a contradiction can be allowed, he was a gregarious recluse. He had to be the one because he loved people and conversation, and the other because his work demanded private thought, solitude and concentration. In the days when I saw him often, between 1943 and 1953, he had no electricity, telephone, radio and running water, but always seemed well-informed and was a fascinating companion. When he went to live in Bombay in 1947 he was perfectly at home with these modern facilities. He gave them up again when he returned to Ceylon. They were irrelevant to him.

In *The Times* London which appeared on 19 August 1993, Russell pointed out, 'Keyt's painting and poetry have not received general recognition outside Sri Lanka and India. These countries are vastly different from the West. Keyt's own originality and his combinations of elements from different historical periods of numerous Sri Lankan, Indian and European traditions puzzled foreign writers, dealers and collectors. And he did not visit the West to promote his art. Nevertheless, he has some significant admirers in England, Germany, Switzerland and the United States.' There were however a few mistakes in the final version that got published about which the daughter Diana protested. Indeed she and her friends planned to bombard the New York office of *The Times* with protests. Martin hastily wrote to the Obituary editor requesting a correction to the incorrect report that George's two wives were dead and only Kusum survived with a son.

While Martin mourned in London, Flavia was to fly to Colombo some time later. She had his ashes placed in a grave next to what would be her mothers' and wrote a moving epitaph for George's grave, 'Separated in life but united forever in death.'

Ruth passed away a few years later in 1998. She had been suffering with strokes for years and the final one ended her life. Ruth had been one of the respected teachers at Trinity. She was already established as one of the leaders of the staff when she met George. Her students still remember her and speak of her with affection. When she finally retired she went to live in her house which she built in Katugastota, a suburb of Kandy. She ended her career as headmistress of the junior boys. During the holidays she went on pilgrimages to Italy and other shrines in Europe for she was always a devout Catholic. Diana's son Gawain was in Colombo when the husband of her colleague came to tell him that she had died.

Of the remaining two partners, Kusum could be considered his second wife since he had married her according to Islamic rites, and George had spent his last years with Kusum, however troubled. He had earlier been very apprehensive about her existence in Ceylon after he had passed away for she had no one there and no one related to her. As he had written to Martin, 'Kusum's own state of health was in shambles and she had very little money.' By all accounts her former husband had died by then, and her only son lived in Pune with his family and Kusum was to join them. Perhaps she was happy living there with her son and grandchildren. Yet it seems to have been a life of isolation as no one seems to have met her and it is possible that she did have one or two breakdowns. On the other hand the life she had lived with George with all its ups and downs was vivid and stimulating and she must have missed it. By all accounts she lived privately and not in very good health in Pune and passed away sometime in the early years of the 21st century.

The one person who had been a source of great solace to George, and was his partner in more ways than one, was Manike. When she passed away on 4 January 2000, Martin wrote one of the most moving tributes on her.

> She was perhaps the most perfect woman I have met. Her face was perfect, with never an ugly expression. Her manner and her

> temperament were perfect, and so was the grace of her movements and gestures. She combined modesty with humour, and decorum with a sense of fun.[34]

He seems to have communicated with her a great deal and found her very knowledgeable on these occasions.

> She must have known English quite well, but never ventured to speak it. I knew no Sinhala, so we never had a conversation in some nine years of frequent association, which ended when I finally returned to England in 1953. But I think we usually knew each other's thoughts, partly because Keyt maintained a lively bilingual conversation.[35]

He describes her extensive knowledge of Kandyan life and even the elaborate process where paddy fields were created in the Kandyan countryside and filtered with a controlled supply of rainwater. His last words about her were:

> Keyt's elopement with Manike – if elopement is the right word – from his own home, from his Roman Catholic wife and his two daughters, and effectively from a European way of life, was, in itself, a momentous sad and tragic event. I am not aware any description of it has been published, although it clearly inspired some of his poetry. . . . Manike was the catalyst which gave rise to these developments. Sinhalese and Indian culture was the beneficiary. In a way, I am pleased Manike never learned English. She was protected from much coarseness in our present civilization.[36]

Apart from Diana and Flavia, George had from Manike two children Prem and Sachin. Prem had taken to drinking and also would turn violent. Eventually he died leaving behind his wife and children. Sachin and his family continue to live in their home near Colombo.

If a man's life is to be judged by his achievements we could say that George's existence had been remarkable for his considerable artistic skill, his legacy to Sri Lanka and to South Asia and his contribution to Modernism. Most of all, his vivid and lively personality outlived his death, and made him into a legendary figure for all times.

Notes

1 Letter to Martin, from Piiyandala, near Colombo, November 10, 1989.
2 Martin Russell to Paddy, Hotel Florida, Zurich, October 13, 1983.
3 Martin Russell to George, Zurich, October 16, 1983.
4 Martin Russell to George from Zurich, October 17, 1983.
5 Martin Russell to George from Zurich, October 18, 1983.
6 Martin Russell to George from Zurich, October 18 1983.
7 Martin Russell to Nail Hobhouse, London, August 8, 1980.
8 Letter by James of James Mayor Gallery, Paris, June 13, 1984.
9 Letter to Martin from Gunnepana, October 10, 1983.
10 Letter to Martin from Gunnepana, January 17, 1984.
11 Letter to Martin from Gunnepana, September 5, 1984.
12 Flavia Keyt in letter to Martin and Anne in London, August 12, 1982.
13 Letter to Martin, Gunnepana, November 5, 1985.
14 Letter to Martin, March 21, 1987.
15 Martin Russell to George, Dungrove Farm House, April 18, 1987.
16 Letter to Martin, from Piliyandala, December 12, 1988.
17 Martin Russell to George, Dungrove Farm House, April 18, 1987.
18 Martin Russell to George, August 13, 1982.
19 Robert Skelton to Martin, August 9, 1982.
20 Tissa Devendra, *The Lives of Keyt*, Observer Pictorial, Colombo, Sri Lanka, 1991, p. 24.
21 Letter to Martin, February 28, 1982.
22 Ibid.
23 Ibid.
24 Letter to Martin, Amunugama, April 27, 1987.
25 Letter to Martin, Sirimalwatta, March 14, 1983.
26 Letter to Martin, Amunugama, Gunnepana, August 5, 1984.
27 Letter to Martin from Gunnepana, August 23, 1984.
28 Letter to Martin, Amunugama, May 13, 1986.
29 Ibid.
30 Letter to Martin, Amunugama, Gunnapanna, October 25, 1987.
31 Cedric de Silva to Martin, Colombo, June 2, 1993.
32 Minnette de Silva at Kandy to Anil de Silva at Cambridge, August 3 1993.
33 Ibid.
34 Martin Russell, 'Tribute to Pilawela Manike,' *Sunday Leader*, Colombo, February 9, 2000.
35 Ibid.
36 Ibid.

12

THE FLAMING TORCH

Events took a contrary turn when the country achieved independence in 1948 for the rise of Sinhalese Buddhism led to a form of majoritinism.

Of course George was aware of the deteriorating conditions in post-Independent Sri Lanka.

> 'austerity measures' as they say in this financially wretched government of ours (which at present, by the way, is resorting to totalitarian methods, military and police, and all that, after the vast crowds tried to storm parliament during the budget speech and the threat of the huge strike due day after tomorrow.) You see, among other *himsa* done to the people, the rice subsidy was done away it, and the price has raised from 20 odd cents to 75 cents a measure![1]

George's misgivings about the government would prove increasingly true and yet he chose to continue living in the land of his birth which had given rise to his art. When in 1961 the government announced a Sinhalese-only linguistic policy most Burghers were to leave the country and emigrate to Canada, Europe or Australia. As Khullar points out,

> Their en masse emigration from the island stemmed from a loss of professional privilege and social prestige as the instruments of their ascendency, the English language and Christian faith, became redundant in a newly-independent nation committed to majoritarian (Sinhala and Buddhist) goals and advancement.[2]

A small group of Burghers stayed on however and some even converted to Buddhism and learnt Sinhala. There was also an artistic and intellectual community of Burghers who retained their own identity and continued to contribute in different fields. Among these would be counted George Keyt and others like Len Van Geyzel, Geoffrey Bawa, Barbara Sansoni and Carl Muller. For George it was inconceivable to leave Sri Lanka and as time passed with all its disadvantages he continued to stay in the country where he had achieved name and fame.

It has often been alleged that George's style was imitative of Picasso. He did admire the great artist and seemed to consider him a genius. In a letter written in the early 1950s he states, 'How fortunate to be able to see the Picasso show – He is at present in the world the greatest.'[3] He goes on to speak in the same letter of his incessant loneliness and states, 'It had even been arranged that I meet Picasso and stay with him in the South of France . . .'[4] But clearly this couldn't take place because of his isolation and lack of means.

Like most modern artists he was influenced by him but to state that he imitated him would be a misjudgement. As W.G. Archer points out,

> The period between 1933 and 1936, however, was nothing if not experimental, and we can see in various pictures the vitalizing shock which Keyt must also have experienced from reproductions of work by Braque and Picasso. Both these artists employed daring distortions. Both were free of tame subservience to naturalism and its conventions. And Keyt must suddenly have realized that a whole new series of idioms lay ready to hand for conscious adoption and that ideas of what was vital in modern art must be sharply revised.[5]

While drawing all the energies of modernism from Picasso he retained his own sensibility and created forms which reflected his own persona and environment. He was as a matter of fact also influenced by Matisse, Braque and Juan Gris and felt himself profoundly in league with the international modernist manoeuvres of the 19th and 20th centuries. Then again his views on Surrealism were discerning,

> Since I wrote my previous letter to you, I have read the Surrealist book you sent me, and I must admit that I was half in love with the movement. But I discovered I could never take to it because as I told you . . . I am not of the literal mind. This movement is such a protestation. Don't you see what I mean? I'm not trying to be paradoxical. I say I am not of the literal mind and cannot

> therefore take to Surrealism. But now I know what the movement means, and I'm grateful to you for sending me the book. Anything which is a 'movement' is false.[6]

A Parisian dealer who was considering having a show of his work in the 1950s felt that it had strong affinities with Asiatic and particularly Indian art. According to Martin Russell,

> Anne and I had brought over to Paris *The First Meeting*, *The Threshing Floor*, and the drawing on rice paper of *Sri Sangha Bohni giving away his head*. Madame Hoenigsberg [the art dealer] was very much impressed by all three works, especially by the drawings. . . . She said that she did not think there was any influence of Picasso in the two paintings, but there were resemblances to the works of Braque and Derain. In the drawings she did see some signs of Picasso's influence also. She also saw at once the Indian and traditional character of the work.[7]

Indeed George himself had felt that the art community in the West found that his work resembled that of Picasso; they were not aware of the works of Kalighat School and miniature paintings in India. To this could be added his considerable affinity with the Indian master artist Jamini Roy whose reuse of the folk traditions of Bengal had resulted in ingenuous modern works in contemporary India. He had also stated his admiration of Jamini Roy and Rabindranath Tagore and he had met the poet and Nobel laureate on his 1934 visit to Sri Lanka. Like Roy his dark calligraphic line swept over the painterly surface detailing the form to which the deep colours were subsidiary. His themes however were often hewn from Indian mythology and had the sensual and erotic content while Roy's endearing paintings dwelt on the ordinary folk and their simple engagements with life. He was likened to M.F. Husain and in his own words, 'M.F. Husain for instance India's leading painter who always, oddly enough, claims me as his guru!'[8] But even more he could be compared with the Goan artist Francis Newton Souza whose strong, energetic line engaged with the woman in all her nudity and with amorous couples. Souza's preoccupation with Picasso made him feel that he had outdone him with his invention of demonic heads. Yet unlike Souza, Keyt seldom engaged with social reality or with corrupt and tainted forms of governance though he was fully conscious of the degradation of life in Sri Lanka. Nor do Souza's edginess and disturbed figures of men and women compare with Keyt's sensual forms always engaged in enraptured love-making. In the end perhaps it would be true to say that he had successfully melded Western forms with indigenous traditions and bought about a synthesis of the two. And yet fundamentally he remained Asian in his sensibility. As a critic pointed out,

> He remains the most outstanding exemplar in Sri Lanka of a truly modern pictorial style, which retains a specifically Asian expression, scorning synthetic folklore, enfeebling tradition, cramping academism, and cloying provincialism, as well as the more outlandish excesses of the contemporary school of European painting.[9]

As far as his own tradition was concerned, Keyt who was said to have been influenced by Ananda K. Coomaraswamy with his scathing reference to the deterioration of traditional arts under unchecked modernism and colonial adminstration and an urging of the Kandyan chiefs in 1815 to restore the temple paintings in their original form had also carefully measured his distance from him. Coomaraswamy had been considerably influenced by William Morris's Art and Craft movement which had been introduced in the late 19th century in the face of increasing mechanization and mass production in Britain. In the different setting of Sri Lanka and India still under colonial rule however, it would have its own disadvantages as somewhat retrograde practices began to be observed. As a critic pointed out:

> The earnest authority of Coomaraswamy's argument, with its unyielding dualities . . . shaped a widespread view of the relationship of Asian/Sri Lankan tradition and Western modernity. This partly explains the mixed responses of the 43Group artists to such issues as the relationship of a Western-inspired artistic modernity to traditional or non-modern social, religious, and cultural values, and the calibration of individual autonomy against the demands of group, audience, community, and nation.[10]

Keyt had great respect for tradition and for Coomaraswamy but was by no means uncritical of him. His modernity created a distance from Coomaraswamy's views which yet formed a component of his work. The essential Kandyan features of painting which are different from the rest of the island are evident in his paintings and would indeed be manifested consistently in all his works. Kandyan art is stylized and its subjects are two-dimensional, with an emphasis on line which does not get blurred by daubs of paint and the colours though limited are brilliant and unadulterated.[11]

Metaphors of modernity

George Keyt's genius lay in melding together the metaphors of modernity in a wide sweep from Picasso and Braque to Jamini Roy and F.N. Souza and envisioning his own text of contemporaneity. He was also one of the few artists who articulated the religious and mythological past of India in modern terms. Yet his interest in Indian tradition was not religious or ritualistic. In an interview he stated, 'If you mean the religious observances, [in India] no – not so much as in the visual and esthetic side of the ceremonies. The ceremonial paraphernalia, the dance. My interest is in philosophy, not ritual.'[12] Yet not unlike a prayer chain the same themes would repeat themselves like a chant and yet it was not repetitive and each one was different. Towards the end, when his energies began to dwindle, the works remained intact in their strong bounding line and colours if without the depth of conviction.

His acerbic views did not spare the Bloomsbury Group though he could not have met Leonard Woolf for he was very young when the latter was stationed in Kandy. The Group was a loosely formed entity without a manifesto or a specific ideology but consisted of an intellectual elite which had liberalized the arts from its Victorian constraints and norms in the early part of the 20th century. In the arts it was the efforts of the influential critic Roger Fry which led to an understanding of Cezanne and the Post-Impressionists which was only by the 1920s and early 1930s. As Spalding points out,

> The distrust of all things French was one of the reasons why artistic developments in France over the last thirty years had largely gone unnoticed in England. Roger Fry's entry into Bloomsbury coincided with the first of his two revelatory Post-Impressionist exhibitions at the Grafton Galleries in London in 1910. While crusading energetically on behalf of Cezanne, Gaugin, Van Gogh and Matisse, he altered the position of Bloomsbury, for he drew his new friends into the furore this exhibition aroused.[13]

As Keyt wrote to Barbara,

> Of course you hear that . . . it always took about thirty years for British people to know and be instilled with the, to them, any new and alien art – safe for acceptance and appreciation – after being acknowledged at once with enthusiastic delight in Paris being

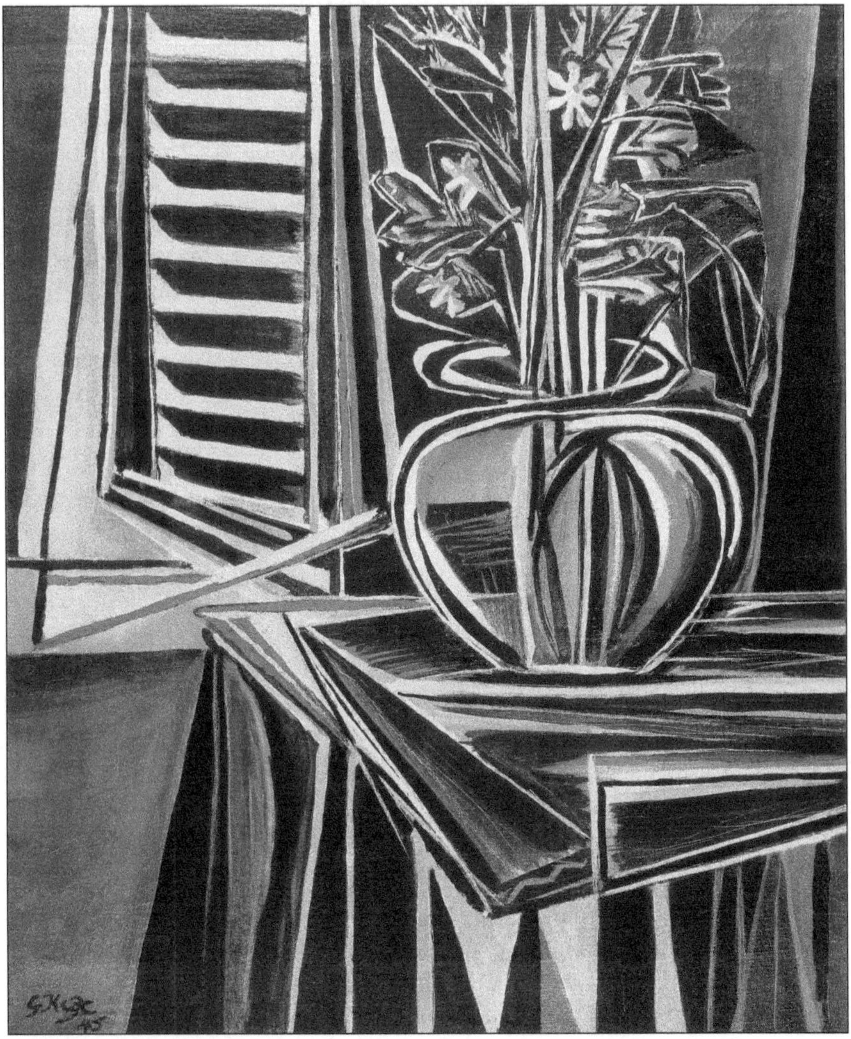

Figure 12.1 Still life with wild flowers.

George Keyt.
Oil on canvas, 1945.
Courtesy: Martin Russell Archive.

known there for a long time. Roger Fry introduced post impressionistic art into England. I've seen his work, and Clive Bell too writing about Cezanne etc. which also I knew at the time in the thirties, and so much more like Cahier d'art etc . . . Picasso was

> in the mid-summit of his fame and Renoir long long before that, like Manet and the rest, when they became known in England.[14]

The '43 Group could be likened in some ways to the Bloomsbury Group which was at the core of modernism in Britain and had caught the attention of the world with its productions of literature, art and theatre and much else. In its heterogeneity and its open-ended membership though not in the daring of its artistic experiments there had been a similarity of intentions if not achievements.

Challenges to academic art

George though part of the '43 Group remained distinctive and different and in fact often felt that he didn't really need to belong to a group. Yet it was as a member of the '43 Group that he first exhibited internationally and came into prominence. The Group increasingly lost its efficacy by the mid-1960s and finally disbanded. As the first group which made a concerted effort in Sri Lanka to challenge academic art it was at the vanguard of art practices and played a crucial role in introducing a new modernist orientation. In a postcolonial situation it also generated a sense of cohesive national identity. The brilliance of artists like George Keyt, Justin Daraniyagala and Ivan Peries could not perhaps have been achieved without the support and encouragements of various members of the Group. Why then did it lose its generative possibilities over the years? One reason for this could be that many of the members like Ivan Peries, George Claessen and Richard Gabriel left the country following the Sinhalese-only policy introduced by the government in the 1960s. But perhaps even more crucially, most of the members of the Group belonged to the upper strata of society which did not attempt an engagement with the people at large. Most of the members with a few exceptions belonged to well-to-do upper classes which rarely had to work for a living and hence art could in some ways be considered an isolated exercise. As a critic ruminated,

> In general, Post-Independence artists, even those of the 43Group and later followers, with some exceptions, have failed to observe the realities of their native experience, and to give expression to the functional needs of a living society outside metropolitan walls . . . The verve and enthusiasm of the forties petered out, perhaps, because they were insufficiently grounded in the bedrock of the cultural patterns of Sri Lanka.[15]

Yet it must be said that for George Keyt who ploughed his own field most of the time, the works continued to engage people at large as in the Buddhist and Indian ethos he grounded his paintings and found a receptive audience. As it is pointed out,

> Keyt soon tired of this cul-de-sac in which he found himself, and decided, once and for all, to arrive at an idealization and articulation of his own historical role as an interpreter of a national heritage and an indigenous consciousness according to his sensibilities, his vision and his needs.[16]

Notwithstanding its historical role, the younger generation of artists in Sri Lanka feel that the '43 Group is like a spreading banyan tree which does not allow anything to grow under its shade. At the same time, it was an important progenitor of modernism in that it broke the shackles of mimetic art. The wave of energy which the '43 Group generated seems to await rekindling. Yet it has to be noted that it was their achievement which gave rise to not just a whole host of younger artists in the island but modernism itself in South Asia. A few years later, in 1947, the Progressive Artists were to form in Bombay declaring that they would break connections with the effete revivalism of the Bengal School and the stultifying practices of academic art. Artists like F.N. Souza, M.F. Husain and S.H. Raza were to carve a bold new path in alternative modernist art which would influence generations of younger artists. Yet it was the '43 Group in Sri Lanka which provided the earliest energetic disavowal of academic art paving the way for the wave of modernism which would overtake the subcontinent in the 1940s.

Notes

1 Letter to Martin, August 11, 1953.
2 Sonal Khullar, Department of Art History, Berkeley University, *The Life of the Buddha and the Art of the Nation: Postcolonial Modernity in George Keyt's Life of the Buddha at Gotami Vihara*, 2004, p. 5.
3 Letter to Martin from Gunnepana, undated.
4 Ibid.
5 W.G. Archer, *India and Modern Art*, Allen and Unwin, London, 1959, p. 124.
6 Letter to Geyzel, early 1936.
7 Martin Russell to George, November 4, 1954.
8 Letter to Martin from Colombo, June 14, 1976.
9 H.A.I. Goonetileke, *George Keyt, A Life in Art*, The George Keyt Foundation, Colombo, 1989, p. 16.

10 Larry D. Lutchmansing, 'Emergent Perspectives in Modern Art: The '43 Group – Formation of a Sri Lankan Avant-Garde', in J.C. Holt (ed), *The Sri Lanka Reader* Duke University, Durham, NC, 2011, pp. 578–579.
11 Refer K.M. de Silva, *A History of Sri Lanka*, Vijitha Yapa Publications, Colombo, Sri Lanka, 2008, p. 274.
12 Interview with Ellen Dissanayake, *Journal of South Asian Literature, Asian Studies Center*, Vol. 12, Nos. 1 and 2, 1976, pp. 91–102, Michigan, U.S.A.
13 Frances Spalding, *The Bloomsbury Group*, National Portrait Gallery, London, 2013, p. 15.
14 Letter to Barbara from Sirmalwatta, October 11, 1982.
15 Goonetileke, op. cit., p. 15.
16 Ibid.

INDEX

Lightning Source UK Ltd.
Milton Keynes UK
UKHW010646270220
359386UK00005BA/413

9 780367 279783